INSTITUTIONS IN TURBULENT ENVIRONMENTS

For Allan Keating
and Jack Darcy

Institutions in Turbulent Environments

A Study of the Impact of Environmental Change Upon Institutions for the Intellectually Disabled

T. P. KEATING
Department of Social Work and Social Policy
School of Public Health
Faculty of Health Sciences
La Trobe University, Australia

Routledge
Taylor & Francis Group

LONDON AND NEW YORK

First published 1999 by Ashgate Publishing

Reissued 2018 by Routledge
2 Park Square, Milton Park, Abingdon, Oxon, OX14 4RN
711 Third Avenue, New York, NY 10017, USA

Routledge is an imprint of the Taylor & Francis Group, an informa business

Publisher's Note
The publisher has gone to great lengths to ensure the quality of this reprint but points out that some imperfections in the original copies may be apparent.

Disclaimer
The publisher has made every effort to trace copyright holders and welcomes correspondence from those they have been unable to contact.

A Library of Congress record exists under LC control number: 99072336

ISBN 13: 978-1-138-31417-7 (hbk)
ISBN 13: 978-0-429-45717-3 (ebk)

Contents

List of Tables and Figures

Acknowledgements

This work developed out of the task of redeveloping one of Victoria's oldest and largest institutions for the intellectually disabled in the period 1987-1993. The task was a pivotal one in the lives of a large number of very committed staff in the institution itself, and in the Department of Health and Community Services. I most gratefully acknowledge the achievements of these staff, and their contribution to the research.

My colleagues in the Department of Social Work and Social Policy, in particular Dr. Martin Ryan, and Mr. Bill Healy provided encouragement and guidance throughout the project. Gaye Neilson, Lisa Doige, Tammy Ebert and Linda Gordes provided invaluable assistance in the preparation of the manuscript.

The patience and support of Irene, Sam, Bridie, Eloise, Declan and Dominic Keating has been essential in sustaining me personally and this research project over five long years. They, as always have my warmest and most grateful affection.

Above all however, this study has been dependent upon Loretta, James, Verna, Jack and many others, for whom the story of Mayday Hills is their story. Their remarkable courage in facing the challenge of building a new life outside the institution provided much of the inspiration for this work. Their contribution to me personally and professionally is warmly acknowledged.

The financial support of the La Trobe University Publications Committee is gratefully acknowledged.

Tom Keating

1 Introduction

A major focus of concern in the study of formal organisations has been with the way in which they change. A great volume of literature concerned with organisational theory and management has in recent years been devoted to the ubiquity of change within the experience of organisations, and with the accelerating pace of that change. On a global scale, the internationalisation of financial markets, ecological threats, rapid technological advancement, and changing perceptions as to the role and function of government have contributed in the later part of the twentieth century to a rapidly changing social and political environment. The formal organisations which populate that environment have faced significant adjustments in their markets, their resources and their legitimacy.

Social policy is concerned with the way in which publicly funded or mandated activity can or should respond to the social environment. As such it has been required to adapt and to change in response to changing attitudes to governmental action, the availability of resources, and to changes in practice technologies.

As social policies have adapted to new and emerging issues, and to changes within the social environment, those organisations which are governed by social policies have themselves had to change and adapt. One of the significant areas of social policy which has undergone dramatic change has been that concerned with the residential care of vulnerable people. These changes are most often referred to as "deinstitutionalisation".

Deinstitutionalisation has been a significant aspect of social policy as it affects a range of vulnerable client groups, in the period from the mid 1960s until the present time. As such, it has been one of the most significant organisational changes undertaken by public sector human services organisations in recent times. In the United States, Britain and Australia, governments have sought during this period to change the models of care for a range of vulnerable or statutorily detained groups in the community, from large scale and segregated congregate facilities to small group care within integrated settings.

The origins of the deinstitutionalisation focus of public policy may be seen in theoretical developments of the 1960s with respect to labelling theory,

1

normalisation, and anti-psychiatry. They may arguably also be linked to the socio-political critiques of capitalist social control mechanisms by the New Left during the 1960s. Civil rights concerns and scepticism about the intentions of the state have been joined in more recent times as wellsprings of deinstitutionalisation by critiques of the Welfare State, and concern about the capacity of the State to fund one hundred per cent of the care of the vulnerable and the disadvantaged in institutional settings.

Deinstitutionalisation has not been without its critics. Questions have been raised as to the quality of the alternatives offered to those no longer having their needs met totally within statutorily controlled environments. There are concerns that the state is effectively transferring responsibility for care to households and communities ill equipped to provide that care. From a political economy perspective, there has been a view that far from disestablishing means of coercive social control, deinstitutionalisation has entailed an expansion of the intrusive and coercive powers of the state; a development of a new mechanism of control, while maintaining the old mechanisms (Cohen, 1985).

In the State of Victoria this direction in public policy may be seen in the redevelopment of the majority of congregate care facilities for children (orphanages and children's homes) between 1972 and 1989; the gradual reduction of psychiatric inpatient services and their replacement with community based service options; the decommissioning of Wilsmere Psychiatric Hospital (1989), St Nicholas Hospital for the Intellectually Disabled (1982), and the Caloola Training Centre for the Intellectually Disabled (1992). The policy directions which favoured alternatives to institutional care were established in legislation by the *Community Welfare Services Act 1978* and subsequently the *Children's and Young Persons' Act 1991*, the *Mental Health Act 1986*, and the *Intellectually Disabled Persons Services Act 1986*.

This study does not focus upon the merits of deinstitutionalisation, but upon it as an instance of major organisational change. It does so with reference to a single detailed case study: the redevelopment of Mayday Hills Training Centre for the Intellectually Disabled. This facility, a large congregate care facility for the Intellectually Disabled located at Beechworth in rural Victoria, was between January 1988 and December 1993 redeveloped and closed. In the process, 178 intellectually disabled people were relocated to community living arrangements.

The study departs from the numerous analyses of individual institutional closures in that it places the redevelopment within the context of organisational change, and, in particular, organisational change in response to major environmental change. The unit of attention is thus the organisation, Mayday

Hills Training Centre, and the formal and informal bodies which represented its environment. The study does not examine in any detail individual changes which took place, but examines the responses of the focal organisation, and the implications of these for the study of organisations and specifically for public sector congregate care facilities.

The study of organisations in this way is important for social work. The majority of social work in Australia takes place within formal organisational settings, very often in the public sector. Social workers have a critical concern with public policies which affect vulnerable and disadvantaged individuals and communities. They have also a critical concern with the institutional means by which these policies are enacted. An understanding of organisational process is thus important for social work both because formal organisations have important impacts upon their clients, and because they themselves must work within these organisations (Jones and May, 1992, 9ff). Organisational change impacts directly upon social workers in their work environment and upon their clients. An understanding of the factors which cause organisations to change, and the ways in which they respond to those factors is critical for effective practice.

The study is organised to reflect a concern with the theory of organisational responses to changing environments. Chapter 2 reviews the body of literature concerned with organisational change and the organisation/environment relationship. This is used to construct a framework for collection and analysis of the data. Chapter 3 provides a description of the organisation under study, while Chapter 4 describes the environment of the organisation. This is analysed in Chapter 5 utilising the theoretical framework developed. Chapter 6 provides in narrative form a detailed description of the responses of the organisation to the changes in its environment. The findings of the study are outlined in Chapter 7. This chapter analyses those organisational responses to environmental change, in the context of the theoretical framework. Chapter 8 discusses the implications of the findings for organisational theory, and their implications for policy, practice and education.

Figure 1.1 Hospital for the Insane, Beechworth (Mayday Hills Hospital) Circa 1910

2 The Literature

This study addresses itself to the process of change within a large human services organisation. Mayday Hills Training Centre, while operating within a large public sector Department and within the broader framework of the public sector of the State of Victoria, may be viewed as an organisation in its own right. Its history was a remarkably stable one. Opened in the latter part of the nineteenth century, it survived with only marginal change to its structure, strategy, and technology for over a century. Beginning in the early 1980s however, and coming to a climax in the period of 1988-1993, it underwent as a consequence of major changes within its environment, a redevelopment which profoundly changed every aspect of its operations, such that the organisation itself was to cease to exist as a separately constituted body.

This study looks to the literature concerned with change as it takes place within complex organisations, and especially that body of literature which is concerned with the changes brought about by the interaction between organisations and their environments. The literature is extensive, and so this review is of necessity selective. **Organisational change** as it will be considered in this study is firstly defined. The literature concerning organisations and their environments is then examined, having regard to **organisational contingency** and **environmental contingency**. This leads to an examination of the range of **typologies** of environments developed within the literature. The alternative theoretical framework for consideration of the organisation/ environmental relationship, that of **population ecology** is examined and its relationship with **adaptation** perspectives considered.

Defining Organisational Change

The reality of change, and its consequence for managers of complex organisations is frequently cited by organisational theorists as being amongst the most significant factors of modern organisational life. Tichy argues that:

....we are proceeding further into the era of discontinuous change brought on by energy problems, finite resources, environmental limits to the absorption of industrial wastes, the cleavage between developed and underdeveloped nations, and a world economy which does not function effectively or efficiently. In this context we encounter ever increasing organisational complexity. (Tichy, 1983, 5)

While there is considerable agreement within the literature as to the prevalence of change there is debate as to how organisational change should be understood. This is not at all surprising given the richness of theory concerning the nature of organisations themselves. Morgan, in arguing for multiple and simultaneous perspectives upon organisations, has identified nine metaphors which offer competing explanations of organisational phenomena (Morgan, 1986). Competing models of organisational change are predicated upon competing conceptualisation of organisations themselves (Clegg, 1990). Organisational change may be understood, for instance as structural adjustment, adaptation, or a response to changed information processing requirements, depending upon whether one understands organisations mechanistically, as being organism like, or as information processing systems.

Before dealing with the issue of theoretical stance towards organisations however, it is worth considering the nature of the change in question.

Following Schein, organisational change may be defined as the induction of new patterns of action, belief, and attitudes among substantial proportions of a population (Schein, 1970). This is problematic however in that change, so defined is a constant phenomenon within social systems. Indeed it may not be possible to distinguish adequately between states of change and stability, since organisations however conceived change continuously, often in subtle and incremental ways. This study will be concerned with organisational change which is large in scale and strategic in nature.

Pullen (1993) takes up the issue of distinguishing between incremental and strategic change. He distinguishes between organisational change which is **continuous** and that which is **discontinuous**; continuous change being the gradual adjustment to evolving environmental circumstances, and discontinuous change being brought about by an abrupt event in the environment for which there is no organisational precedent. Discontinuous change represents a rapid and fundamental shift in the basic circumstances of the organisation and requires a redefinition of its internal logic. Pullen argues that the models and strategies usually associated with organisational change are of limited utility because they assume relative continuing stability and gradual evolution of internal arrangements, and that managers can predict future states with reasonable accuracy.

Appropriate strategic responses, Pullen suggests are either **structural** or **power related;** they require either transformation and reconfiguration from the ground up with a new mission, constituency, product and value set, or alternatively they consist of attempting to influence the future through strategies which shape and form the environment. The second of these, he suggests is arguably not open to public sector organisations for which the environment may be largely determined by extrinsic political processes.

Klein (1980) similarly identifies both the transformational and the normative aspect of organisational change. He writes that it consists of a process or series of events occurring over a period of time, usually involving a more or less orderly and somewhat predictable sequence of interactions. Though it involves the reactions of individuals, it also entails the reorganisation of group, organisational, or even community behaviour patterns and requires the alteration of social values (Klein, 1980).

Strategic change is defined by Tichy as "nonroutine, nonincremental, and discontinuous change which alters the overall orientation of the organisation and/or components of the organisation" (Tichy, 1983, 17). This definition allows for change which is both intentional, (that is explicitly planned for) and that which is "realised" (that is, emerges out of circumstances).

He argues that strategic change is triggered when problems, crises, or opportunities are identified through information which exceeds the thresholds established by historical, planning, comparative or scientific data. Problems, crises, or opportunities emerge as a consequence of **environment, diversification, technology,** and **people**.

Surveying organisational theory, Tichy argues as is noted above, that the way change is understood is predicated upon the model adopted for organisations. He distinguishes between a **classical/mechanistic** model which assume that technical considerations will be paramount, the **human resources organic** model which gives primacy to issues of culture and the relationship between staff and the organisation, and the **political** model, which understands organisations in terms of the exercise of power.

He argues that organisational change is brought about as organisations are continually required to make adjustments to resolve three problems: the **technical design problem,** the **political allocation problem**, and the **cultural problem**. The technical design problem emerges because all organisations face a production problem. In the context of organisational threats or opportunities, social, financial and technical resources must be arranged to produce some desired output. In order to solve this problem, management engages in strategic planning and organisational design and redesign. The political allocation problem emerges as organisations face the problem of allocating power and resources. The cultural problem reflects the demand upon the organisation to determine the values, objectives and beliefs which will form the "normative glue" of the organisation and to communicate these.

Tichy proposes the metaphor of a strategic rope; constructed from technical, political and cultural strands. From a distance the strands are indistinguishable, but if unravelled, weaken the organisation. At any time, one or a combination of strands may require adjustment as a consequence of changed internal or external circumstances, but in doing so, may prompt adjustments in the other strands. Systems generated separately to deal with the technical, political and cultural are interdependent and in a well managed organisation are congruent. Managing change, Tichy argues:

> ...involves making technical, political, and cultural decisions about desired new organisational states, weighting the trade-offs and acting on them. (Tichy, 1983, 12)

Tichy's representation of the relationship between the strands of the strategic rope is reproduced as Figure 2.1 below:

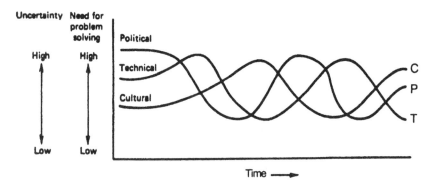

Figure 2.1   Relationship between Political, Technical and Cultural Cycles
Source: (Tichy, 1983, 12)

Adjustments in each of these three problem areas are conceptualised in cyclical terms. Organisations vary over time in the amount of energy they commit to adjustment in technical, political and cultural cycles. Cycles overlap and interact with each other.

This study then addresses itself to strategic change (so defined) as it occurred within the Mayday Hills Training Centre. Its concern is with major non-routine, non-incremental discontinuity which prompted adjustment of the technical, political and cultural systems of the organisation

Organisations and Their Environments

This study is principally concerned with the relationship of Mayday Hills Training Centre, as focal organisation, with its environment. As such, it focuses upon the body of literature dealing with the organisation/environment relationship, and does not address itself to the larger body of literature concerned with organisational change.

In the period following the mid 1960s, a considerable body of research and theoretical literature has been developed addressing the organisation/ environment relationship. Much of the literature has its research origins in the industrial production sector, through the work of Burns and Stalker (1961), Woodward (1965), and Lawrence and Lorsch (1967). It has its theoretical origins in open system theory and, in Morgan's terms the "organismic metaphor" of organisations (Morgan, 1986). Consideration of the models derived from this literature for human service organisations is relatively recent, and largely derivative (Hasenfeld, 1983).

An important beginning point for consideration of a theoretical framework for the organisation/environment relationship is with the work of Lawrence and Lorsch, and their conception of organisations as contingent upon environmental variables.

Organisational Contingency

Lawrence and Lorsch (1967), have identified some essential aspects of the relationship between the internal structure and processes of organisations and their technological and economic environment. They do so in the context of identifying that the tasks facing an organisation in one set of technological or economic conditions, may be very different from those when faced with different circumstances. They ask the question: what types of organisation does it take to deal with different environmental conditions?

The principle dimensions upon which they examine organisations are their state of **differentiation** and their state of **integration**. As organisations deal with aspects of their environment, they become segmented into units, each dealing with part of the outside conditions. These units must then be unified in order to ensure that the organisation is able to act in a coherent manner. **'Differentiation'** is defined as the cognitive and emotional orientation among managers in different functional departments, while **'Integration'** is defined as the quality of the state of collaboration that exists among departments that are required to achieve unity of effort by the demands of the environment.

In examining six organisations operating within a dynamic environment, Lawrence and Lorsch found high levels of differentiation between functional units within those organisations, with respect to formality of structure, interpersonal orientation, time orientation and goal orientation. This differentiation was highly correlated with environmental requirements. In the case of the more highly performing organisations, i.e. those which are most well adapted to the requirements of their environments, the degree of differentiation between units was most pronounced as was the degree of integration (the capacity for cooperative action) between them.

Examining the paradoxical presence of high levels of differentiation with similarly high levels of integration, they found that high performing organisations in the specific dynamic environment they were examining, had effective conflict resolution procedures based upon the utilisation of "integrators". Effective integrators had an appropriate interpersonal and goal and time orientation, had authority based upon hierarchy and knowledge, and were given incentives to identify the task of joint decision making as important. These organisations had a clear preference for confronting differences in opinion as they appeared rather than avoiding them or resolving them by hierarchical command (Lawrence and Lorsch, 1986, 54).

Extending their analysis to other industries with less dynamic environments, they established that the status of integration and differentiation in effective organisations differs depending on the demands of the particular environment (Lawrence and Lorsch, 1986, 108). The more diverse and dynamic the environment, the more differentiated and highly integrated the organisation was required to be. Thus the structure and processes of organisations are **contingent** upon aspects of their environment.

Expanding upon this work and addressing the issue of factors upon which an organisation's structure is contingent, Mintzberg (1979) identifies as pre-eminent; **age** and **size**, **technology** and **environment**. With respect to age, he suggests that older organisations are more formalised in their behaviour and that their structures reflect the age of the foundation of the industry of which they are a part. Larger organisations, he argues, are more elaborate in their structures, having greater specialisation of tasks and greater differentiation of units. As they become larger, they tend towards a larger average size of work units and towards greater formalisation of behaviour:

> ...increased size leads to greater job specialisation within units and both of these factors lead to more differentiation between units, then to more levels in the hierarchy. Job specialisation reduces the need for intra-unit co-ordination, which allows for an increase in unit size. But job specialisation, together with unit differentiation also increases the need for inter-unit co-ordination, which causes the organisation to formalise its behaviour and make greater use of planning and control systems. Finally, more formalised behaviour and greater use of planning and control systems means more standardisation, which means increased bureaucratisation of the structure. (Mintzberg, 1979, 234)

As they increase in size and complexity, organisations change in a discontinuous and non-linear manner over time through patterns he describes as craft\entrepreneurial, bureaucratic, divisionalised and matrix stages.

Technological systems, in Mintzberg's view, vary in their impact upon organisational structures and functioning along the dimensions of **regulation** and **sophistication**; where regulation refers to the extent to which operators' work is controlled or regulated by their instruments; and sophistication refers to the intricateness or complexity of the system (Mintzberg, 1979, 250).

A regulating technical system bureaucratises the operating core of the organisation since it is possible to define output more generally and with less specificity and hence also the operating tasks. A sophisticated technical system elaborates the support staff structures, placing greater emphasis upon design, technical support and supervisory functions. Automated technical systems have the effect of debureaucratising the structures above the operating core, since control and supervision are diminished in importance (Mintzberg, 1979, 266).

Importantly for the purposes of this study, Mintzberg identifies four characteristics of an organisational environment which impact significantly upon that organisation's structure and processes. **Stability**, the degree to which changes which occur in the environment do so unexpectedly; **Complexity**, the comprehensibility of the environment; **Market Diversity**, the degree of integration within the organisation's markets; and **Hostility**, the degree of competition and conflict between the organisation and its environment, including the availability of resources within that environment (Mintzberg, 1979,

268). Mintzberg develops a two dimensional matrix which identifies the intersecting impact of the first two of these variables. This is shown as Table 2.2 below.

Table 2.2   Environmental Variables

	STABLE	DYNAMIC
Complex	Decentralised Bureaucratic (Standardisation of work skills)	Decentralised Organic (Mutual Adjustment)
Simple	Centralised Bureaucratic (Standardisation of work processes)	Centralised Organic (Direct Supervision)

Source: (Mintzberg, 1979, 286)

Simple, stable environments give rise to centralised, bureaucratic structures in which the principal mechanism for co-ordination is the standardisation of work processes. This is because the more an organisation is able to predict its environment, the more it is able to insulate its operating core and standardise its activities. Complex, stable environments similarly lead to structures which are bureaucratic but which are also decentralised, allowing greater scope for operators to make decisions in response to the complexity they encounter. Co-ordination is achieved by the standardisation of the operator's skills, and greater emphasis is placed upon staff training and the provision of requisite skills.

When the organisation's environment is dynamic but simple, it can combine a centralisation of decision making with the flexibility of an organic structure. In this structure, direct supervision becomes the principal means of co-ordination. The more difficult environment however, that which is both dynamic and complex, requires that the organisation decentralise power and authority to managers who can comprehend the issues and also allow them the flexibility through organic structures, to respond to the unpredictable. Mutual adjustment brought about by integrative mechanisms is the principal means of co-ordination.

Mintzberg's remaining variables **Market Diversity** and **Hostility** act as an overlay upon this two dimensional matrix. In a diverse market place he argues that the organisation must co-ordinate its work through the standardisation of outputs. Extreme hostility, he suggests, will cause an organisation to centralise its structure temporarily.

Of greatest significance, in Mintzberg's view, is the presence of a dynamic environment:

> ...dynamic environments seem to drive the structure to an organic state no matter what its age, size or technical system. Likewise, complex conditions seem to require decentralisation, and conditions of extreme hostility, centralisation, no matter what other contingency factors are present. (Mintzberg, 1979, 287)

The final variable upon which Mintzberg argues that organisations are contingent is that of power. The presence of a dominating **external control** in the form of government or parent company for instance will have a bureaucratising and centralising effect. Predominant **fashions** in organisational structure or management theory can have the effect of overriding the imperatives of the organisation's actual operating environment. The **power needs of the members** to influence or control their own workplace can be such as to impose structural requirements upon the organisation, generally because of the greater influence of line managers, requirements towards greater bureaucratisation and centralisation. In each case, these factors may lead the organisation to adopt structures that the other contingency factors of age, size, technical system and environment deem inappropriate (Mintzberg, 1979, 296).

This study is particularly concerned with the contingent responses of organisations to changes within their environments. Hage and Aiken (1980) have examined the relationship between a range of organisational properties and their responsiveness to change. Defining program change as the number of new program initiatives adopted by the organisation over a five year period, they examined the behaviours of sixteen health and welfare agencies. Specifically they tested the correlation between the variables of **complexity**, **centralisation**, **formalisation** and **job satisfaction** with the rate of program change within these organisations.

Their results were generally consistent with those of Mintzberg. They found that the rate of organisational change is positively correlated with the degree of centralisation and formalisation. Within this however, particular indices were found to be stronger predictions of likely program change than others. The number of occupational specialties in the organisation (one indicator of complexity) was found to be a better predictor of program change in the organisation than professional training or professional activity. Participation in agency-wide decision making was found to be a more powerful index than the degree of hierarchy of authority; and the degree of job codification (formalisation) was a more powerful predictor of program change than role observation (Hage and Aiken, 1980, 177).

In their view then, those organisations are disposed towards the adoption of innovation in the form of program change, which are more complex by means of being multiple disciplinary, which provide a means by which employees are able to participate in organisational goal setting, and in which roles and functions are clearly defined.

Environmental Contingency

Lawrence and Lorsch (1986) and Mintzberg (1979) have identified the environment of the organisation as primary amongst factors upon which organisational functioning is contingent. A considerable body of literature seeks to elucidate the nature of this contingency.

Miles (1980) adopts an approach to organisations which emphasises relationships between sub-units and systems and the external environment. An organisation may be defined, he says, as "a coalition of interest groups, sharing a common resource base, paying homage to a common mission and depending upon a larger context for its legitimacy and development" (Miles, 1980, 5). Interest groups are created by the division of labour and work tasks, but are mutually dependent. They are associated by the requirement to formally adhere to the goals of the organisation as a whole, though the common mission may be displaced by more individual goals. These factors, together with their common dependence upon a limited resource base, and the consequent competition, may create tensions which must be balanced and managed. Finally, an organisation is an open system, which is dependent upon its environment for both legitimacy and needed resources. Organisations confronted with hostile, dynamic, or uncertain environments, must exert considerable energy in managing the relationship.

In dealing specifically with the fourth of these characteristics, the relationship between the organisation and its environment, Miles distinguishes between "contingency" approaches, those which are concerned with how organisations can most closely conform their structures and their processes to the nature and dictates of their confronting environments, and "processes" approaches, which are concerned with the strategic choices required to achieve such a relationship (Miles, 1980, 10).

Environments are distinguished by Miles as either **general**, that is, consisting of whole classes of conditions including technological, legal, political, economic, demographic, ecological and cultural conditions; or **specific**, that is those organisations with which a focal organisation is in direct interaction. The specific environment, Miles also refers to as the "organisation-set" (Miles, 1980, 195).

A major task of complex organisations, is coping with environmental uncertainty since paradoxically, complex organisations are open systems which are constantly adapting to changed environmental circumstances, but also require determinence for the purposes of internal rationality and efficiency. Uncertainty exists in relation to information, causal relationships, organisational preferences, time spans for effective feedback and the assignment of probability to events. Miles, following March and Simon (1958), argues that typically organisations cope with uncertainty, and the reality of limited resources and decision making capability, by means of **bounded rationality**. Bounded rationality refers to the process of satisficing; pursuing satisfactory rather than optimal solutions to problems (March and Simon, 1958, 165).

Hasenfeld focuses upon the specific nature of the relationship between **human services organisations** and their environments (Hasenfeld, 1983, 50ff). A key characteristic of human service organisations is their degree of dependence upon mandating organisations (governments, benefactors, etc.) for a steady flow of resources and support. As such they are extremely vulnerable to external influences and a potential loss of autonomy. The relationship between such an organisation and its environment is thus ambivalent:

> The environment is both a set of resources that the organisation must mobilise to survive and carry out its activities and a set of constraints to which it must adapt when operationalising service objectives. The patterns of service delivery reflect the organisation's strategies to manage its relations with the environment. (Hasenfeld, 1983, 51)

Hasenfeld similarly distinguishes between the **general environment** of a focal organisation; the economic, demographic, cultural, politico-legal and technological conditions which are common to all organisations and are not amenable to change, and the **task environment**; the specific set of organisations with which the organisation exchanges resources and services. The general environment determines the range and type of human service organisations it can sustain. It "differentially supports the emergence of organisations and differentially selects those that will survive on the basis of the fit between their structure and activities and the environment's characteristics" (Hasenfeld, 1983, 51). The conditions relevant to the general environment, and which he identifies as differentially "supporting" organisations, he identifies as **economic, sociodemographic, cultural, political legal** and **technological**.

The **task environment** of the organisation is determined by its **domain choice** which is itself a function of the resources available to it:

> ...the organisation's domain identifies the point at which the organisation is dependent upon inputs from the environment. The composition of that environment, the location within it of capacities, in turn determines upon whom the organisation is dependent. (Hasenfeld, 1983, 60)

The task environment, in Hasenfeld's view, consists of the set of all external groups and organisations controlling access to potential and actual resources required by the focal organisation. It may comprise: (1) providers of fiscal resources; (2) providers of legitimation and authority; (3) providers of clients; (4) providers of complementary services; (5) consumers and (6) competing organisations. Any specific organisation may represent multiples of these categories.

Human service organisations, Hasenfield suggests, seek to enhance their autonomy and secure some control over their task environment. This requires the reduction of dependence upon specific elements within the environment, since such dependence generates uncertainty, increases vulnerability to external pressures and may ultimately jeopardise internal integrity and survival. He identifies four major types of strategies utilised by such organisations to negotiate favourable relations within their environments: those are **authoritative, competitive, cooperative** and **disruptive**. Cooperation strategies, those most used by human service organisations, he further divides into strategies of **contracting, coalition** and **cooptation** (Hasenfeld, 1983, 70).

Carlson in considering the relationship between public school organisations and aspects of their environment, provides two additional important aspects for consideration; the relationship between the organisation and its **clients** (as environment), and the particular circumstances of **public sector** organisations (Carlson, 1964, 262ff).

Carlson argues that a critical dimension of the organisation/environment relationship is the relationship between the organisation and its clients. He differentiates possible relationships between them according to the level of choice which they each may exercise with respect to entering the relationship and constructs a two dimensional matrix accordingly. His interest is in particular with those in the quadrant defined by voluntary participation by both the organisation and its clients; the environment of the **wild** organisation, and contrastingly, that characterised by non-voluntary participation of both; the environment of the **domesticated** organisation. Domesticated organisations, as defined by these relationships, do not have to compete for clients and so have a guaranteed existence. Further they are protected from the ordinary and usual needs of organisations in that while their resourcing may be restricted, it is not tied to performance. Wild organisations, in contrast are not protected in any way and in consequence display much greater adaptive capability.

Carlson argues that domesticated organisations face a major problem in motivation of both organisational members and clients, since neither is participating voluntarily. Adaptive responses of the organisation to this environment are such as to protect valued resources by the segregation of non-preferred clients and the preferential treatment of preferred clients. In institutional settings, this can lead to the isolation of clients within "back wards" and goal displacement where discipline or control are substituted for treatment. Clients similarly may adapt to the non-voluntary nature of the relationship by adaptations which redefine their experience of the organisation, leading similarly to goal displacement.

Defining Environmental Types

Emery and Trist (1965) in a work which has been seminal within the literature, have constructed a model of organisational/environmental relations which seeks to predict the adaptive response of organisations to the uncertainty to which Miles refers. This model identifies types of interdependencies between an organisation (or its component parts), and its environment, as **Internal Dependencies**, **Transactional Interdependence** - either of an input or output type, and **Environmental Interdependencies**.

These relationships are represented graphically as Figure 2.3 below.

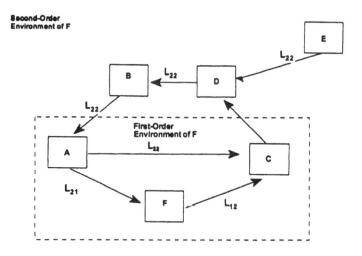

Figure 2.3 Organisational/Environmental Interdependencies
Source: (Miles, 1980, 204)

Internal dependencies are entirely contained within the focal organisation (F) and present at least theoretically, the least threat to the organisation, since conflict within relationships between Departments or other components can usually be resolved by recourse to a mutually recognised source of power and decision making. Nevertheless organisations which are highly differentiated may experience significant conflict over such matters as resource allocation, performance measurement, autonomy and responsibility.

Transactional interdependencies (L_{12}, L_{21}) may be more difficult to manage because of the absence of third party intermediaries, but because they involve mutual linkages and place the parties in close touch with one another, they offer the prospect of mutual problem solving. Conflicts between the focal organisation and those elements of its environment with which it enjoys transactional interdependency, may be resolved by voluntary restrictions upon competition, by cooperation, or by reciprocal arrangements which optimise the interests for both parties.

Of greater threat to the organisation, and likely to tax more severely the adaptive capacity of the organisation, are environmental interdependencies (L_{22}). These are concerned with the linkages which exist between elements of the environment, and which have an indirect impact upon the organisation. It is these relationships which Emery and Trist refer to as the **causal texture** of the organisation. Because the relationship between its causal texture and the organisation is indirect, changes are less likely to be detected or monitored effectively. Yet changes in the causal texture may pose major challenges to the adaptive capacity of the organisation because they are essentially independent of the organisation and less amenable to its influence. The potential impact of the causal texture of the organisation upon it may be anticipated within the Emery and Trist schema according to the position of that environment along a continuum of high to low causal texture. The position on the continuum is determined with reference to the **strength of connectedness** between demands of the environment and the **movement** or rate of change within elements of the environment. Four environmental types are hypothesised which are fixed by their position on these dimensions. These are shown in Table 2.4 together with the predicted organisational response to each setting.

Table 2.4   Environmental Types and Predicted Organisational Responses

Environmental Types	"Causal Texture"		Appropriate Coping Techniques
	Movement	Connectedness	
I	Placid	Random	Tactics
II	Placid	Clustered	Strategies
III	Disturbed	Reactive	Operations
IV	Turbulent	Mutual-Causal	Multilateral agreements

As can be seen from this table, as the environment becomes more turbulent and interconnected, the threat to the organisation increases. Decision making uncertainty increases, and organisational coping responses will move from unilateral, short-term tactics to multi-lateral long-term agreements.

In this framework, **Type I** or **Placid-Randomised Environments** are marked by low degrees of movement and an absence of connectedness. The environment is not formally organised and transactions are largely initiated and controlled by the focal organisation. In these circumstances, the focal organisation can confidently deal unilaterally with elements of the environment in the knowledge that this will not effect other relationships. The principal means of dealing with the environment is tactical.

Type II or **Placid-Clustered Environments** are relatively stable but consist of potentially powerful coalitions. Strategic decision making replaces tactics as key adaptive responses, and problem solving takes on a long term rather than short term focus. Information about the environment and potential coalitions of interests becomes critical for organisational management and survival.

Type III, Disturbed-Reactive Environments, are those occupied by competitor organisations, in which the focal organisation is driven "not only to make sequential choices, but to choose actions that will draw off the other organisations" (Emery and Trist, 1965, 26). The primary adaptive response is described as operational in that it is calculated and tactical, but highly reactive and counter-reactive. It is an environment in which intelligence and information concerning changes in the environment can become critical to the survival of the focal organisation.

The final environmental type, **Type IV** or the **Turbulent Field**, is one in which the rate of change, and the connectedness of the elements of the environment is such that the focal organisation has little influence over the environment. The accelerated rate of change exceeds the capacity of the organisation for prediction and hence control, and changes within the organisation are induced by elements of the environment rather than the organisation itself. The connectedness of the environment is such that changes are seen to come from the "environmental field" rather than individual elements. This is the experience of organisations faced with simultaneous and inter-related changes in relevant technology, market structure and consumer preference.

For Emery and Trist, relevant uncertainty may be reduced through two principal means; the emergence of values which have significance for all members of the field and the development of intra and inter organisational matrices which limit, using value criteria, the character, and by extension the membership of the field (Emery and Trist, 1965, 29). They thus propose that as a pre-requisite of stability, organisations must seek a high level of goal congruence within themselves and a high level of convergence with other organisations.

Miles, referring to the Emery and Trist typology, argues that increasingly the experience of complex organisations is of operating within a turbulent field; in which there is a high level of connectedness and an accelerating rate of unpredictable change. In these circumstances, decision makers are faced with decreasing choices in organisational directions, reduced time frames within which to take decisions, and the likelihood of conflict being generated within internal and transactional inter-dependencies, in Emery and Trist's terms, a high level of "relevant uncertainty" (Miles, 1980, 216).

The Emery and Trist schema has been elaborated upon extensively within the subsequent literature. While the literature suggests further dimensions upon which environments may vary, and more complex classification systems for environmental types, with the exception of the literature concerning environmental ecology, it does not offer a significant conceptual advance upon the Emery and Trist framework. Terreberry (1976) focusing on Emery and Trist's delineation of the 'turbulent field' goes further in arguing for an evolutionary account of organisational environment, akin to that applied to biological science. He describes the turbulent field as one in which the accelerating rate of complexity of interactive effects exceeds the component systems' capacity for prediction, and hence control of the compounding consequence of their actions (Terreberry, 1976, 178). His evolutionary perspective rests on the assertion that: a) contemporary changes in organisational environments are such as to increase the ratio of externally induced change to internally induced change; and b) that other formal organisations are, increasingly, the important component in the environment of any focal organisation. This evolution of organisational environments, he argues is accompanied, among viable systems, by an increase in the system's ability to learn and to perform according to changing contingencies in its environment (Terreberry, 1976, 177).

Motamedi (1976), also utilising the Emery and Trist typology of organisational environments argues for an approach which balances **adaptability**; defined as the system's ability to interact with the environment in such a way as to ensure its survival, with **copability** (the system's internal ability to maintain its identity and to solve the problems created for it by the need to adapt) (Motamedi, 1976, 186). Typically organisations respond to the requirement of adaptability with strategies of **conforming**, **controlling**, **resisting** or **repressing** the problems generated by change (Motamedi, 1976).

Motamedi introduces a further differential in the dimensions of **static** and **dynamic** responses to the adapting and coping tasks. Static responses are those which while accommodating the requirements of the environment or the implications of adaptations do so without systemic modification. The changes may require different positioning, or the development of new products or responses, but do not modify the nature of the focal organisation. Dynamic responses bring about fundamental and systemic modications to the organisation. Constructing a matrix which links the Emery and Trist typology with the critical tasks of adaptation and copability, he identifies the differential nature of required organisational responses to environment types (Motamedi, 1976, 192).

A placid, randomised environment requires adaptability and copability effects which are low. A placid, clustered environment requires adaptability and copability levels which are statically high, but dynamically low in that resources, goals and values are relatively unchanging but are clustered, and so require organisational responses which are differential according to the cluster.

A disturbed reactive environment requires a capacity on the part of the focal organisation to understand and respond to the reactive behaviour of the many social systems which exist within its environment. In consequence, it may be associated with adaptability and copability efforts which are statically low but dynamically high. A turbulent field environment, in which the organisation must respond not to the activities of organisations within its environment, but to the at times unpredictable properties of the environmental field, requires adaptive and coping responses which are both statically and dynamically high.

Katz and Kahn in their elaboration of Emery and Trist's typology of organisational environments propose a matrix based upon the functional relationships which organisations establish with different sectors of the environment and the dimensions which may be applicable to those sections (Katz and Kahn, 1978, 122ff). Following Emery and Trist, they identify the relevant dimensions on which environments may vary as **Stability/Turbulence**, **Uniformity/Diversity** and **Clustered/Randomised**, to which they add a fourth; **Scarcity/Munificence**. "The niggardliness or the abundance of the natural environment", they argue, "is the ultimate determinant of necessary input for any organisation" (Katz and Kahn, 1978, 127). These environmental dimensions may be variously applied to the environmental sectors of: (1) value patterns of the cultural environment; (2) the political structure or pattern of legal norms; (3) the economic environment; (4) the informational and technical environment, and (5) the natural environment of geography, natural resources and climate. Utilising this matrix, they suggest that an organisation's environment may be described by a score in each of the 20 cells created.

A further elaboration of the dimensions identified by Emery and Trist for the classification of organisational types, has been constructed by Jurkovich in his "Core Typology of Organisational Environments" (Jurkovich, 1974). This typology adds a static/non static dimension to the factors already identified associated with environmental complexity, the routineness or predicability of organisational environmental relations, the inter-connectedness of environmental components, and the remoteness, or the extent to which important environmental elements are in direct or indirect contact with the focal organisation; and dynamic dimensions (those factors associated with the rate and predicability of change within key environmental variables).

Amongst the **static** dimensions of environmental variability, **complexity** refers to the number of different organisationally relevant attributes or components. Increased complexity clearly places additional strain upon organisational management and adaptability by placing additional strain upon information processing capacity, by the diversion of organisational resources from production processes and by increasing the probability that errors will be made in the processing and interpretation of information about the environment.

Jurkovich's major contribution to the classification of organisational types lies in his identification that low and high change rates can be dichotomised further into stable and unstable rates. On this dimension it can be seen that environments may be not only changing at variable rates, but may also be unstable in that rate. He identifies four types of environmental movement; low, stable change; high, stable change; low, unstable change; and high, unstable change. Each of these has particular impacts upon the organisation, and in particular upon its capacity for planning.

To the **static** and **dynamic** clusters of elements of organisational environments, Miles suggests a further cluster which he describes as **environmental receptivity**. This set of dimensions, drawn from the work of Howard Aldrich (1972) includes the factors of **resource scarcity, output receptivity**, and **domain choice flexibility**. **Resource scarcity** refers to the availability of resources required by the focal organisation, within the input environment. **Output receptivity** refers to the willingness of elements within the environment to accept the products of the organisation, including by-products and wastes. **Domain choice flexibility** is the capacity of the focal organisation to alter its sphere of activity by expansion or contraction in the face of internal or external factors. Environmental receptivity is in his view, a cluster of dimensions which will serve to modify the influence of the static and dynamic factors. Thus, the relative availability of resources may dramatically effect the influence of the clustering of environmental elements or their rate of change. A high level of domain choice may mitigate the effects of environmental turbulence by making possible the adoption of less turbulent market or spheres of activity.

Miles, bringing together these cluster of dimensions of organisational environments, forms a typology of "Core Environmental Dimensions as Sources of Decision-Making Uncertainty", which is reproduced as Table 2.5.

Table 2.5   Core Environmental Dimensions as Sources of Decision-Making Uncertainty

Source: (Miles, 1980, 222)

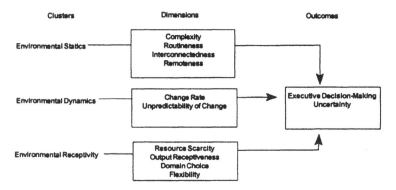

Schmidt (1992a) brings together consideration of organisational structure and strategy in responses to environmental conditions, in his consideration of the differential environments of three types of human service organisations in Israel. In doing so, he has particular regard to the value choices which may govern the domain availability of organisations, and also their resource dependency. He argues that:

> Human Service organisations operate as open systems, adopting strategies aimed to achieve a fit between opportunities and risks in the task environment, the resources and their disposal and the values of their executive leadership. (Schmidt, 1992a, 173)

The strategic choices available to organisations in response to characteristics of their environment are between **cooperation** and **competition**, and between **generalism** and **specialism**. The structural choices as between **formalism** and **informalism** and between **centralisation** and **decentralisation**. These choices are elaborated with reference to environments which are variously turbulent or placid, uncertain or predictable, rich or impoverished, homogenous or heterogenous.

Organisations operating in a turbulent task environment, characterised by uncertainty, few available resources and a relatively hererogenous target population, he suggests, tend to adopt competitive and generalist strategies. Their structures tend to be less formal or rigid and they tend to have decentralised authority. In environments characterised by a higher degree of stability and homogenous target population, relatively high levels of certainty and a steady flow of resources, organisations tend to develop strategies of cooperation and specialism. Their structures are relatively mechanistic and centralised (Schmidt, 1992a, 182).

Schmidt's analysis is highly consistent with that of other writers, but is distinguishable particularly for the emphasis it places upon the determinative effect of resource availability. The amount of resources available or potentially available to the organisation, as well as the demand for the services which the organisation produces, is in his view critical to both the structure and strategy it develops. Organisations faced with uncertainty of resource availability are more likely to choose competitive over cooperative strategies and seek to ensure certainty in resource supply. The relative richness of the resource environment has a direct impact upon structure in that relatively rich environment tend to encourage a focus upon production functions, while relatively poor environments tend to create a focus upon the boundary systems of procurement and disposal. When uncertainty prevails, the most developed subsystems become those concerned with planning, research and development.

Population Ecology Models

The literature thus far examined is concerned to define the dimensions upon which organisational environments vary, and the nature of organisational responses to that variability. An alternative model for examining the nature of the organisation/environment relationship however, is one in which the focus is not upon how the organisation adapts to changed environmental circumstances, but upon how it may fail to adapt.

Hannan and Freeman propose an alternative conceptualisation of organisation/environment relationships in that it is a "population" based rather than an individual organisation based perspective upon the relationship. In so doing, they propose a **population ecology** model which seeks to explain the **selection** of organisational types in response to environmental factors, as well as the **adaptation** of single organisations to those factors. The adaptation perspective, they describe as one which sees "sub-units of organisations, usually managers or dominant coalitions, scan the relevant environment for opportunities and threats, formulate strategic responses and adjust organisational structures appropriately" (Hannan and Freeman, 1978, 132). This, they believe, is inadequate to explain the structural variability amongst organisations. To do so, a perspective is required on the way in which the environment itself selects organisations for survival.

There are, they suggest very substantial constraints upon the capacity of organisations to adapt to changes within their environment. These constraints, which arise from internal structural arrangements as well as environmental constraints they call **inertial pressures**. Specifically they include from an internal perspective; **sunk costs**, availability of **information**, internal **political opposition**, and the organisation's own **history**. Externally, they include; **legal and fiscal** barriers, **information** about the environment, **legitimacy**, and the "**collective rationale**" - the consensus that exists between organisations which may be variably affected by the environment or the organisation's response to it (Hannan and Freeman, 1978, 134).

Their focus is upon aggregates of organisations (populations) rather than members. **Populations**, are defined as classes of organisations that are relatively homogenous in terms of environmental vulnerability. Within populations, organisations are distinguished by their **organisation form** or **blueprint**. Their blueprint consists of the roles or procedures for obtaining and acting on inputs in order to produce an organisational product or response. The organisation's blueprint can be inferred from (1) its formal structure, (2) its pattern of activity, and (3) its normative order (the ways of organising that are defined as right and proper). **Organisational ecology**, as defined, is concerned with the "distribution of organisational forms or blueprints across environmental conditions and the limitations on organisational structure in different environments" (Hannan and Freeman 1978, 140).

Hannan and Freeman argue for the application of a principle of **isomorphism**; that in each distinguishable environmental configuration, one finds, in equilibrium, only that organisational form optimally adapted to the demands of the environment. To support this they propose a resource dependence theory of **competition** between organisational forms, and a **niche** theory, which proposes that social organisations in equilibrium will exhibit structural features that are specialised to select features in the resource environment.

Their competition theory proposes that as long as the resources that sustain organisations are finite and populations have unlimited capacity to expand, competition must ensue. Organisational forms fail to flourish in certain environments because other forms successfully compete with them for resources. In this situation, non optimal forms are selected out (Hannan and Freeman, 1978, 144).

Niche theory addresses itself to the fit between the organisational form of the population and the environmental type. Principally their concern is with the **specialist** and **generalist** organisational form and its applicability to stable and unstable environments (Hannan and Freeman 1978, 151). An organisational population niche is that area in which the population out competes all other populations, and consists of all those combinations of resource levels at which the population can survive and reproduce itself. A distinction may be drawn between whether a population of organisations flourishes because it maximises its exploitation of the environment through specialisation and accepts the risk of having that environment change or because it accepts a lower level of exploitation in return for greater security. This latter form requires a generalism in organisational form, with simultaneous reliance upon a wide variety of resources, and maintenance of excess capacity within internal resources. Excess capacity enhances adaptability in uncertain environments by allowing a capacity for redeployment to emergent needs and for enhanced coordinative capacity.

The success of generalist and specialist strategies is affected also by the time frame of environmental variability. A distinction is made between **finegrained** variation where the typical duration of variations in environmental states are short relative to the lifetime of organisations, and **coarsegrained** variations, in which they are typically longer. Changes in demand for supply of goods and services are typically finegrained, while changes in legal structures are typically coarsegrained. Such changes in the duration of variation are important for the consequences of sub-optimal strategies. Poor choices or responses to finegrained variations are likely to do less damage than when the variation is coarsegrained since the period of decline may exceed the organisational capacity to sustain itself under unfavourable conditions (Hannan and Freeman, 1978, 158).

The Hannan and Freeman approach is significant in two critical respects. It shifts attention away from the specifics of single organisation/environment relations and the strategic responses of such organisations to changes within their environments, to the study of classes or populations of organisations, which are defined by their organisational form. Secondly, it seeks to relate specific aspects of organisational form, that is the level of structural specialism, to the nature of the environmental uncertainty.

Also supporting a population ecology approach, Aldrich argues that the organisational theory literature attributes too much to strategic management of organisations:

> Purpose is deeply embedded in current models of business strategy and organisational transformation, but such veneration of purposeful behaviour has blinded us to other forces: chance and necessity. Population thinking helps

correct this bias by directing our attention to models of random or stochastic change, by noting the tenuous link between intentions and outcomes, and by emphasising the limited degrees of freedom available to many decision-makers. (Aldrich, 1986, 71)

The key to understanding the variability of organisational forms across environmental types, he suggests, is in understanding **constraints**. Organisational opportunity structures are defined by the intersection of unique resource constraints which constitute a viable niche for an organisational form. Whilst some properties of environments are open to manipulation by organisations, others are given or **necessary**.

Aldrich does however concede some place for strategy. The distribution of organisational forms is brought about by (1) the **creation** of new organisations, (2) the **disappearance** of existing organisations and (3) by organisational **transformations**. Transformation takes place in times of **disequilibrium**, and is, in population ecology terms, the occasion of meaningful strategy. To create real advantage to an organisation, strategies must be valuable, ie they must work and lead to a more efficient use of resources or more effective exploitation of a niche; they must be rare, and most of all, they must not be entirely imitable. Organisations which adopt such strategies, by means of entrepreneurship, modification or organisational culture and technological breakthrough, are themselves a source of disequilibrium.

Reconciling Adaptation and Ecology Models

Astley and Van de Ven provide a useful framework for viewing the theoretical perspectives upon the organisation/environment relationship examined above in their identification of four central perspectives upon organisational theory (Astley and van de Ven, 1983). They use these four perspectives to examine critical debates within current organisational theory; three of which concern the organisation/environment relationship.

They identify as critical theoretical perspectives; the **system-structural view**, the **natural selection view**, the **collective-action view**, and the **strategic choice view**. These are arranged diagrammatically in a four quadrant matrix in which their position is determined by whether the unit of concern is at the micro level (individual organisation) or macro level (population and communities of organisations) and whether their orientation is deterministic or voluntaristic. This matrix is reproduced as Table 2.6.

Table 2.6   Perspectives and Debates in Organisational Theory
Source: (Astley and van de Ven, 1983, 247)

MACRO LEVEL (Populations and communities of organisations)	NATURAL SELECTION VIEW	COLLECTIVE-ACTION VIEW
	Schools: Population ecology, industrial economics, economy history.	*Schools:* Human ecology, political economy, pluralism
	Structure: Environmental competition and carrying capacity predefine niches. Industrial structure is economically and technically determined.	*Structure:* Communities or networks of semiautonomous partisan groups that interact to modify or construct their collective environment, rules, options. Organisation is collective-action controlling, liberating, and expanding individual action.
	Change: A natural evolution of environmental variation, selection and retention. The economic context circumscribes the direction and extent of organisational growth.	*Change:* Collective bargaining, conflict, negotiation, and compromise through partisan mutual adjustment.
	Behaviour: Random, natural, or economic, environmental selection.	*Behaviour:* Reasonable, collectively constructed, and politically negotiated orders.
	Manager Role: Inactive. Q3	*Manager Role:* Interactive. Q4
	Q1 SYSTEM-STRUCTURAL VIEW	Q2 STRATEGIC CHOICE VIEW
	Schools: Systems theory, structural functionalism, contingency theory.	*Schools:* Action theory, contemporary decision theory, strategic management.
	Structure: Roles and positions hierarchically arranged to efficiently achieve the function of the system.	*Structure:* People and their relationships organised and socialised to serve the choices and purposes of people in power.
	Change: Divide and integrate roles to adapt subsystems to changes in environment, technology, size, and resource needs.	*Change:* Environment and structure are enacted and embody the meaning of action of people in power.
MICRO LEVEL (Individual organisations)	*Behaviour:* Determined, constrained, and adaptive.	*Behaviour:* Constructed, autonomous, and enacted.
	Manager Role: Reactive.	*Manager Role:* Proactive.
	DETERMINISTIC ORIENTATION	VOLUNTARISTIC ORIENTATION

The **System-Structural** View brings together the diverse schools of structural functionalism and systems theory, through a common deterministic orientation. Organisational behaviour is seen as a response to impersonal mechanisms which act as external constraints. Organisational change is viewed essentially as **adaptation** and occurs as "the product of exogenous shifts in the environment" (Astley and van de Ven 1983, 248).

The **Strategic Choice** View stems from a more voluntaristic perspective, but one nevertheless which has as its concern individual organisations. According to this view, organisations are continuously constructed, sustained and changed by actor's definitions of the situation. Strategic choice is seen as available to organisations with respect to their structure and strategy, and may extend also to their environment. The environment exists not as a set of intractable constraints, but can be changed and manipulated through political negotiations (Astley and van de Ven 1983, 249).

The **Natural Selection** View focuses not upon single organisations, but upon the structural and demographic characteristics of total populations of organisations and industries. It posits that environmental resources are structured in the form of "niches" whose existence and distribution across society are relatively intractable to manipulation by single organisations. There are thus severe limitations to the possibility of strategic choice. Organisations either "fit" into a niche or are "selected out".

The **Collective Action** View in contradistinction suggests that rather than organisations being collectively determined environmentally, they may be guided by collective purpose and choice. In this view "collective survival ... is achieved by collaboration between organisations through the construction of a regulated and controlled social environment that mediates the effects of the natural environment" (Astley and van de Ven 1983, 251). These organisations are viewed as symbiotically interdependent, yet semi-autonomous.

Astley and van de Ven seek to reconcile these competing views of organisations, with reference to the dialectical tension between "structural forms" and "personnel action" perspectives and "part" and "whole" perspectives (Astley and van de Ven 1983, 267). Reciprocal relations exist, they suggest, between structural forms and personnel actions:

> Organisations are...neither purely objective nor purely subjective phenomena. They are objective systems insofar as they exhibit structure that are only partially modifiable through personnel actions, but they are subjective insofar as these structures are populated by individuals who act in unpredictable as well as predictable ways. (Astley and van de Ven, 1983, 266)

Similarly, with respect to part/whole relationships:

> organisations...are regarded as constituent parts of the wider patterns and forces that unfold in society at large...but also capable of partially autonomous action in their own right... (Astley and van de Ven, 1983, 268)

They conclude that to adequately appreciate organisational theory it is necessary attend to the field's basic antithetical nature. The four perspectives they identify are sources of tensions within the field because they are seen as mutually exclusive rather than understandings of phenomena which emerge as the perspective is widened or narrowed.

Framework for the Study

In examining the literature, it can be seen that there is a preponderance of views that change has a high level of prevalence within contemporary complex organisations. Tichy places this within a macro-organisation and global context, relating it to trends in resource availability and the globalisation of economies. Others have dealt more specifically with the extent and frequency of fundamental change within organisations. Motamedi argues that change within organisations should be seen as analogous to that occurring with evolution in the natural world. Evolving organisations will be those which are adaptive to change, and will be characterised by their capacity to process information about their environment.

This study focuses, because of the case at hand, upon contingency theories of organisations; those which argue that the organisation determines its design parameters in response to the characteristics of its environment. In this the study draws in particular upon the work of Lawrence and Lorsch which identified the relationship between an organisation's levels of diversity and integration and its environment; and upon that of Mintzberg, which identifies the contingent variables upon which an organisation's structures and processes might be based. It notes however, that this material is drawn from areas of study other than that of Human Service Organisations. The study seeks to adapt and to modify this theoretical material with reference to that field.

In examining organisational responses to differential environmental conditions, the study notes the centrality within the literature of Emery and Trist's typology of environmental types and the elaborations of various writers upon this schema. It notes the recurrent concern of these writers with organisational responses which are contingent upon changeable or turbulent environments.

Finally, this review has examined the body of literature which focuses upon the prevalence of particular organisational forms in the context of changing environments. This literature is concerned not only with the adaptive responses of individual organisations, but also with the ways in which environments themselves determine the survival of populations of organisational types.

This study addresses itself to the changes which took place within a major institution for the intellectually disabled between 1988 and 1993. In doing so, it assumes that in major part these changes were associated with changes within the environment within which that organisation functioned.

The study seeks to answer three questions, firstly, how did this organisation try, in Tichy's terms to solve the technical production, resource allocation, and cultural problems posed for it by the changes within its environment. Secondly, the study asks: why the organisation responded in the way it did. Thirdly, in a more speculative mode, the study examines the implications of this analysis for theory about organisations and their environments. In doing so, it addresses itself to the place of institutional models of care within the current social and political environment, i.e. what are the implications of contemplating organisational environments for the design of these organisational types?

In order to answer the first of these questions, the study draws upon the theoretical material discussed in Chapter 2 to construct a framework within which the organisational changes might be viewed.

Following Tichy (1983), the framework addresses itself to three core organisational problems: the cultural problem; the political allocation problem; and the technical design problem. It assumes that these problems must be addressed within the political, technical and cultural systems of which the organisation was a part. While acknowledging that some simplification is required for representational reasons, this may be represented as follows:

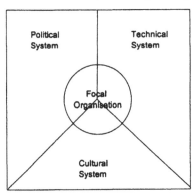

Figure 2.7 Organisation/Environment Systems

This representation acknowledges both the relationship between the elements of the focal organisation and their continuity with and connectedness to elements within the environment. It suggests also a segmentation of the environment, though it should be acknowledged that elements of the environment may operate within more than one system.

In this the study follows closely also, the framework utilised by Katz and Kahn (1978). A comparison of the two frameworks identifies their essential similarity as Table 2.8

Table 2.8   Comparison of Organisational Systems Frameworks

Tichy	Katz and Kahn
Cultural System	Values and Culture
Political System	Political Economic
Technological System	Technological and information related Geographic

The element of geography identified in the Katz and Kahn typology is excluded in this case as it is not clear that this is a relevant contingency variable in this instance. The geographic location of the institution was significant with respect to isolation and the dependance of the local economy upon it, but these factors may be addressed in the context of political and cultural factors.

Within this broad framework the environment of the organisation, both specific and general is described and classified. The dimensions utilises for this description are those identified within the literature. A comparison (Table 2.9) of the major typologies developed within the literature identifies their essential consistency and their derivation from the initial Emery and Trist (1965; 1973) analysis.

Table 2.9 Comparison of Major Typologies of Environmental Dimensions

Emery & Trist	Katz & Kahn	Jurkovitch	Miles
1 Movement	Stability/Turbulence	Movement - Static dynamic	Movement
2 Connectedness	Clustered/Randomised	Connectedness	Connectedness
3	Uniformity/Diversity	Complexity	
4	Scarcity/Munificence		Environmental Receptivity

Consolidating these typologies, a matrix can be developed which links the interrelated systems identified by Tichy, and the four most commonly identified dimensions upon which organisational environments vary. This matrix may be represented as follows:

Table 2.10 Framework for Analysis of Environmental and Organisational Contingency Factors

Environmental Contingency Factors

		Movement	Connectedness	Complexity	Environmental Receptivity
Environmental Organisational System	Cultural System				
	Political System				
	Technical System				

Completion of this matrix provides a detailed description of the environment and its key linkages to aspects of the focal organisation. Further, changes over time may be noted, in order to provide a dynamic representation of changes within the environment and key linkages with the organisation.

Classification of the environment may be achieved utilising the Emery and Trist high/low characterisation and their four component typology of environmental types. This may be used to describe the "causal texture" of the organisation as defined by Emery and Trist, although some modification to the typology may be required in the context of the two additional dimensions within the framework being utilised.

Having described the environment of the formal organisation, the study proceeds to analyse the changes within the organisation brought about by the factors within that environment. In this instance, the framework utilised that of Emery and Trist, whereby the organisation is described in terms of the **internal dependencies, transactional dependencies,** and **environmental dependencies**. Of these, internal dependencies are discussed in terms of the dimensions identified in the literature: **differentiation** and **integration** (Lawrence and Lorsch), and **power distribution**, **structural arrangement**, and **mechanism for coordination** (Mintzberg). As the study is concerned with organisational change, the emphasis is upon the modifications in these relationships over time.

3 Description of the Organisation

The following chapter provides a description of the focal organisation as it operated prior to the commencement of the institutional redevelopment. It does so in terms of the cultural system, the political system and the technological system of the organisation.

The Cultural System

Edgar Schein suggests that organisational culture may be analysed at three levels where level refers to the degree of visibility of the phenomena in question (Schein, 1992, 16ff). These levels, which range from very tangible, overt manifestations, to deeply embedded unconscious assumptions; he describes these as **artefacts, espoused values**, and **basic assumptions** (the essence of culture). Artefacts include all the visible behaviour of the organisation, together with the organisational processes by which such behaviour is made routine. Espoused values reflect the individual values which have assumed a social validity because of their proven utility to the organisation. They reflect what the organisation says it believes or does, rather than what it actually does, and may or may not be congruent with basic assumptions. These last are those beliefs that have become so taken for granted that little variation in them is encountered within a cultural unit. They tend to be neither confronted nor debated because to modify them is to destabilise the cognitive and interpersonal world of organisational members. Rather than modify them, organisations may distort new data by denial, projection or rationalisation.

With these levels of perception in mind, Schein defines organisational culture as:

> ...a pattern of shared basic assumptions that the group has learned as it solved its problems of external adaptation and internal integration, that has worked well enough to be considered valid and, therefore, to be taught to new members as the correct way to perceive, think, and feel in relation to those problems. (Schein, 1992, 12)

This framework provides a useful mechanism through which the culture of Mayday Hills Training Centre may be understood.

Artefacts

Artefacts, as described by Schein, consist of the phenomena which one sees, hears and feels when encountering a new group. They also include the visible behaviour of the group and the organisational processes by which such behaviour is made routine.

While the history of institutional care within Australia may be different in its detail from that of the United States, Mayday Hills Training Centre resembled in its major aspect, the institutions which grew out of the period Wolfensberger (1975) describes as "the indictment". The facility was isolated geographically within the State, but also within the community of Beechworth. The residents seldom went off campus and no more than a few percent were engaged in off campus day activities. The facility was large in scale, having in July 1988, 178 residents, who lived in overcrowded dormitory style accommodation. The largest of these units, Grevillea House, housed 38 profoundly disabled and frail aged people, who remained essentially inactive through most days. The facility itself was located on a large farm which by 1988 had ceased production.

Mayday Hills Hospital was constructed during the 1860s and reflected architecturally the prevailing perceptions of intellectually disabled persons and the appropriate services responses to their needs. Those perceptions remained in force well into the 1980s; a testimony to the strength with which they were held, and the manner in which archaic structures, both physical and programmatic, continued to have pervasive effect upon the services delivered.

> Mayday Hills was absolutely appalling. I have this vignette: I saw someone being hosed down in a courtyard - it was the harshness of it.
>
> (Scovell interview)

The first and most striking artefact of the Mayday Hills Training Centre as it existed in 1988 was its physical environment. The facility was located on a hill above the town of Beechworth. Beechworth is located 190 kms from Melbourne in the North East of Victoria. It is a township rich in history, having been a centre for goldmining activity between 1850 and 1860. Much of its architecture reflects a colonial and Victorian history. It has a stable population of approximately 5,500 and an economy premised upon public service employment in the health sector. Mayday Hills Hospital, which stood high on a hill on the southern outskirts of the town, was in 1987 the major employer.

Albert Road, which climbs the hill and gave access to the centre, ended at the hospital gate, so that it was not travelled unless to visit the hospital. The immediate neighbours of the hospital/training centre, were another large institution, the Ovens and Murray Hospital for the Aged and residential properties which had been purchased over the years by the hospital itself for either staff or client accommodation. While the perimeter wall of the hospital had been largely dismantled in the 1970s, the hospital, and the Training Centre within it remained locationally isolated.

Within the hospital itself, the Training Centre was physically and metaphorically isolated. The residential units which made up the Training Centre were located on the southern and eastern side of the property, at the most extreme distance from the entrance to the hospital and behind and out of sight of the imposing architecture of the administrative centre. The high profile, and clinically more interesting acute psychiatric unit, Kerferd Clinic, was located on the north western boundary. A wide and elegant driveway linked it, the administrative centre and the gateway. Close by were the more recently built geriatric psychiatry wards.

Mayday Hills Hospital itself was made up of a mixture of imposing Victorian architecture, functional buildings constructed towards the end of the 1950s and some modern psychiatric facilities. It stood on 80 hectares of landscaped gardens. The idyllic beauty of the ornamental gardens which covered the major part of the hospital property, masked the drabness and frugality of the training centre units. All accommodation was of a dormitory style. Toileting facilities were primitive and there was little capacity for personal belongings:

> The principal environment that staff had to work with clients in was very very poor and when you have got large dormitories and large communal living areas, and very little access for people in terms of making their own cup of tea and those sorts of things. To be fair to the staff at Mayday, I think that there really wasn't, the environment wasn't conducive to assisting people to move on.
>
> (Lindley interview)

Prior to the separation of the intellectual disability and psychiatric programs within the Health Department in 1967, no distinction had been made between client groups within the Hospital, as it was then titled. There had been one "ward" only which was identified for the care of the intellectually disabled.

This ward, known as the Children's Cottages was used to accommodate profoundly retarded adults, and was located in the Unit which came to be known as Myrtle House.

The Training Centre residential units were identified as "Gatehouse", a Victorian residence and two other houses located at the entrance to the Hospital, "Carinya", "Myrtle", "Grevillea", "Wattle", "Banksia" and "Jarrah". All but the last three of these units were Victorian cottages which were part of the original 1867 construction. They were generally dilapidated, but structurally more sound than the other three, which were temporary buildings constructed after a major fire in 1951.

The "Gatehouse" acted as a program for the development of independent living skills. The program was created by a group of staff who had been frustrated by the lack of attention to the Training Centre by Hospital management. Left to themselves, they developed during 1987 the Gatehouse program, and secured access to a house owned by the Hospital in Graham Avenue, Wangaratta. This was an important initiative, but one which demonstrated the programmatic isolation of the facility. While contemporary practice would suggest that residents would best receive training within integrated rather than segregated environments, this program assumed training within the institution for up to two years. Further, it was providing training in independence for residents who had little prospect of gaining actual independence, since no plans existed for their re-accommodation.

"Carinya" provided accommodation for eight residents who were to all intents and purposes independent. They were elderly people whose disability was at most borderline and whose reason for institutionalisation was not clear. They received and required little in the way of staff support.

"Myrtle House", formerly the Children's Cottages, was one of the most notorious closed wards in the Victorian institutional system. The Unit acted as repository for those residents whose disturbed behaviour was unacceptable elsewhere in the Institution. Its wire grate was constantly locked and its windows boarded up or replaced by perspex. The Unit was putrid with the smell of urine and the faeces which were daubed on the walls. Aggressive and disturbed clients aggravated one another's behaviour, such that staff and residents alike were constantly subject to assault. A senior officer within Community Services Victoria described the response to Myrtle House by the then Minister, the Hon Race Mathews:

> I was informed by one of Matthews' advisors that he found the intellectual disability field one of the most distressing of all, and that the unit that distressed him most of all was Mayday Hills; that he actually (according to this advisor),

cried after leaving Mayday Hills and he described the locked ward at Mayday Hills as being the most distressing unit he had ever seen at all. I was talking about how terrible Caloola was, and this person said no, no, Mayday Hills is worse than that and the Minister was even more upset by that.

(Anonymous Respondent I interview)

"Grevillea House" provided accommodation for the most profoundly disabled of the Institution's residents. Many were bedridden or non-ambulant and required constant nursing care. The overcrowding in the unit and the pressure of constant care meant that residents lived most of their lives in a single room, frequently sleeping, eating and recreating in the one place. Toileting and bathing facilities were primitive:

> The technology around toileting as recent as 1990 in Grevillea, which was where the most severely disabled clients were; they were basically lined up and commoded communally in the same room that they ate, the same room that they spent their leisure time. Those clients in 1990 were in hospital gowns, with back openings and only done up at the neck and no underwear because that made life easier for the staff in order to be able to clean the incontinence. So the technology had not even gone as far as recognising that these clients should have been dressed in everyday clothes and they should be toileted with some dignity and pride.

(Hind interview)

"Wattle House" and "Banksia House" were located in the "temporary" buildings and provided accommodation for mainly middle-aged to elderly women. Very little day activity was available, and most time was spent sitting in a large lounge area watching television. "Jarrah House" was also located in a temporary building. Its residents were middle-aged men, many of whom had difficult behaviours. A number were heavily medicated and secluded at night to avoid them doing damage to the premises.

The division of labour within the hospital was a critical artefact of the organisation's culture. The structure of the organisation was determined by occupation and by function. Rigid separations existed between administration, the nursing division, allied heath and non-direct care. Each had separate management and communications took place formally. Unlike many institutions at this time, industrial power was held by the nursing division rather than by non-direct care staff, and the industrial organisation represented an organisation itself within the hospital structure. In the face of absent administrative leadership, and weak and ineffective management through nursing administration, the union sub-branch became the effective means by which communication took place and direction was given.

The relative status of organisational units, and their attendant occupational groups was reflected in employment practices within the hospital. Minimum staffing agreements were established for nursing and direct care and these were rigidly enforced by management and the union, irrespective of actual work demands within units. Non-direct care positions were also filled but with less priority. Allied Health positions were accorded the lowest priority. Staffing positions had been progressively reduced over time. Those positions which existed were seldom fully staffed, and this group of employees was seldom consulted on developments within the Centre. In its assessment of day program provision within its institutions in 1978, Community Services Victoria concluded that Mayday Hills Training Centre provided one of the lowest levels of program activity of any institution. These day activities were provided intermittently by the "occupational therapy" department, which was staffed by a single occupational therapist and a small group of unqualified "craft supervisors".

A compelling artefact of the organisational culture was the industrial apparatus which had developed. As indicated above, the union sub-branch provided the effective leadership within the institution which it did with aggression and a contempt for management. Further, the union had gathered to itself legitimacy as the body which spoke on behalf of client issues. Demands made by the sub-branch were frequently couched in terms of supporting quality client care, and were believed by union members to be so.

> I think the union stuff was based on a whole lot of power base and anger. I think what they were after was control over what they saw in the Health Department was a fairly vicious uncaring regime. ID staff never had a sense that anybody cared about them or their client group or that any money was put into it, and so they were depressed, depressed or angry. They were either depressed and doing next to nothing with their client group or very angry and very politically motivated in the union.
>
> (Hind interview)

The sub-branch, ably led locally and aligned factionally with the right wing leadership of the union's state branch, negotiated fixed staffing agreements for each work unit within the hospital, generous rostering arrangements, and strict demarcations between levels of staffing positions as well as occupational groups. A cleaner could not do the work of a "heavy duty cleaner" whose duties were prescribed as including cleaning above shoulder height. In a crisis, an artisan or food and domestic services worker could not come to the assistance of a nurse. Roles were reflected strictly in colour and cut of uniform.

The industrial history of the institution was legend. The story was told that the conditions of the employees were hard won by the union and vigilance was required if they were to be retained. This contributed to a fierce loyalty to the union, which was tinged with more than a little fear. At times of industrial dispute, solidarity was policed with threats to the families of waverers and the slashing of car tyres. Steve Menzie described the power of the union in the institution:

> There was the union based power, and it was very militant really. A good union, but it was run by people who could only see the union's point of view... there's no doubt that the union to a large degree were running the place.
>
> (Menzie interview)

Espoused Values

The espoused values of the Mayday Hills Training Centre in 1988 are difficult to glean from official publications, since the Centre was near completely integrated with the psychiatric hospital. In order to identify the stated values of the organisation, it is necessary to draw upon documentation concerning the hospital as a whole.

The Health Services Agreement established for the total Mayday Hills Hospital for the 1988/89 year represents the final point at which specific objectives were established for the Training Centre. The Agreement, for the first time acknowledged that the context within which the Training Centre operated was established through the Community Services Department and summarised the policy context of the Training Centre in terms of the responsibilities set out in the Community Welfare Services Act and the Intellectually Disabled Persons Services Act. It summarised these as follows:

- to facilitate the development of community services and the administration of community service programs at the regional and local level in cooperation and conjunction with government departments, municipalities, non-government organisations and community groups;
- to ensure that community and other services are fully accessible to all persons and that information concerning all services is readily available by cooperation with government departments, municipalities, non-government organisations and community groups;

- to promote coordination of community services planning and delivery through cooperating with providers and consumers of community services and to encourage voluntary participation, self-help and consumer involvement in the planning development and carrying out of community services;
- to assist communities to identify and to meet the continuing and emerging needs of families and individuals within their communities;
- to establish, maintain and develop consultative and cooperative arrangements which promote the coordination of social resources in Victoria in conjunction with government agencies, municipalities, non-government organisations and community groups;
- to integrate social planning with economic and physical planning in conjunction with other government agencies; and
- to promote, assist and encourage community consultation in social resource planning.

> Health Service Agreement 1989/90
> Beechworth Corporation
> (Mayday Hills Hospital)

This summary reflected the broad provisions of the *Community Welfare Services Act* of the day, and addressed issues of service planning and social planning which were prominent goals of the community services department prior to its substantial expansion in 1985 to form Community Services Victoria. While not in conflict with them, this summary did not reflect the very specific objectives and principles of the *Intellectually Disabled Persons Services Act*, which had been proclaimed the year before.

The specific objectives proposed for the Training Centre, within the Agreement in part reflected the principles of the Act, but were very operational, and did not espouse a particular value stance. In particular the following objectives were significant:

- develop plans and costings to transfer Myrtle House program to a less restrictive and more attractive environment (objective 2.1);
- development of a plan to reassess living standards, accommodation and day activities of on campus based residents (objective 2.5);
- extend community based residential program for both on and off campus clients (objective 2.6); and
- to establish a regional approach to service provision and development. (Objective 2.13).

> Health Service Agreement 1989/90
> Beechworth Corporation
> (Mayday Hills Hospital)

Figure 3.1   A photo taken in the early 1970s from the rear of hospital, looking from the "back wards" of Myrtle House and Grevillea towards the impressive mid-Victorian architecture of the administration block

These objectives were very measured and designed to reflect the resources, level of flexibility and also the level of commitment of the institution to normalisation values. They proposed to "develop plans" for Myrtle House and the "assessment" of accommodation and day programs, extend in unspecified ways community housing, and "develop a regional approach" to service development. While they failed to expose a defined value position, they nevertheless reflected one.

The staff orientation handbook for the institution gave some expression to the goals of the institution, again without espousal of normalisation values:

> A fine tradition of care for the people who are the responsibility of the institution has been built up over the years by our staff... Our number one goal must be to provide the finest possible standard of care consistent with our resources and to continually seek ways of bringing improvement to the conditions of our patients and residents... In the foreseeable future this institution will continue in the tradition of the past 122 years. It will be a considerable residential agency as well as the major resource for psychiatric and intellectual disability services in the region. (Staff Handbook, Mayday Hills Psychiatric Hospital and Intellectual Disability Centre, Beechworth, July 1989)

Basic Assumptions

The artefacts of the organisation's culture, its physical aspects, its mode of operation, the relationships between its staff, together with the absence of espoused values, give an indication of the basic assumptions of the organisation. While such assumptions were not uniformly held within the institution, it is possible to identify those which were most potent in determining the life of the organisation. These assumptions were: that intellectually disabled clients are incapable of self-care; that Mayday Hills Training Centre existed to meet the needs of staff and would always remain unchanged; and that the interests of employees would always be in conflict with those of management.

It was a deeply held conviction amongst the staff of the institution that intellectually disabled clients were incapable of living in other than very dependent ways. This was reinforced by the fact that the largest number of residents of the Training Centre had remained there, in unchanged circumstances for in excess of 30 years. Unlike the psychiatric patients of the hospital, particularly those within the Acute Unit, they did not "recover" and their conditions were untreatable.

In keeping with this assumption, few attempts were made to improve the capacity of clients to care for themselves. Developmental programs were not a priority for management or for the majority of staff, since it was assumed that these could not be effective. Behavioural difficulties with residents were managed by means of isolation or medication, both of which tended to reduce client capacity for self-management, rather than increase it.

Many of the staff of the institution had worked at Mayday Hills for most of their working lives. For many, employment there had been generational, with parents and even grandparents having worked there previously. It is not surprising then, that for many, the institution was a fixture and they could not imagine it not continuing:

> ... the place is here for the benefit of the people of Beechworth as a place of employment and it has got a long history of that and many of the people who have worked there as psych nurses or MRNs did so because... it meant that they didn't have to leave Beechworth. It was ideal to just walk up the hill and get your training, get paid while you get trained.
>
> (Lindley interview)

More than this however, it was widely believed, that not only would the institution continue, it would do so unchanged:

> ... the small town syndrome worked. Mayday Hills clothed and fed a lot of families as did some of the other large institutions, and I think that people felt the sense of security that it was there, it was always going to be there... I think when the change was starting people just brushed it off... I think people didn't believe it because they didn't want to believe it. They were very much attached. It was their workplace, they were very much attached to a lot of clients there and it was more like home.
>
> (Menzie interview)

It was a view which was in some respects at odds with the actual experience of the organisation, since while much remained unchanged between 1867 and 1987, there was much which had changed within the memory of the staff concerned. The introduction of psychotropic medication had, during the 1950s, a dramatic impact upon the psychiatric services which were provided within the wider hospital, replacing much of the mechanical restraint previously utilised and making possible the discharge of many patients. Many staff were able to recall the discontinuation of the farm and the consequent change in activity level amongst residents. Most were able to recall the height of admissions during the 1960s when the total population of the hospital exceeded

1,000, and the impact of restricting admissions which reduced the population by 50 percent over the ensuing decade.

The assumption was however, entirely consistent with the day to day experience of most staff whose work routine remained extremely constant. Each day, direct care staff would provide care in the same setting to the same clients. They seldom had contact with other agencies or personnel, and seldom had reason to leave the campus. Their responsibility was to ensure that when they ceased duty at the end of their 12 hour shift, the unit was in the same condition in which they found it when they commenced, that clients were safe, and that nothing untoward had occurred. Their work life was one which promoted an assumption of inertia.

Not only was the institution assumed to be a continuing fixture, its assumed role was to provide for the needs of staff and more generally for the community of Beechworth. Beechworth was a public service town which had been reliant for generations upon the employment within its health institutions:

> It seemed to me it was very much seeing the place as employment for people in the town and one of the assumptions would be that it would be for the benefit of the staff rather than for the benefit of the people who lived there all their lives. And I think that was borne out through anytime you would walk into any of the units, seeing staff sitting around in the tea room, or in the staff room, not interacting with clients on the ward and the union wanting to stop any change to the twelve hour shift that was up there. And it couldn't have been good for the clients but was just there for the benefit of the staff.
>
> (Lindley interview)

Jim Kesselschmidt, Manager of Direct Care in the Training Centre in its last year described what he saw as the dynamic which created this situation:

> ... when you stay at one place all of the time, but particularly when everyone is at the one place, you develop unusual cultures. When you are cut off, when you're up on a hill surrounded by a wall, you develop your own sub-culture and over time part of that sub-culture is the reason for being there. I think it is highlighted in ... when it is more efficient for staff to have a break at a certain time, and therefore client meals are organised around that. So that you get the perverse situation of clients having to have their main evening meal at 4 or 5 o'clock in the evening and really not much until breakfast the next day, so staff can get their break at a reasonable hour... The whole rhythms of an institution are there; ultimately the needs of staff became superordinate, the needs of clients became sub-ordinate.
>
> (Kesselschmidt interview)

A third basic assumption concerned the essential antagonism between the interests of staff and senior management of the Department of which they were part. In early 1988 effective local management of Mayday Hills Hospital was by the industrial body representing staff. The nominal management openly sought approval for the most basic decisions from the sub-branch of the union. The union maintained an office on the campus, and up to three staff and at a time were released from duties, on full pay, to pursue union duties. Nevertheless, discussions between management and the workforce took place with an air of confrontation, reflecting an underlying assumption that, despite weak local management and an essential collusion concerning the preservation of the institution, the relationship between employees and the department was inevitably adversarial.

It was the belief of the workforce that the favourable conditions it enjoyed had been won for it by militant industrial action. Any management initiative was viewed with suspicion, and in principle resisted.

The Political System

The political system of Mayday Hills Training Centre may be considered in terms of the **interests** represented within organisations, the **conflicts** which arose between those interests, and the **sources of power** which were available to them. This framework has been developed by Morgan (1986) to elucidate the metaphor of organisations as political systems.

Under this metaphor, organisations are seen as intrinsically political. They are viewed as loose networks of people with divergent interests, who gather together for reasons of expediency. Viewed in this way, organisational life is concerned with the ways in which interests seek to optimise their goals. Organisational analysis is concerned with mapping these interests, identifying their points of potential conflict as well as coalition, and understanding the sources of power which might be utilised by them to resolve conflicts.

In the Morgan framework **interests** are a complex set of predispositions, embracing goals, values, desires, expectations and other orientations and inclinations that lead a person to act in one way rather than another (Morgan, 1986, 149). Interests are understood in terms of three interconnecting domains; organisational task, career, and personal life. Such domains operate for each individual, and the political content of organisations is increased as a function of the multiple individuals and multiple interests represented in an organisation. Conflict arises where these interests collide.

Interests

Within Mayday Hills Training Centre prior to the redevelopment, three sets of interests may be identified: staff, union and management (including nursing administration). These categories were in some senses distinct, but were linked by overlapping membership, and a convergence of goals. Within the staff category, further distinctions may be made between nursing staff, non-direct care staff, and allied health staff, whose task interests were dissimilar. They shared however, a high level of convergence with respect to career interests.

The task interests of the staff of Mayday Hills Training Centre were defined by the daily routine of the institution. These routines provided an essentially static and predictable framework to the everyday life residents. The tasks of direct care staff included toileting, feeding and supervising residents. It did not include training or developmental activity, which was generally outside the skills and training of the staff employed. Community services program adviser, Rob Macdonald, described the absence of program activity within the institution at the time of his commencement there in 1988:

> In the two years I worked there, I did not see one staff member at any time, involved with delivering a program, or doing training in a unit.
>
> (Macdonald interview)

Non-direct care staff similarly worked to routines within the institution which were invariable. Their status within the organisation was lower than that of direct care staff because their level of skill was considered lower and they were more easily replaced. Allied health staff were small in number, and entirely lacked political power. They consisted of a small number of professional (usually occupational therapy) staff and a group of unqualified "craft supervisors". No social workers were employed. They had little in the way of resources available to them, and in times of financial stringency, were the first group to suffer through reductions in resources or the non-replacement of staff.

Management consisted of senior administrative staff and nursing administration staff. Administration staff were responsible for the management of the resources of the institution and were very powerful in their ability to provide or withhold resources. This group directly supervised non-direct care. Until formal separation from the psychiatric hospital in December 1991 there was not a separation of administration of the two facilities. While there were separate facilities prior to this time, the workforce was not clearly separate and staff could be rostered across either facility. There was a distinct nursing administration for the Training Centre from 1988 but this was, until 1991 subservient to nursing administration for the psychiatric hospital.

The distinction between nursing administration and direct care staff was not a strong one:

> ... most of the nursing administration had come up through the ranks themselves and they weren't very removed from being unit staff themselves... I don't think there was a great deal of drive from nursing administration but that was also about knowledge and being resourced too, and being exposed to another way of doing things. I think there wasn't a lot of that in the period of time before we got up there and probably the time when we were up there.
>
> (Lindley interview)

The major industrial body operating in the institution was HEF(2). This powerful public sector union had coverage of all public psychiatry and intellectual disability services and institutions. It had aggressively asserted the entitlements of its members at the statewide level and had at Mayday Hills established a position of pre-eminence over management. Its interests were defined in terms of the protection and extension of the rights of its members, but it frequently took the view at Mayday Hills, that it represented also the interests of clients. Many of the union's arguments for additional resources or benefits for its members were couched in terms of client interests. The argument concerning minimum statfing levels on residential units was framed in terms of maintaining adequate levels of care. (Industrial Agreement: Department of Labour/Hospitals Employees Federation No 2 Branch/Health Department Victoria/Community Services Victoria, February 1989).

The three interest groups identified however, had convergent career interests, since this was intimately related to the continuation of the institution. The majority of staff, irrespective of position, were long term residents within the region. They were not career bureaucrats or professionals in the sense of people who might be prepared to relocate to other areas to further their careers or preserve their employment. The maintenance of the institution gave them stability of employment in the location of their choice, and whatever other differences existed or arose, were ultimately subsidiary to this over-arching common interest. This developed over time, into an informal alliance between all parts of the institution to preserve the status quo. Attempts by the central office of the Health Department to reduce expenditure at Mayday Hills were responded to by the industrial organisation rather than local management. For its part, local management tended to promote the extension of the power of the union:

> ... there were lots of mini power plays going on but staff would be critical of management and would see them as outsiders at certain points in time but at other times when it suited them they would align themselves in fact with management within the hospital against the regional office, or against our unit for example.
>
> (Lindley interview)

Steven Menzie, a long term employee of the institution, was conscious of this relationship, but also aware of some of the external forces which would affect it:

> I think what seemed to be happening was that there was collusion between administration and the union and it looked as though they were working together quite nicely. But there was other stuff slowly happening, and changes were happening and I think probably about the mid 80s there was certainly a lot happening and was just landing on the doorstep, so to speak, and some of us were saying, well hang on!
>
> (Menzie interview)

The extra-mural interests of the parties are beyond the scope of this study as the methodology does not provide a means by which this might be assessed. It can be noted however, that there was strong anecdotal evidence that the "two on - two off" rostering system created a situation in which many staff were able to maintain multiple forms of employment. This system involved the rostering of staff on two consecutive days for twelve hour shifts, with a subsequent two day break. It was subject to abuse as staff could arrange "sick leave" for one of these rostered days, and have a colleague work that day at penalty rates. They could then reciprocate the arrangement. The roster concentrated work over a small number of days in the week, allowing the opportunity for other employment, particularly in rural or farming industries. This created a lifestyle interest in maintaining both the institution and the forms of employment it involved, and increased the resistance to change.

Conflict

Conflict between the interests which have been identified occurred on a regular basis, but did so within the limits prescribed by the over-arching common interest in preserving the facility, and in the case of industrial disputes had a ritualistic quality. On a regular basis the union would raise a matter of local dispute and on occasion would bring strike action. This had the effect of reinforcing union authority as disputes were invariably resolved in its favour (Jones interview). Should a more serious dispute arise, as it did in February 1989, the ultimate recourse was to the power of the union at the State level, and its capacity to bring strike action in every institution in the State.

Mr David Jones, the first chief executive officer for psychiatric services in the region, and responsible for the institution, described the relationship between local management and the union at the time of his appointment in 1988:

> I think I would characterise it as a balanced interaction between a management and union who were stuck with each other and who had a joint interest in perpetuating the organisation; therefore getting along with each other; therefore making all kinds of compromises. The technology of management was without strategy. It was based upon day to day management of functions. There were assumptions by management and other people that the organisation would continue in perpetuity. There was very little need to adopt strategies for effective resource management. I think this is also illustrated by the arrangements for the large number of artisan staff; which numbered over 200. There was a lot of make-work jobs done by artisan staff where they patched up old facilities in which there was absolutely no provision of care, and where they beautified the garden outside the front door where very few intellectually disabled clients ever went.
>
> (Jones interview)

Conflict also arose when the small number of staff who were trained in intellectual disability nursing sought to implement programs for clients. This was not supported by the administration of the institution which saw this as an unnecessary use of resources. It was responded to by the denial of access to resources such as vehicles, without which the programs could not be delivered.

> ... the mentality of the day was money went to the gardens... I mean the gardens were beautiful, and money went to those sorts of things - the doing up of the hall, we never got a red cent for the wards and things like that... nothing for the person, not a bit of partitioning... and you look around the grounds, and what was in the grounds, and the hall and the painting in the office space, and they always had the best of it and we didn't have any, and the ward suffered, and I think that alone was pretty awful.
>
> (Menzie interview)

The Technological System

The technology of an organisation may be described as the procedures utilised by that organisation to produce its goods or services. In the case of human services organisations, the technological system must take particular note of the complexities associated with human behaviour. Hasenfeld, seeking to capture the specifics of these organisational settings describes human service technology as:

> a set of institutional procedures aimed at changing the physical, psychological, social or cultural attributes of people in order to transform them from a given status to a new prescribed status. (Hasenfeld, 1983, 111)

Hasenfeld has developed a table of components of human service technologies which provide a useful means of describing the technological system of Mayday Hills Training Centre, and of indicating the nature of its changes over time. This table is reproduced as Table 3.3.

The framework differentiates as components of human service technologies the following: **Client attributes**, are the range of attributes considered by the organisation to be relevant to its functions (including their extensiveness), their degree of variability and their stability. **Knowledge technology** includes both the techniques of intervention and their believed completeness in addressing the client's service requirements. The knowledge component may be classified as **environmental** in that they seek to manipulate the biological or physiological attributes of clients; **cognitive**, seeking to manipulate the perception or cognition of clients, or **affective**, manipulating client affects or feelings.

Table 3.2   Summary of the Components of Human Service Technologies

Source: (Hasenfeld, 1983, 133)

CLIENT ATTRIBUTES	KNOWLEDGE	INTERACTION	CLIENT CONTROL	OPERATIONS
a. Interest in client biography b. Client variability c. Client stability	a. Techniques of intervention: • Environmental • Biophysical • Cognitive • Affective b. Cause-effect relations	a. Medium • Equipment • Information • Interpersonal b. Pattern: • Activity-passivity • Guidance-cooperation • Mutual participation c. Communication net	a. Reinforcement mediation b. Overtness of control	a. Task inter-dependence • Independent • Sequential • Reciprocal • Team

Interaction technology within the framework refers to the **medium** of intervention, including the use of equipment, information processing and/or interpersonal relations, the **patterns of interaction** including whether the exchanges between the intervener and the client may be described as activity/ passivity, guidance/cooperation or mutual participation, and the **communication pattern**; whether communication typically takes place on an individual to individual, individual to collective, or collective to collective basis. **Client control** refers to whether the techniques utilised by the organisation to prevent the undermining of intervention, are overt or indirect, and whether they are directly administered by staff. **Operational technology** refers to the connectedness between aspects of the service production. Tasks may be fully dependent, sequentially related, reciprocal or contingent upon one another, or may be in a team relationship. This last indicates a reciprocal interdependence and a requirement to work together.

These attributes of technology must be placed within the context of the purpose for which the organisation utilises them; the desired product or projected impact of the organisation's output. In this Hasenfeld distinguishes between **people processing** technologies, **people sustaining** technologies, and **people changing** technologies (Hasenfeld, 1983, 134ff).

People processing technologies are concerned with the conferring upon clients of a particular social label, position or status, in order to bring about a particular response to them by social groups or organisations. They are based upon systems of client classification and require minimal staff/client interaction. People sustaining technologies aim to prevent, arrest or delay deterioration of a person's well being or social status by removing or minimising the effects of conditions that threaten that well being or by compensating for deficits in personal resources. They have as an underlying assumption that clients have little potential for change that will improve their social functioning. Their core activities are custodial care and sustentation and are characterised by staff-client interactions of an activity-passivity type. People changing technologies are concerned to directly alter client biophysical, psychological or social attributes in order to improve well being. This is achieved by removing or reducing deficiencies, barriers or incapacities or by the enhancement of personal capacities. They assume that the client has a significant capacity for change and is amenable to it. They require intensive and extensive relationships between staff and clients.

The Technological System of Mayday Hills Training Centre

The technological system of the Training Centre is described using the Hasenfeld framework as it provides a useful means of providing an overview.

Within the context of Mayday Hills Training Centre clients were viewed in a static way. While extensive client histories were maintained, in keeping with medical frame of reference of the hospital, these were not significantly utilised (Lindley interview). As the majority of clients of the service were long term residents, or had long term residence within other training centres, the case histories were frequently extensive. Despite this, they were viewed within the institution as having very little variability in their requirements for care, and as requiring little change in their care over time, because of their presumed stability of condition. Programs were not individualised, and the routine of each day was consistent for all residents of each residential unit, and from day to day. Thus the data concerning individuals which were collected on a day to day basis, consistent with the organisational requirements of the Health system, were not significantly utilised in determining client care, and were largely immaterial to the technology of care. Julie Hind, Regional Coordinator for Intellectual Disability Services and later Chief Executive Officer of the Training Centre described the essentially static nature of the care available:

The care was based on a very old technology of custodial care, to a level which shocked me because the technology I understood was very different - around individualised working with clients, quality of life, doing developmental programming and the sense that everybody was able to learn or grow and develop. The technology in there was to leave them be. They controlled clients either through heavy doses of medication or through bribery with cigarettes, so that we had many people who were addicted to tobacco. They managed them by locking doors or locking up those people who had less severe disabilities but higher challenging behaviours. Basically the world wasn't allowed into Mayday and Mayday didn't go out to the world.

(Hind interview)

The knowledge utilised by the institution in the care of its clients was a combination of biophysical and environmental. The organisational history of the Training Centre was within the psychiatric system, and the majority of direct care staff were trained in psychiatric nursing, with its heavy emphasis upon drug treatment. Few were trained specifically in mental retardation nursing, which has a strong behavioural orientation. This bias towards biomedical intervention may be seen in the 1987 survey of the use of chemical restraint within intellectual disability institutions (Community Services Victoria, 1987). This indicated that the highest usage was at Mayday Hills and Aradale, the two institutions which had continued to operate within psychiatric services. One of the implications of the use of high levels of medication, and of chemical restraint was that the likelihood of behavioural modification or training related interventions being successful, was significantly reduced. Clients whose cognitive functioning was reduced by excessive exposure to medication could not effectively be trained by behavioural means.

Jim Kesselschmidt described the difficulties of confronting the dependencies upon medication for client control:

... one of the first things that we asked for [was] the name of each client, what medication they were on, now, six months before and twelve months before that and then went individually to each unit manager and asked them why they were on that medication... And of course they were on major tranquillisers... and when we talk about restraint, seclusion and aversive therapy in terms of client rights; they were being chemically restrained out of their brains. I remember one of the classic reasons was, I said why is this client on X [medication] for night time, and I was told "Oh Jim this guy's got nocturnal restlessness". I said "well have you tried Milo or Horlicks, you know let's do a progression, is it documented anywhere?..." for a lot of people it was like releasing them into another world.

(Kesselschmidt interview)

The utilisation of medication aside, the principal means of intervention within the institution was environmental. The training centre sought to provide a safe and secure environment within which the basic needs of clients for shelter, nourishment and safety were met. Little in the way of developmental programing was provided, since it was not believed the clients could attain increased skill levels, or would have the opportunity to practise them. The 1988 survey of levels of day programs provided to training centre clients indicated the institution had amongst the lowest levels of programming available in the State (Community Services Victoria, 1988). David Jones described the technology of care in the institution in 1988:

> The technology of care in the Training Centre was undeveloped in relation to the directions that care technology was taking elsewhere within the State system. The principal means of care was congregate accommodation; the product of long term institutional arrangements. There was very limited input of allied health professions; very limited rehabilitation programs. Principally it was nurse driven, with an emphasis on maintenance of ward order, so the technology bore very little resemblance to normalisation, least restrictive form of care and merging with the community.
>
> (Jones interview)

Steve Menzie, worked in the Training Centre for twenty-five years, and was a unit manger at the time of its closure. He described the technology of care of the facility:

> ... the model of care was based on custodial care. It was a matter of you went in each day and you did the very basic things; you cleaned floors, you got people up and dressed and bathed and all that sort of thing, and you fed them. And really that was the model. There was very little, there was no occupational therapy, there was basically no community access... So it was very, very basic and we just didn't have any resources there and because of the large numbers and the very low staff ratios, everything you did was custodial care.
>
> (Menzie interview)

It was believed within the institution that these interventions were causative of client responses. As changed behaviour or improvement in level of functioning was not anticipated, effective client care was believed to be completely provided for by benign containment and the utilisation of medication to control the extremes of behaviour.

Interaction as it took place within the training centre was interpersonal, activity-passivity based, and largely entailed communication between individual staff members and clients as a collectivity.

The principal mechanism for the provision of care within the institution was through the agency of the direct care staff member. This staff member was employed to work in the residential units of the institution; to provide basic nursing care, to supervise meals, to dispense medication and generally to supervise the lives of the residents. Generally these staff worked alone or in small numbers, on rostered shifts within the institution. As such they related to groups of clients of between 28 and 35. Apart from limited participation in housekeeping and personal hygiene tasks, clients were essentially passive. Communication took place for the most part from the carer to the client as a group, though some individual communication was required.

Clients were controlled by direct rather than indirect means. Their daily routine, their medication, their meals and their clothing, were directly controlled by their carers. Some indirect control was exercised through the use of incentives such as access to cigarettes, to reinforce or modify behaviour. This needs to be understood however, in the context of an environment which was completely in the overt control of the carers.

It can be seen from this analysis that the purpose of the technology utilised by Mayday Hills Training Centre was predominantly "people sustaining" as described by Hasenfeld. It sought to ensure that the incapacities of clients, which were not seen to be amenable to change, had a reduced impact upon their physical well being. The nature of the care then was essentially custodial or directed towards ensuring that basic living requirements were met. Staff/client contact which existed, assumed that staff would perform active roles in caring for clients, but that clients themselves would be essentially passive (Menzie interview).

The operations technology of the institution was a function of the hierarchial administrative and occupational structure, and the location of service delivery on a single site. Occupational and status boundaries were rigorously enforced, such that there was very little exchange between staff performing different functions. This meant that the organisation tended towards an independent mode of task interdependencies, i.e. tasks were performed independently. Nursing staff were not dependent upon artisan or occupational therapy staff in order to perform their basic nursing duties. Coordination was provided however, by virtue of the unchanging routines of everyday institutional life. The institution provided "whole of life care". The majority of client needs were met on campus, and most personal care needs were met by unit nursing staff. At certain times during the day, particular duties were to be performed, and both staff and residents moved according to these familiar rhythms. While care tasks then were not explicitly related, the all encompassing nature of the institutional environment, ensured a high level of integration of tasks.

Summary

The dominant purpose of the technology of Mayday Hills was people sustaining. This reflected the underlying assumption of the organisation that residents were incapable of self care. Utilising Hasenfield's summary of components of human service technologies (Table 3.2), the technology of the training centre is summarised as follows:

Table 3.3 Summary of the Components of the Mayday Hills Training Centre Technology (1987)

Client Attributes	Knowledge	Interaction	Client Control	Operations
• clients viewed as static • client histories as official record rather than care plan • clients viewed collectively rather than individually	• bio-physical intervention through medication • environmental intervention through provision of a safe environment	• interpersonal - reliant upon staff/client interaction • activity - passivity. Clients as passive recipients of care • communication from individual staff member to groups of clients	• control exerted directly by carers	• independent task dependence reflecting rigid occupational hierarchies • coordination achieved through the "whole of life care" on a single site

As can be seen from this table, the specifics of the organisation's technology of care develop logically from the cultural assumption about client capacities. Where clients are not expected to change, develop, or move on, relevant knowledge concerns the means of providing secure care for them and of maintaining their behaviour within the limits of tolerance of the care system. Having little capacity for self care, they are the passive recipients of the care of others, and they exert little influence over their own living circumstances or futures. They can be appropriately dealt with as a group, since their principal need, that for sustenance, is one they share with their peers. It is not an individualistic one such as the realisation of their personal potential, aspirations or happiness. The provision of care at a single location ensured an all-encompassing environment in which residents had limited social networks.

The basic underlying assumptions which formed the core elements of the culture of the organisation are summarised in figure 3.4 below:

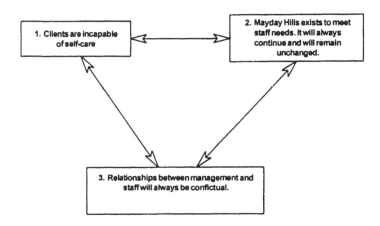

Figure 3.4 Core Elements of the Culture of Mayday Hills Training Centre (1987)

The assumptions of client incapacity and organisational inertia directly reinforced each other. Because clients were incapable of independence, the organisation's role would continue unchanged, as a means of providing for them.   The fact of the organisation's persistence was evidence of client incapacity, since otherwise it would be unnecessary.   Any attempt by management to change aspects of the organisation was: (1) evidence of management antagonism towards workers; (2) doomed to failure because the organisation existed to meet staff employment needs, would always continue unchanged; and (3) antagonistic towards the interests of clients because their incapacity required the persistence of the organisation as unchanged.

The three principal interest groups identified - staff, union and management - have been distinguished by their divergent task interests. The staff were principally concerned with the operational activity of the institution, the union with the preservation and extension of its members' rights, and management with the overall conduct of the institution. These distinctions were blurred to some extent however, with an increasingly powerful and authoritative union assuming management functions.

The differences between these interests were substantially reduced by their convergence with respect to career and lifestyle (or extra-mural) interest. Each of the groups concerned, while they might differ on elements of policy or practice, were united in their concern to preserve the institution and the employment lifestyle of their members which was tied to that preservation. This meant that individual conflicts were submerged in the face of a significant external threat to the institution.

Conflicts occurred between interests, generally as the union sought to extend its members entitlements through demarcation disputes and the establishment of minimum staffing requirements, management attempted fiscal restraint, and staff became frustrated at not being able to improve client care.

Conflicts between management and staff were resolved with reference to authority and the use of organisational structure, rules and regulation (Morgan, 1986, 159). Access to vehicles or other resources could be denied, and activity generally made more difficult. In the case of conflict between management and the union, where this could not be resolved through negotiation, it was inevitably resolved with reference to the superior statewide power of the union.

4 The Environment of the Organisation

Mayday Hills Training Centre for the Intellectually Disabled operated during the period from 1988 to 1993 within a complex and changing environment. Utilising the data collected through this study, this chapter identifys the major aspects of this environment, and those which were subject to the most significant changes within the period.

Following the framework developed in Chapter 2, the study discusses the environment in terms of the **Cultural, Political** and **Technical** Systems. The key elements of these systems, as identified from the data, are as follows:

- Cultural System
    - the philosophical basis of care
    - the model of public administration
- Political System
    - administrative arrangements
    - resource availability
- Technical System
    - the legislative and policy basis of care
    - the technology of care.

These elements of the environment are described below.

The Cultural System

The Philosophical Basis of Care

The changes which took place in the care of the intellectually disabled in Victoria during the 1980s relied upon the emergence of a competing perspective of the intellectually disabled person and upon appropriate models of care. The Canadian sociologist Wolfensberger, elaborating upon earlier Scandinavian perspectives, proposed in the late 1970s a view of the intellectually disabled which assumed a capacity to learn and viewed the environments within which they lived as disabling. In Wolfensberger's view, it is the way in which care is provided to the disabled person which defines the way in which he is perceived by society. The principle of "normalisation" was proposed whereby disabled individuals are provided with the same environments and opportunities which are available to the non-disabled.

"Normalisation", developed firstly in Scandinavia (Perrin and Nirje, 1985), and modified and codified by Wolfensberger provided a conceptual framework within which the movement from institutional settings to community based ones might be understood. It identified the tendency to "warehouse" and segregate people, and sought to encourage a coherent model of services being offered, the planning necessary to ensure comprehensiveness of service, and the centrality of the evaluation of services in terms of networks, roles, contacts and activities which they make available for service users (Brown and Smith, 1992).

Whitehead has identified the social origins of normalisation in the confluence of international political developments concerning the rights of minorities, and the emergence of the "new sociology" of the 1960s (Whitehead, 1992, 47). The experiences of deprivation during the 1930s depression, followed by the Nazi atrocities against minorities during the Second World War, gave rise, in his view, to a widespread concern within developed countries with the protection of the rights of disadvantaged and marginalised social groups. This was given strongest expression in the black civil rights movement in the United States during the 1950s and 1960s, which in turn provided a model for activity on behalf and by other minorities.

The "new sociology" which emerged in the United States during the 1960s was concerned with social processes rather than institutions and social functions. In particular, labelling theory elucidated by Goffman and others concerned itself with the ways in which people are defined by others and the effect this may have upon their subsequent behaviour (Goffman, 1968; Pearson, 1975). Whitehead argues that these developments underpin the theoretical framework of normalisation and contribute to the social environment in which it would become accepted and promoted.

Emerson (1992) has identified the origins of the normalisation principle in the application of civil rights to the field of mental retardation in Denmark and Sweden in the late 1950s. These early formulations advocated that services should seek to maximise the quality of life of service users by reproducing the lifestyle experienced by non-disabled citizens. Their intent was to ensure that people with learning difficulties enjoyed the right to the same quality of life as non-disabled community members. This did not however imply that segregated settings were unacceptable. In these early formulations, integration was not a requirement of equality.

A more elaborate definition of normalisation was first proposed by Wolfensberger in 1972, and was further developed by him in the subsequent decade. His early formulation defined normalisation as the:

> ...utilisation of means which are as culturally normative as possible, in order to establish and/or maintain personal behaviours and characteristics which are as culturally normative as possible. (Wolfensberger, 1972, 28)

As Emerson points out, this underwent two major modifications, reflecting a growing concern about the public perception of the disabled person, and the reformulation of the aims of normalisation in terms of socially valued roles rather than culturally normative practices (Emerson, 1992, 5).

Wolfensberger and Thomas (1983) have identified the major themes which are the theoretical underpinning of normalisation. These are: (1) **the social intent of historical and social processes**, whereby social policies reflect an unconsciously destructive intention towards marginalised groups. In consequence, normalisation as defined by Wolfensberger places emphasis upon raising the consciousness of those involved in human services. (2) The importance of **role expectation** in defining deviance. In this they support the premises of labelling theorists who assert that the characteristics and behaviours of members of deviant social groups is largely determined by the way in which society responds to and "labels" them, rather than to biological or psychological attributes (Emerson, 1992, 6). (3) **Devaluing characteristics** have a **cumulative and multiplicative** effect, such that the more devalued a person (or the greater the number of devalued people in a setting) the greater the impact of further devaluing characteristics. (4) The **developmental model**, which stresses the capacity of all individuals for growth and development. (5) The importance of **imitation or modelling** as methods of learning. (6) The importance of **social imagery** whereby stereotypes of disabled people are perpetuated through the transmission of potent social symbols; and (7) the importance of **social integration** through socially valued roles.

This last is of particular importance in understanding the movement through the 1980s in Victoria, away from segregated institutional settings for the intellectually disabled. Wolfensberger and Thomas argue that:

> normalisation requires that, to the highest degree and in as many areas of life as feasible, a [devalued] person or group have the opportunity to be personally integrated into the valued life of society. This means that as much as possible [devalued] people would be enabled to: live in normative housing within the valued community, and with [not just near to] valued people; be educated with

their non-devalued peers; work in the same facilities as ordinary people; and be involved in a positive fashion in worship, recreation, shopping, and all the other activities in which members of society engage. (Wolfensberger and Thomas, 1983, 27)

The Wolfensberger formulation of normalisation thus addressed itself in a broad way to the way in which disability is defined by and perpetuated by society, as well as prescribing service responses which at once minimise the devaluing of society members and maximise the personal functioning of individuals through developmental training and modelling. This formulation was widely adopted and provided the theoretical and philosophical underpinnings of the development of intellectual disability services in Victoria during the 1980s.

Among activists and educationalists in the field of intellectual disability, **normalisation** became during the late 1970 and early 1980s, the dominant model in the consideration of the care of the intellectually disabled. While it took pre-eminence in the intellectual consideration of the care of the disabled, its impact upon actual service delivery was much slower and the major service delivery mechanisms for the client group, the institutions, remained largely unchanged through to the mid 1980s. The impact of new models of care was felt however at a policy level, with the "Rimmer Report" on Intellectual Disability Services (Rimmer 1984) which proposed alternative models to the Minister for Healh, and the White Paper on Mental Retardation Services. A separate Mental Retardation Division of the Health Department was established, and had as its first Director, Dr Errol Cox an activist and proponent of normalisation.

Cox, rather than attempt significant reform of the large institutions of the State, concentrated on the development of alternative models of community based care. Again the institutions, while facing a declining resource base and a lower priority in service development terms, remained largely unaffected by changes in the technological environment. They continued to be the major source of employment within the field. They involved labour intensive and socially unattractive work, and were highly unionised. As such, they were able to exert a political pressure in resistance to change which was not available to proponents of more progressive approaches. This was borne out in 1982 following the election of the first Cain Labor government, when Cox left his position following conflict with his Minister.

Errol Cox's policy was to let the institutions wither on the vine. The institutions felt it intensely. But he wasn't going to throw good money after bad. That was

part of the reason he left, and one of the main criticisms of him. He thought that
you could put millions and millons into the institutions and not see a difference.
Errol was an ideologue, and he recruited people with strong ideology. Ideology
drove the whole thing - but that can only be sustained for so long.

(Scovell interview)

While the institutions, as bulwarks against change, remained politically
and industrially powerful, reform became firmly established through the regional
teams which Cox had initiated, and was furthered by the sympathetic public
response to the celebrated Annie Macdonald case. In 1977 Ms Annie
Macdonald, a profoundly disabled child who was a resident of St Nicholas
Hospital in Carlton, had made application to the Supreme Court to be discharged
from care on the grounds that her intelligence had not been properly assessed.
Ms Macdonald, supported by a former employee of the institution, Ms Rosemary
Crossley, was successful in her application, and also succeeded in drawing
sympathetic public attention to the issue of the functional capabilities of disabled
people and the poverty of their institutional environments (Crossley and
Macdonald, 1981; Community Services Victoria, 1988a).

In 1981 the Victorian Government, in the face of a sustained public
campaign, decided to close St Nicholas Hospital. Its one hundred and two
residents were relocated to dispersed residential units across Victoria between
April 1983 and March 1985 (Community Services Victoria, 1988a). These
Community Residential Units operated as small institutions with little
interaction between the residents and the communities in which they operated
and the staff were employed on conditions borrowed from the institutional
environment which inhibited effective community contact. Nevertheless, the
closure of St Nicholas Hospital marked the first triumph of those who strongly
opposed institutional models of care for the intellectually disabled, and who
advocated normalisation as the principle upon which services should be based.

These developments within the State were mirrored at the Commonwealth
level, with the federal Government passing, also in 1986 the *Disability Services
Act* (DSA). The DSA provided a policy statement on the rights of people with
disabilities as well as a set of principles and objectives to apply to service
provision. This Act sought to develop new and innovative services that would
meet individual needs and also provide a transition program to assist "older-
style" services that existed prior to the Act to become "quality services"
(Conway, 1992).

While this was the case, the implementation of the broad vision of
normalisation was limited by the inability of Government to deliver on its

comprehensiveness, and the tendency to focus upon realisable goals and targets. While the major policy document embodying the normalisation principles, the Ten Year Plan for the Redevelopment of Intellectual Disability Services (1988), gave clear expression to the goals, in practice the plan became one largely of addressing the issue of institutional settings.

By the early 1990s the influence of normalisation, as the prevailing ideology in the intellectual disability field had diminished. Academically it was being rejected as societal reaction theories of deviance were themselves being rejected (Emerson 1992, 11). Increasingly, practitioners were becoming concerned at the absence of choice on the part of consumers of services themselves as to their preferred living arrangements (Wolfensberger, 1980, 92). Civil libertarians in the field were becoming concerned at what Dalley has described as the moral authoritarianism and conservatism inherent within Wolfensberger's theories (Dalley, 1992, 103ff). In placing its emphasis upon socially valued roles and the reduction of the devaluing of groups and individuals by the modification of behaviours which attract labelling, it was argued that Wolfensberger's theory of normalisation was in danger of assuming the norms of the dominant societal group with little regard to the values of diversity or difference.

The normalisation principle, as elsewhere, had been taken up by practitioners in the field of Intellectual Disability Services in Victoria with an evangelical fervour, and between 1982 and 1990 was the dominant ideology within the field (Anonymous Respondent I interview; Scovell interview; Green interview):

> There was a passionate commitment to reform. This was the best era of my professional life. We felt we were bringing services to local communities; people were getting respite in their own communities.
>
> (Scovell interview)

It utilised a technical language of its own and initiated neophytes through "Passing Workshops" which taught conformity to the principle in all its elaborations. No deviation was permitted and its internal coherence and monolithic nature, initially strengths, progressively became liabilities:

> I did a couple of short "Passing" experiences, and then undertook the five day one... It was much more like propaganda than education and coming from an education background, I couldn't believe the teaching technique they used in their lectures, because there was no way you could question, no way you could debate, no way you could discuss, it was just basically hear this, believe it...

having gone beyond the first couple of days which were lecture based, into having to place yourself in the shoes of a person with ID and live the next few days from that mind set, shadowing people through a facility that you were given to look at fairly closely and assess and evaluate....

(Hind interview)

Through the later part of the 1980s, the debate within the field of social administration moved from a concern with institutional and non-institutional forms of care, and towards a concern about the application of market mechanisms to the field. Trapped within a restricted language which carried with it strong moral undertones, and no longer setting the terms of the critical policy debates, the adherents of normalisation progressively lost political influence.

The major changes in the prevailing ideology associated with the management of intellectual disability services which took place in the early 1990s came about not through a re-evaluation of normalisation as a model for service development, but as a consequence of the supplanting of welfare based models of service more generally by economically defined models (Bryson, 1992, 43). This took place in the disability field earlier than in other fields of welfare within the state, and entailed the removal from the Disability Services Division of the Department of Community Services (CSV) of all those with a background in service delivery, and in particular, the majority of those with an adherence to the principles of normalisation.

The Model of Public Administration

In addition to changing policy and practice with respect to disability, the redevelopment of Mayday Hills Training Centre also took place during a time of two significant environmental changes; one in policy and the other administrative.

The first concerned itself with changing perspectives on the Welfare State, by which the social reformist orthodoxy which had hitherto dominated Australian politics was supplanted by what Bryson has described as an individualist or anti-collectivist perspective (Bryson, 1989, 43). The second concerned the changes in the focus of administrative activity which commenced with the election of the Cain Labor Government in Victoria in March 1982 and was made most explicit in the Health and Community Services portfolio with the appointment of Dr John Paterson as Director General of the Department of Community Services in July 1989.

In his analysis of the major changes which took place within the Australian political environment during the 1980s, Kelly argues that the period saw the fundamental renegotiation of the pillars of Australian social and public life (Kelly 1992). These he describes as: White Australia, industry protection, industrial conciliation and arbitration, dependence upon allies in foreign affairs, and state paternalism. These taken together, constituted he argues, the Deakinite settlement upon which public policy was built for the first eighty years of the country's history. The 1980s represented, he claims, an "end of certainty" whereby each element of that settlement was modified or abandoned.

The last of these, the dismantling of the functions of the State in meeting the basic economic and social requirements of its citizens through institutionalised provisions, or the Welfare State, occurred concurrently with similar developments within other OECD countries as internationally countries have moved towards more market oriented policies (Pusey, 1991; Bryson, 1992). Henderson has identified the common elements of these policies as: taxation reform, towards broadening the base of taxation and reduction of marginal rates; loosening of financial markets through freer international capital flows; loosening of product markets by means of deregulation and privatisation, and labour market reform through enterprise bargaining (Henderson, 1989).

The intellectual disability field, and the welfare sector generally, was to some extent insulated from these developments within Victoria by a neo-Keynesian state Labor government between 1982-1992. It could not entirely be so as the Commonwealth government's control over financial matters ensured that the State's finances and hence its policy choices were determined within an increasingly market oriented and deregulated environment. The capacity of the State Government to pay for social programs during its final term was influenced by the deregulated finance market. Changes in industrial union behaviour as a consequence of changed Commonwealth government approaches to labor market regulation weakened the position of public sector unions during the late 1980s and influenced important relationships in the delivery of social programs. Most significantly however, was the growing discordance through the late 1980s between the implied intent of the *Intellectually Disabled Persons Services Act* to expand the client group and to make comprehensive a service delivery system, and the emergent policy imperatives towards reduced government outlays and responsibility.

During the 1980s and early 1990s, the period which provides a backdrop to this study, public administration in the State of Victoria underwent profound change with respect to government as policy maker, and in the technology of management.

In the period which immediately preceded this time, the public service had been characterised by the emergence of the functional expert as manager, and by Government as a passive recipient of policy. Senior management of functional departments were increasingly, through the 1970s, drawn from professional ranks within the functional departments. They were frequently highly motivated and with a vocational commitment to their area of speciality. In the specific case of the community services department this was explicitly the case with the emergence of social work as the dominant profession, and the advancement of social workers to positions of administrative prominence and ultimately control (Markiewicz, 1988; Bryson 1992; Hough, 1994).

Beginning in the late 1970s but becoming explicit with the election of a Labor Government in Victoria in October 1982, a different approach to public sector administration emerged in Victoria and also at a Commonwealth level. Bryson describes this change in culture as "managerialism" which she suggests "essentially implies a focus on technocratic matters and formal structures with management techniques cast as value free" (Bryson, 1992, 362). Amongst the administrative changes which marked this development, she lists, in addition to the reorganisation of the functional responsibilities of Departments:

> ... the development of extensive new rules about parliamentary interaction and interaction with cabinet: the institution of program budgeting; the establishment of a senior executive service with incentive payments and a management appraisal and improvement scheme; establishment of management by objectives; the development of elaborate information [EDP] systems; the development of corporate plans and of a range of strategy plans for the economy, poverty, urban development, culture and social justice to name a few. (Bryson, 1992, 363)

Alford, O'Neill, Maguire, Considine, Maetzelfeldt and Ernst (1994) refer to this period as the second stage in the evolution of public sector management in Victoria. The first stage or **conventional** model extending to the early 1980s was characterised by direct public sector production, organisational hierarchy and control through standardised work. Its principles were procedural equity, due process and the avoidance of waste, corruption or systems disaster. The second stage, or the **managerialist** model, entailed a modest amount of transfer of production from the public to the private sector, and a retention of hierarchy as the essential organising principle. It sought however, to transform the means of control from standardised processes to an emphasis on outputs and outcomes (Alford, O'Neill, McGuire, Considine, Maetzelfeldt, and Ernst, 1994, 5).

They identify the ideological antecedents of managerialism, and its later manifestations in the "contract state" of the Kennett government, in Simon's work on bounded rationality, contingency theory, and the public interest theory. Bounded rationally supported the division of organisations into autonomous components which were comprehensible to the limited cognitive capacity of individuals (March and Simon, 1958). Contingency theory encouraged the tailoring of organisations to suit task and environmental circumstances and legitimised the shaping of organisations to serve goals (Lawrence and Lorsch, 1986; Mintzberg, 1979). Public interest theory, mediated through popular discussions about the role and functioning of government (Osborn and Gaebler, 1993), proposed the utilisation of market tools to manage non market political decisions (Stretton and Orchard, 1994; Self, 1993).

The full effect of the changed focus to which Bryson refers was felt with the appointment of Dr John Paterson as Director General of Community Services in 1989. Paterson indicated his fundamental concern with the administrative processes of the Department in his forward to the Department's Annual Report for 1990/91:

> Whether the product is physical objects or human services, the logic of organisation and control is identical. When the logic is violated, things go wrong. In CSVs case they go wrong for people: the unit cost goes through the roof, service quality suffers and service backlogs grow. You read about it in the papers. (Paterson, 1991, 5)

The impact of this change of focus of public administration away from substantive policy goals and towards the processes of administration may be seen in the 1992 paper by the Director General of Community Services Victoria, Dr John Paterson, entitled **Evaluation and Welfare Programs.** This paper indicates the abandonment of the rights based normalisation perspective which had hitherto underpinned the operation of the services (Paterson 1992).

Paterson argued that the evaluation of programs within the welfare field is bedevilled by the inherent difficulties in measuring effectiveness, tension between individual as distinct from social goods as goals of programs, and fragmentation and lack of management sophistication within the field. These are not unfamiliar observations within the literature concerning Human Services Organisations (Hasenfeld, 1983, 110ff; Jones and May, 1992, 86ff). Paterson's comments however concerning the mismatch between client rights as defined by statewide law and the capacities and imperatives of administrative systems constitutes a critique of earlier approaches to service management and an assertion of an alternative and more administratively determined framework.

Paterson argued that the principles established within the IDPS Act, and in particular those set out in s.5 do not recognise the reality of rationing for services within a fixed and parliamentary determined budget:

a)   Intellectually disabled persons have the same right as other members of the community to services which support a reasonable quality of life; and

b)   It is the responsibility of the State of Victoria to plan, fund, ensure the provision of and evaluate services to intellectually disabled persons according to the principles stated herein. (IDPS Act, 1986, s.5)

Further, they leave unanswered fundamental program definitional issues such as the criteria for determining priority of access for services. The Act, together with the *Guardianship and Administration Act*, in providing mechanisms for constraint upon the executive capacity of the Department, he argued "...provides multiple avenues for statutory queue jumping", and fails to account for the rights to services of those other eligible clients whose needs are not met in consequence. He argues that the "rights" perspective of the legislation effectively disempowers family members who provide the large amount of care to clients. In summary, he argued:

> the marked disjunctions between a statute centred on individual rights, a received service system which is out of kilter with the Act, unspecified value weights for allocation of services under a budget constraint, and 'all or nothing' queuing systems, make definitive evaluation impossible in other than the narrowed terms. (Paterson, 1992, 24)

The impact of Paterson's critique can be seen in changed approach to the administration of intellectual disability services from the early 1990s. The program became more administratively determined, with the development of manuals and guidelines which prescribed administratively the nature of care to be provided:

> ...emphasis was very much about using all of these economic mathematical formulae and looking at unit cost of service, unit outputs ... and I just felt that it started to change the culture. Started to talk with agencies much more about

productivity and issues to deal with efficiency, and I am not denying the need to do that and perhaps the system hadn't sufficiently addressed those issues.

(Bartholomew interview)

This can be seen most clearly with the case management guidelines which sought to codify the practices of casework, but gave little guidance in the making of complex case decisions (Community Services Victoria, 1992). A senior manager within the Department at this time described the impact of these changes:

I saw [the Director, Disability Services] bringing in people who were managers who would develop and implement manuals, structures, processes, without the background and experience of the issues and would particularly take very strong centralised lines in relation to head office and Regions... what came through was very much a strong central controlled, central discipline about implementing certain tasks and certain responsibilities; client services manuals and a range of things that had been implemented at that time. Again without a great deal of knowledge of the framework of the Act; but the manual work was done and implementation of it was done as if we were implementing product lines.

(Anonymous Respondent I interview)

A Regional Manger of Disability Services saw both gains and loses in the approach taken:

...it was driven by other things than practice, around trying to get common procedures at a statewide level and I think for a number of years it was absolutely and utterly content free. Now that is not to say it shouldn't have had a procedural [focus]; the common procedures and standards across the State, but it was almost as though that era had gone from one extreme where you had the ideologues who gave no attention to things like common procedures or dollars, but were focussed purely on a human rights zealous approach to increasing services and getting things changed, and quality of life, but the pendulum swung right over to the other extreme where it was very hard for a number of years to find any people who actually had any content knowledge at all at a senior level.

(Hind interview)

Another senior manager, one who was strongly supportive of the new order, described the loss of the creativity and commitment to the client that characterised the old order:

the thing that's in my head that characterises what killed it was disrespect. There was absolutely, you know, sweeping clean stuff, the past is just not how to do it. But it was complete disrespect for what came from that period.... there were things seen that could be done. There were ways in which, even in that appalling institutional setting, major change could happen which could improve the life of people living there, but there wasn't support from Head Office to follow through at all, and there was often blocking of it... It wasn't because John would have blocked it... but he wasn't giving that leadership and the people in charge couldn't understand, didn't have the content, and were very controlling.

(Anonymous Respondent II interview)

The election of the Kennett conservative government in October 1992 brought with it a radical agenda of reduction in public outlays, privatisation of services, and reduced governmental activity. It provided a discontinuity with the policy framework which had operated for the previous ten years. In particular the policy of deinstitutionalisation which had become identified closely with the outgoing Labor Party Minister Setches, while still endorsed by the government, was generally given a lower status relative to the goals of restructuring the relationship between government and services provided in the Health and Community Services field, and industrial reform more generally.

The government moved quickly to collapse the former departments of Community Services and Health into a single government agency. The financial position of the State at the time of the accession of the new government, was particularly parlous. The new government immediately placed severe restrictions on expenditure and froze all capital expenditure, putting at risk many developments within the disability field, including the final stage of the Mayday Hills redevelopment.

The Political System

Administrative Arrangements

The Political Environment, as outlined in the Morgan (1986) framework, is concerned with dominant interests, and the distribution of power and resources within the organisation's task environment. This section will outline the critical components of that environment and the ways these changed during the redevelopment period.

Principal amongst the formal organisations within Mayday Hills Training Centre's environment was the public service department of which it was a part. At times during the redevelopment period, this was variously the Health Commission, the Health Department (HDV), Community Services Victoria (CSV), and the Department of Health and Community Services (H&CS). Mayday Hills Training Centre was at once formally a part of these organisations, and separate from them, since the Training Centre's longevity, geographic and programmatic isolation ensured that it had a organisational life separate to, and sometimes opposed to, its parent organisation. Until the transfer in December 1990 to the line management of Community Services Victoria, and the eventual merging of the Health and Community Services departments, the Training Centre owed its formal organisational allegiances to a statutory department other than that which was responsible for its programmatic direction. During this time, the organisational arrangements were strongly linked and yet separate.

The other major grouping of formal organisation within the Training Centre's political environment was represented by the industrial bodies which had coverage of its employees. These were through various titles the Hospital Employees Federation No. 2 Branch (HEF2), later the Hospital and Community Services Union (HACSU), and the Victorian Public Service Association (VPSA), later the State Public Service Federation (SPSF). Both these organisations were engaged in a complex relationship with the Training Centre and between themselves, as the nature of industrial relations underwent significant change during the late 1980s.

Community Services Victoria/Health Department Victoria

Community Services Victoria was established as an agency by the Victorian Government in March 1985 following the election to a second term of the Cain Labor Government (Solomon, 1987). The new Agency brought together the welfare functions of the former Department of Community Welfare Services, the children's services functions of the Health Commission and new Commonwealth/State Home and Community Care program. In October of that year, following considerable debate, the Government also transferred to the new Department, the Mental Retardation Division of the Health Commission. That Division was entitled the Office of Intellectual Disability Services (OIDS) in the new Department.

For many in the field of intellectual disability, the move to the new organisation was welcomed as the completion of the long struggle to free the field from the control of the medical profession and the "medical model" of practice. For others the absorption into a broadly based human services organisation represented a frustration of the desire to be established as a

Department in its own right, and raised the fear that the hard won priority focus upon intellectual disability services would be lost within a more broadly focused organisation. Heather Scovell, a senior officer in the Office of Intellectual Disability Services, and later a Regional Director in CSV, expressed the feeling held by many:

> I remember feeling some of the opposition to integration. It was inevitable, but not attractive. Our hard won status would be absorbed and lose its status.
>
> (Scovell interview)

Julie Hind described the anxiety about these changes held by many in the field:

> There had been, with the Act in '86, a period of a sense of intellectual disability finally making it in its own sense and the client groups actually having a profile in the Health Department that it hadn't been previously because it had been swamped by psych services. With the mooted changes into community services, and the implementation of that, I think many in the field thought that it had gone from being swamped by psych services into being potentially swamped by welfare services and therefore people with ID would actually... this new era of life for them would be swamped and lost.
>
> (Hind interview)

A view frequently put was that the intellectually disabled, when required to compete for attention and resources with other client groups, invariably lose. This tension between the appropriateness of integration into broader based and more generic service systems and the desire for separateness in order to protect advantages for the client group was to characterise debates about intellectual disability services at both a policy and service level for the next five years.

The compromise accepted by the then Director General of Community Services Victoria, Mr Peter Johnstone, was an uneasy one. It allowed intellectual disability services to maintain separateness within the broader Department as an Office, to be known as the Office of Intellectual Disability Services (OIDS) with a Deputy Director General responsible to him for its operations. This could not be sustained since it ran counter to the intent of Government in establishing the Agency. It did however have the effect of encouraging the view within OIDS that separateness was possible.

Johnstone finally achieved the integration of the operational components of the Department through what he called the regional coordination project.

This project involved extensive planning and consultation with all parts of the Department and in the end justified the appointment in October 1987 of Regional Directors to manage the Department's 18 regions. Johnstone was unwilling in the end however to force any further structural integration. The researcher was responsible within the Department for the management of this program of coordination and integration at the regional level.

Of greater concern than the structural integration however was the conflict in cultures between the parts of the department; conflicts which were perpetuated in the program development functions of the Department long after successful integration of the operational functions had been achieved. Those parts of the Department which had come from the Department of Community Welfare Services did so with a strong tradition of regionalised operationally driven management. That Department had been regionalised beginning in 1972 and had been driven by goals of closure of large congregate care welfare institutions and latterly the development of community control of welfare resources on a regional basis (Keating, 1983). The intellectual disability services component of the Department had a history of struggle for attention to the needs of their client group, and a strong sense of oppression by mental health professionals. They were inspired by the "normalisation" and "social role valorisation" theories of Wolfensberger, and had a zealousness about the rights of the intellectually disabled. It was ironic that their fervour led them to support segregative service development which ran counter to the theories they espoused (Anonymous Respondent I interview):

> It was being driven strongly by ideologues who were absolutely and utterly committed to that sense of client rights and a new order of quality of life for them. And I think the rest of us in the field were pretty much smitten by the same sort of zealous fire in the belly stuff.
>
> (Hind interview)

> Cultural change occurred with the merger with CSV. It changed to a management expertise. The Department was looking for people with really good management skills, beyond people with the right ideas and a good heart. After about nine months the cultural shift to management expertise came. In I.D. if you had the right ideas you were okay. Later there came an acceptance that you could come from another field and bring skills. There was less emphasis upon content, and a few people from other areas.
>
> (Scovell interview)

The Office of Intellectual Disability Services (OIDS) or the Division of Intellectual Disability Services as it became had two Directors between 1987 and 1991. David Green, formerly a Director within the Department of Community Welfare Services prior to becoming Associate Director of the Brotherhood of St Lawrence brought to the position, a commitment to broadening the base of services and reducing the ideological narrowness which had reinforced separateness. Allan Rassaby, Director from 1989 to 1991, had been an architect of the *Intellectually Disabled Persons Services Act* and a recognised reformer in the field.

They managed the Office during a time of major change in which the Department was commencing to understand its changed role as a consequence of the IDPS Act, and OIDS was seeking to come to an understanding of its changed role relative to the operational or regional areas of the Department. During their periods as Director, the Ten Year Plan for Intellectual Disability Services was prepared, the Intellectual Disability Services Redevelopment budget of 1988/89 was brought down, and the first two years of the State Plan for Intellectual Disability services were implemented. The Intellectual Disability Services Program at this time thus experienced a crisis of leadership as its senior managers changed and were replaced by new managers with different visions of the future of the program. It was fundamentally reshaped by a major legislative change, the impacts of which were not well understood. It underwent a major policy development exercise which would seek to define its future, but would ultimately have limited impact. It experienced a major expansion of resources for services, which was superimposed upon an ill-defined service system. The program was, in short, chaotic, as successive Directors sought to give definition to, and in some respects, reform the existing service structure, define the identity of the program, and shape its future both in policy terms, and in practice through major budget initiatives.

> ... in that period of time Allan Rassaby was running disability services and was involved in writing the Act. In a very strong and very ideological way he was promoting service development and redevelopment. There was lots of tension about Allan's approach, that he was promoting changes in the system without, I think, a real understanding of how you manage that change. He had a commitment to it and a belief in it, but I think he was almost an academic as opposed to being able to translate that belief and that thinking into day to day practice.

> On the ground it was reflected by staff members who believed in it and were implementing parts of the Act in great detail in regional teams without any

understanding about how it could be integrated holistically across the whole region. The regional team was almost standing apart from the institution; there was almost two separate codes of practice.

Allan was replaced by Terri Whiting who I think really didn't understand a great deal of the issues at all. She was one of the new broom who talked of what was required but I don't think had any detailed understanding of what it actually meant on the ground for the staff, the residents, and their families. She was followed by, I think Paul Bartholomew, who was the ultimate pragmatist. Paul was very nuts and bolts, and was interested in results. He was going through some personal organisational trauma fairly quickly... and wasn't in the position all that long... fairly soon after he moved into the position, he and John Paterson exchanged roles.

(Anonymous Respondent I interview)

Despite the chaotic nature of the policy and administrative environment, the Division continued to be highly motivated and cohesive. Paul Bartholomew joined the Department in 1988, as Deputy Director General, and from September 1990 was General Manager for Disability Services. He described the ethos at that time:

I felt that the people who worked there at that time had, as you do normally find in those areas where people have worked with people with disabilities for a long time, an enormous commitment to what they were doing, and an enormous sense of trying to actually improve the lives of people with disabilities. They might not have been doing things as economically and smart and as technically well as we could have been doing, but I felt we had a tremendous relationship with the field and there was a really shared common set of core values about people with disabilities being encouraged and supported to take their rightful place in the community.

(Bartholomew interview)

John Paterson, appointed in 1989 as Director General, did not view the administration of the program as positively. From his perspective, a refocusing was required as much for ethical reasons as for reasons of administrative efficiency:

I found as I got to know more about that program that it was full of anomalies and full of wishful thinking and double talk. I went and acted in Allan Rassaby's Division Head job for a month or so while he was on leave, and I conducted a kind of *action audit* of how it was working. I found that many of things that were being done there were very illogically driven and had very little actual connection with reality. For example, the big drive was to get a General Service Plan for every registered client; it had become a big *production line* operation. All the Divisional targets were attached to that, and the Act, which Rassaby had largely written, called for it. But when we actually put those completed plans to scrutiny and weighed up a sample of them, it turned out that the cost of actually doing, the resources involved, was several times greater than those then available. Those then available were far greater than had ever been available before. So there was a whole lot of kind of celebratory stuff and work that was basically ritualistic rather than directly involved in services. That satisfied the needs of the reformist group and did very little for the clients.

I was also *very* affronted by the *kind* of dissonance between the mission as conceived, which was to do good, and what I saw as a wanton neglect of all the evidence that things were not even acceptable let alone good in the *actual* institutions that we *actually* ran. There was plenty of evidence, and there was much folk lore which these people would actually talk about: "Oh terrible things happen at Caloola." And then I would say, "But you're responsible for Caloola. How can you say that? What are you doing about it?" I'd be told, Oh you can't do anything about it." I was shocked by the resigned abrogation of management responsibility, by the self proclaimed idealists and reformers. If something you're running is rife with crime and abuse, rape, brutality and endemic theft and god knows what else, which is precisely the situation then prevailing, *and* you know about it, *and* you're not doing anything about it, then to me you are as culpable as the thieves and bashers. So I was very offended by what I saw. The rhetoric and the idealism in which some of these people clothed themselves, was totally separate from what they actually *did* when faced with systemic abuse, which was precisely *nothing*. They went on consulting respectfully with the HEF2 leadership.

(Paterson interview)

The Upper Murray Region of Community Services Victoria was established in September 1987 with the appointment of the researcher as Regional Director. Prior to this there had existed separate regional arrangements for Community Welfare Services and Intellectual Disability Services. The Intellectual Disability Services regions had been co-extensive with Health Department Regions which covered the area of two CSV regions. The new regional arrangements thus required the separation into two units of the regional intellectual disability team.

Historically the involvement of the Office of Intellectual Disability Services (and its predecessors) in North East Victoria had been minimal. Mayday Hills Training Centre represented the largest service, but was owned and managed by the Office of Psychiatric Services (HDV). A non-government Residential Association (NERCA) operated in Wodonga and Wangaratta, providing four Community Residential Units. Also Day Training Centres located in Wodonga and Wangaratta provided funded day activity programs for the intellectually disabled. The regional team of the Department was small in size, had been located in Benalla, a small municipality located at a distance from the major population centres of the region, and so had had little impact upon service delivery in North East Victoria.

The new regional team for the Upper Murray Region consisted of only two members for much of its first year of operation. On the advice of the then General manager of the Office of Intellectual Disability Services, the Regional Director instructed that a major priority of the team would be Mayday Hills Training Centre. The motivation for this was in part the Director's own deep sense of shock at the poverty of the environment for residents of the Training Centre when he first visited it in April 1987. It was also in part the belief that the Region's credibility with respect to the institution had to be established at an early point, negotiation of entry at a later time would be difficult to achieve.

Dr John Paterson was appointed Director General of Community Services Victoria in July 1989. Paterson had previously been Director General of the Department of Water Resources in Victoria, and had established his reputation as an organisational reformer as chief executive of the Hunter Water Board. Paterson come to the position of Director General of CSV with a mandate for change, as government had come under repeated public criticism of the Department's performance in Child Protection Services. He built upon this mandate with extravagant and public descriptions of the paucity of management expertise he found in the Department when he commenced (Paterson, 1990; Hough, 1994).

Prior to Paterson's time CSV provided an environment which enhanced the position of the entrepreneur, and promoted a culture of innovation at the periphery. The structure of the organisation, divided as it was between the Program Directions divisions and Regional Services Division encouraged a culture with two realities: a central culture which was policy and program focussed but lacking a concern for or capacity to understand operational realities, and a regional culture which was dismissive of all things central, and which had the potential for lawlessness. This was aggravated by the structure of Regional Services Division in which eighteen Regional Directors reported to a single Deputy Director General. This ensured that while collegiality was strong within the Division, and there was a strong sense of operational reality, Regional Directors were effectively answerable to no-one, since their manager could not possibly know what was happening in 18 major work units.

Entrepreneurial managers were able to maximise the opportunities created by what was a very fluid environment. They controlled the information and Program Directors controlled the resources. By responding to the key interests and pet projects of Program Divisions, Regional Directors could "sell" their capacity to deliver the outcomes wanted, with few central constraints. Thus innovations could be mounted which linked the Region's capacity to provide operational skill, with the resources which could be gleaned from the Program Divisions.

Paterson immediately restructured the Department to end the arrangement whereby all eighteen regions reported to a single Deputy Director General, and the other Divisions had program design but no operational responsibilities. He abolished the Office of Intellectual Disability Services and established in its place the Intellectual Disability Services Division. He subsequently further restructured the organisation in September 1990 to reduce the number of regions from eighteen to thirteen by combining pairs of rural regions, and by reordering the responsibilities of Program Divisions to reduce their number by one. He established a Disability Services Division which combined responsibility for intellectual disability services and physical and sensory disability services. In March 1991 he vacated the position of Director General in order to directly manage the Division of Intellectual Disability Services. His stated reason for this was to observe at first hand the management of the program and better understand its demands.

Paterson described the state of the program at the time of his review of it, in the foreword to his Annual Report to Parliament for 1990/91. There were, he said, fundamental flaws in IDS case management practice, the symptoms of which were: difficulties in identifying the nominal IDS case management system; parent complaints about lack of follow-through on individual general service plans; regional discontent with head office program design, standards and support; endemic conflict between the program and the Department's training branch about training priorities, unevenness in regional performance; lack of confidence amongst senior managers in aspects of program operations; and the absence of useful performance indicators (Paterson, 1991). He took decisive action to reshape the administration of the program:

> Since the completion of the review in April, the head office of Disability Services Division has been restructured, and new appointments made to all management

positions including general manager, program director and section heads. The work program of the Disability Services Branch has been reconstructed primarily to meet field demands for specific products. (Paterson, 1991)

Following the resignation of Rassaby in early 1991, one of Paterson's protégés, Karen Cleave, was appointed as Director of the Disability Services Division reporting to the Division's General Manager, Paul Bartholomew. Cleave had little grasp of the service issues within the program, but a strong sense of administrative procedure, and the capacity to deliver completed administrative tasks which Paterson had found lacking in the program. Under her leadership the program became more ordered and many of the essential tools required by staff, such as practice manuals, were completed. Doug Dalton, a long time senior officer of the Department who occupied executive positions in both the Office of Intellectual Disability Services and Regional Centres, and who was Chief Executive Officer of Caloola at the time of its closure, these changes represented a rebalancing of the competing interests within the program:

> I think what happened then there was a shift towards a more managerialist approach to it which de-emphasised some of the more radical approaches that were being advocated. And said there are other interests, there are other stake holders in this game that whilst the clients are paramount there are the Parents Associations, there is the unions, there are our staff, there are the communities into which these people will be moving in which we will attempt to maintain. And all of those interests have somehow to be managed. The competing demands on us have to be responded to in some reasonably consistent way.
>
> (Dalton interview)

For many however, while the program became less chaotic at this time, it also lost much of its creative and innovative force. Central management of the program was less tolerant of variation and less supportive of operational attempts to reform the system:

> ... she was very clear that that [the centre] was where the direction was coming from and it was the Region's job to implement those directions rather than to be doing what they should have been doing which was looking at how you actually develop programs at a local level to better suit people's needs and then share that expertise around. I felt that we had at that time, an extremely competent group of people as Regional Directors, ... and they really did drive the whole service delivery framework of the organisation and we started to lose that. I don't think that was just related to disabilities, I think it was a general shift.
>
> (Bartholomew interview)

... the Head Office stuff became so unrealistic. Their model of care, was so theoretical and so unrelated. Like for instance, there was this big push on foster care and I used to think, "what is the message that you are giving a parent who is ultimately feeling like they have failed because their kid has to go into care and you have to pay the foster carers money that you were never prepared to pay to parents"... it reflects where they were coming from in Head Office. It was a design - "we're designing a product" but the bit that's missing in the product design is the content.

(Anonymous Respondent II interview)

Paterson was responsible for two very significant reforms within the intellectual disability field, both of which were of immediate relevance to institutional management: the adoption of a hard line approach to the enforcement of discipline procedures, particularly with regard to abuse of clients, and the streamlining of management reporting lines within institutions. Prompted by the adverse findings of an enquiry into allegation of abuse at Pleasant Creek Training Centre (Wallace, 1991), Paterson initiated procedures for the vigorous prosecution of breaches of discipline (Paterson, 1991, 1992). These, together with external scrutiny brought to light further extensive corruption and abuse, at Caloola, Janefield, and Aradale training centres. It was clear that the isolated and enclosed cultures of the institutions coupled with the industrial protection afforded offenders, had led at least in some places to the entrenchment of abusive and exploitative practices:

I was appalled by the near total lack of basic management skills in the dreamers occupying the key management roles in the program. They were dangerous not only to the clients, but also to well intentioned staff. They presided over a system where there were decent kids coming out of the MRN qualification, terrific youngsters in most cases. The new graduates were there with a mission, they wanted to serve and do good things. Then they went into *our* institutions, which were being run by a corrupt and oppressive system. They discovered that if you bucked that system you placed your career, and in many cases even your physical safety in jeopardy as well. But they were trapped, and if they cried out they would not be heard in the dreaming tower of head office.

The whole institutional racket was under-written by a structural flaw, in *our* system. The redundant levels of hierarchy within the MRN arrangements made it possible to ensure that anyone on the inside that was caught doing anything bad could always report it to someone sympathetic to the culprit, who would then make sure the report went *nowhere*. The person making the report would be punished, not the offender. How it could happen was fairly clear, simply by looking at the *structures*. As far as I was concerned anyone with even the most elementary management orientation would try to understand how bad things could happen and go on happening for long periods. Our dreamers had not bothered - abuse was some kind of god given constant to them - not their business. I was sickened by this lethal form of impotent idealism. Meanwhile there they were, solemnly consulting away with the HEF2, the main entrepreneur and guarantor of this vicious system.

(Paterson interview)

Paterson's uncompromising approach and willingness to expose abuse rather than cover it up, did much to improve accountability within the institutions, though they failed to address the isolation which enabled abusive practices to take hold:

Paterson did some good things. I think the issue about cleaning out the institutions and really taking on the issues of rorts and abuse of staff and some of the malpractice issues that I think were more endemic in the system than many of us would realise, was a good thing that he did. There are some situations like that where his total unyielding attitude actually produced results.

(Bartholomew interview)

Two senior managers in the Department, both of whom had institutional management responsibilities described the impact of this approach:

Reform of the institutions took really strong leadership. John Paterson said he was going to kick the shit out of people who did the wrong thing - you don't hit, steal or rape. It was very symbolic. One of the most successful things he did was to demand a standard of behaviour that was the same as other work places.

(Scovell interview)

... he said, "We will not tolerate abuse, we will not tolerate fraud. People's rights will be respected and institutions will be managed in a way where people are accountable." He conducted the investigations, and they were conducted effectively compared to the Health investigations of psych facilities. John personally led the introduction of unit managers, and made sure that it happened and that there was training in place. That was about having each person in the institution having a staff member ultimately, finally accountable for their wellbeing, which was an essential move because this was at a time when nobody was accountable... He introduced very strong organisational approaches to discipline... I'm absolutely certain that there is cruelty, incidents of cruelty, and people there who shouldn't be there, and maybe times when people rip off money and so on, but a systematic way of life, it is not institutionalised... I think that it stopped at that point.

(Anonymous Respondent II interview)

As this last quotation indicates, the second major reform was linked to the first, in that Paterson attributed the disciplinary problems in the institution to the failure of management accountability. The fact that unit supervisors in training centres were rostered to, "two-on, two-off" shifts in the same way that other direct care staff were, meant that units lacked management continuity. Night shifts were managed by night supervisors (also on revolving shifts) which meant that any residential unit had four supervisors in any week, who had very little contact with one another:

Henceforth one line of accountability will connect senior management with the individual client, replacing the six or more channels that inevitably exist when the first and second lines of supervisory or management staff work the two-on, two-off roster... Under the old arrangements no-one was fully responsible, no-one was accountable, and unchecked corruption was the result.

(Paterson, 1991)

The place of institutions within the Department's operations was to change markedly between 1985 and 1992. Under the Mental Retardation Branch (HDV) managed by Errol Cox, institutions were anathema. Left to themselves, they were expected to decay:

The early days didn't hit the institutions. The Regions had to be set up separately to create a new ideology; we were going to do things differently, create a different ethic. It would have been compromised by the ethic of the institutions. At the time there were the institutions with appalling conditions, and Regions with all the new resources. Modern management techniques didn't hit the institutions until much later; their hierarchies and power bases weren't focussed on quality care.

(Scovell interview)

They were poorly understood in the early days of Community Services Victoria, but under Green and Rassaby's direction, there had commenced an attempt to reform them by integrating them with broader service systems, while working towards their elimination. Following the institutional scandals of 1991, the institutions increasingly became the focus of Departmental management attention. The principal management task was defined less in terms of their closure, and more in terms of improving their operations and avoiding the repetition of scandals.

The administrative arrangement for the joint facilities at Warrnambool, Ararat and Beechworth which emerged from the machinery of government changes of 1985, were confused and the source of much inaction in the years to come. The arrangements were determined by an industrial agreement in which HEF(2) had a strong view about the interests of its members, and the departments concerned did not have a strong view. In particular, the Department which would be responsible for the service system to be transferred, Community Services Victoria, had little knowledge of joint facilities, and no understanding of the significance of the issues.

The decision of Government was that the Joint Facilities would remain within the line management of the Health Department (Office of Psychiatric Services), and that Community Services Victoria would be responsible for providing the direction of the program to be provided at the facilities for the intellectually disabled. In the words of the Order of the Governor in Council which effected the transfer:

> Nothing in this will diminish the responsibility of the chief General manager of the Health Department Victoria, for the management of the services within the facilities. (Administration Order of Governor in Council, 1 Oct 1985)

The nature of the responsibility of CSV to provide programmatic advice was not made explicit in the Order, nor in the subsequent working party report of the Public Service Board which spelt out the implementation arrangements for the transfer of services (Public Service Board's Report on Administration Transfers, 1985). This report specified that the two Departments should enter into an agreement concerning the services to be provided at the facilities. It required that CSV should provide funding for three positions at both Aradale and Mayday Hills to enhance their management infrastructure, and it provided that Post Basic Mental Retardation Nursing Training would be provided at these two institutions. The crucial issues of who would ultimately be responsible for the quality of the care provided, who would direct the utilisation of resources at the facilities, and the ultimate powers of each organisation to direct activities in the institutions were indeterminate.

That authority in the facilities was muddled may be seen in the actions of the two Departments in the subsequent twelve months. In 1986 Community Services Victoria submitted to the Office of Psychiatric Services a draft agreement concerning the joint facilities. This proposed agreement was inadequate on any assessment in that it dealt only with existing services, did not deal with resourcing issues, and made no attempt to clarify control. The Director of the Office of Psychiatric Services (HDV), refused to sign that agreement, however inadequate, as it could limit his authority with respect to the facilities. The authority then, of CSV to even propose an agreement concerning service provision at the facilities was repudiated.

In the State Budget of 1986/87 provision was made for the three senior management positions in each of Aradale and Mayday Hills. In the event, the General Manager, Office of Intellectual Disability Services, CSV, chose not to allocate more than one of these positions to each of the facilities. He claimed that the facilities were being managed by Health and that they were not fundamentally of concern to CSV. A Director of Nursing position was created in each facility and the remaining four positions for which Government had appropriated funds, were absorbed into his Divisional budget. In this CSV made clear its view that the joint facilities were not of major concern to it.

Between October 1985 and September 1987 there was inaction on the part of both Departments with respect to authority and responsibility for the joint facilities. The Office of Psychiatric Services was attempting to regain budget control of all its facilities, of which Mayday Hills was one of the most seriously out of control (Jones interview). It acknowledged no interest on the part of CSV in the outcome of this struggle. CSV was distracted throughout this time by the internal power struggles which emerged from the 1985 restructure, and made little impact upon the management of its own facilities. Aradale and Mayday Hills, at arms length from the Department received even less attention. The Minister for Community Services visited Mayday Hills once, as did the Director General. They were impressed with the tranquil grounds and ornamental gardens and their attention was not drawn to the impoverished environments of the Myrtle and Grevillea Units.

A further complication to the confused management arrangements was added by the proclamation in October 1987 of the *Intellectually Disabled Persons Services Act*. This had the effect of giving to the Director General of CSV powers and responsibilities with respect to services provided to registered eligible clients under the Act, including those services provided by other parties. This had the potential of affecting responsibilities of the Departments as established under the Administrative Order of October 1985. This fact was not registered however, and no legal advice was gained by CSV concerning the impact of the legislation on its responsibilities for the joint facilities. The argument was put in 1991 by the Health Department however, that following the proclamation of the Act, CSV had been responsible for the quality of services to residents of both Mayday Hills and Aradale, and that the abuses identified in an inquiry into Aradale at this time were at least partly, if not entirely, the responsibility of CSV.

The appointment of Regional Directors of CSV in September 1987 and the subsequent appointment of Regional Chief Executive Officers of the Office of Psychiatric Services in September 1988 moved the locus of the debate concerning authority and responsibility from the central to the regional level. The Regional Director, CSV, for the Upper Murray Region, (the researcher) took the view that Mayday Hills was the most significant service delivery outlet within his region and the one in which there was most serious problems in service quality. He believed that it was critical that he assert a position of influence with respect to the facility at an early stage as this would become progressively more difficult. The Regional Director CSV, for the Central Highlands Region (including Aradale) took the view that the Department had not provided him with resources to deal with Aradale and so he could not be expected to deal with what he knew to be a major problem in service delivery quality.

Through most of 1988, the Regional Director, Upper Murray focussed attention on Mayday Hills which was not welcomed either by the management of the institution or the Department centrally. The credibility of the regional team was low; a product of a protracted dispute between a former Psychiatrist Superintendent, and the former Coordinator of Regional Team in Benalla (Brookes interview). CSV was an outsider in the very insular and inward looking facility and community of Beechworth. Institutional management provided little information, and where it was pushed to agree on changes to practice, failed to act on agreements:

> ... the Training Centre was with Health and we were at CSV, and we were trying to implement the Act and start some of those things... the first two or three years of the redevelopment phase, I guess were the most difficult years of the lot because we were not only doing it from outside the Department that ran the Training Centre, we were doing it inside a political environment in which Health certainly didn't care about the ID side of the facility, that it was happy enough to bleed the Training Centre dry in order to pay for its own reforming platform in psych services. I think we had a fairly antagonistic set of colleagues in the Health Department at the facility at that stage.
>
> (Hind interview)

Within CSV centrally there was strong resistance to the view that the Department had responsibilities in the joint facilities. Two staffing positions were provided for each of Aradale and Mayday Hills for the implementation of the IDPS Act, the development of General Service Plans, staff training, and review systems. This was seen as the extent of the responsibility and, in particular, no responsibility was acknowledged for the resources of the facility. This issue came to a head in April 1988 when the Regional Directors of both Upper Murray and Central Highlands sought recognition within their administrative structures for the resource management responsibilities in the joint facilities. These pleas for assistance were rejected.

Despite the absence of central recognition of the joint facilities as part of the disability services system, negotiations proceeded locally concerning the relationship between CSV and HDV in the management of the centre. This continued because of CSV regional officers' concern about the quality of services being provided, and their compliance with the IDPS Act, and because of the Psychiatric Services Regional Executive Officer's perception that his organisation lacked the expertise to deal satisfactorily with intellectual disability issues. In May 1989 the Regional Director CSV put to the CEO Psychiatric Services a statement delineating the role of CSV in relation to the centre. This statement expressed the responsibilities of the Regional Director CSV as follows:

- planning and developing an integrated regional program for intellectually disabled persons;
- ensuring that intellectually disabled persons receive a high quality of care and that services are provided consistent with the Act;
- promoting the integration of intellectually disabled persons into the community; and
- setting standards for agencies providing services for intellectually disabled persons and monitoring performance against these standards.
  Minutes, Training Centre Liaison Committee, May 1989

That statement was accepted, and in keeping with the then prevailing management ethos, was endorsed by the sub-branch of the union. It formed the formal basis of intervention by CSV in the institution until December 1991 when the Training Centre was formally transferred to CSV's administrative authority.

An opportunity to assert a community services perspective in the management of the training centre came with the negotiation within the hospital of a Health Service Agreement. The purpose of this agreement, ostensibly an agreement between the central office of HDV and one of its own hospitals, was to agree budget targets and priority goals. As the training centre was formally part of the psychiatric hospital it was incorporated within the agreement, to which CSV was expected to be a signatory.

The negotiation of the Health Services Agreement, while not fulfilling the Health Department objectives of bringing Mayday Hills under control, did have some important implications for the ultimate redevelopment of the Training Centre.

- It acknowledged, albeit imprecisely, the authority of CSV at the Regional level, to establish the strategic directions of the facility.
- For its part, CSV insisted that it would not sign an Agreement which did not have as a service goal the redevelopment of the accommodation provided in Myrtle House, and which did not include a statement of the resources committed in the Training Centre part of the Hospital. This was the first strong statement of CSV's authority and the first placement of these critical issues on the agenda between the two Departments.

A further Health Services Agreement was attempted during 1989, but aborted at an early stage. It was clear, following a large scale industrial dispute in February 1989 that the critical management tasks were financial and industrial and the elaborate pretences of the service agreement process were unlikely to have an impact upon these. The second Health Services Agreement did not proceed beyond the first draft stage, but by this time the importance of program direction being provided by CSV for the Training Centre was well established.

Through early 1989 and early 1990, CSV regional staff sought to assert a directive role within the Training Centre. This occurred through the Training Centre Liaison Committee, consisting of the Regional Director CSV, the Regional Chief Executive Officer, Psychiatric Services, the Manager, Intellectual Disability Services and the Director of Nursing (later, Manager Direct Care) for the Training Centre. It occurred through the insistence of CSV procedures for such matters as incident reporting, and in the provision of training opportunities for staff. The most significant opportunity arose with the announcement of the State Plan for the Redevelopment of Intellectual Disability Services in May 1989. The Region was able to use the possibility of additional resources for service development as an incentive to staff for change.

Resource Availability

Funding for services for the intellectually disabled was provided through the Victorian State budget. Budget responsibility was transferred as a result of the 1985 machinery of government changes to Community Services Victoria from the Health Department. This was an acrimonious process which resulted in both Departments feeling aggrieved. The budget allocations for the joint facilities however were not transferred, and HDV continued to have budget responsibility for them.

Following the election of the Cain Labor government in March 1982, all government departments were required to improve the productivity of their administrations, and to delivery to government a "productivity premium" equivalent to a 1½% reduction in recurrent expenditure. The funds thus generated were used to fund new policy initiatives. By this means the government was able to reshape public expenditure. Those areas which were not favoured by the government were progressively reduced, and those favoured were expanded over time through policy initiatives. The new government took much of the policy development responsibility which had been the exclusive preserve of the public service and invested this in Policy Committees made up of interested party members. The government also closely vetted new legislation through Bills Committees to ensure consistency with party policy.

The intellectual disability field received bi-partisan support in the Victorian parliament in the early and mid 1980s. The processes of reform, in what was acknowledged by both major parties to be a rundown and neglected area, was commenced during the administration of the previous Liberal government under Minister Borthwick. It was continued by the first Labour minister, Mr Tom Roper. This included the decommissioning of St Nicholas Hospital and the establishment of the Committee on a Legislative Framework for Service to Intellectually Disabled Persons which reported in 1984 (Rimmer, 1984):

> ...the government I think to its credit, at that stage was doing a few things that were pushing the implementation of the principles that were [later] encompassed in the Act and some of the requirements, and they included a significant investment in training of staff, the funding of advocacy groups and the creation of formal advocacy structures, like the Office of the Public Advocate, Community Visitors Program and the Guardianship Board. And at the same time they were making the structural alterations to the organisation to enable the implementation and the shift away from the old style institutional centralised planning and management of services for people with an intellectual disability to a much more decentralised model.
>
> (Dalton interview)

Because of the level of support within the Parliament for the intellectual disability field, that program area received continuing budget support through the period of the first Cain government (1982-85). This took the form of support for additional community residential units (CRUs) and expansions to regional teams, at a time when most government departments received little growth (Scovell interview). This took place in the form of incremental growth, and without a consistent policy or service development framework.

This commenced to change with the 1987/88 state budget which foreshadowed the release of the Ten Year Plan. The community consultations which took place across the state in the development of that plan had created an expectation that substantial resources would be provided to augment services. Anticipating the plan, the 1987/88 Budget provided an injection of funds into strategic service developments known to be consistent with the evolving policy document. This budget, commonly referred to as the IDS redevelopment budget provided an increase of $8m.

The major injection of resources came in the following year with the beginning of the State Plan for intellectual disability services. This was a budget plan designed to give force to the Ten Year Plan, which was, in essence, a policy document. The State Plan was staged to coincide with the three year term of the fourth Cain (Kirner) government (1989-92). It provided $50m over the three years for the expansion of family and childrens services, alternative accommodation and care, community support and vocational services (Resource Allocation of State Plan Resources to regions, 1 November 1989). It represented a major expansion in service availability and was one of the most significant policy undertakings of that government.

While the State Plan was a three year budget commitment, it was subject to the annual state government appropriations process. This meant that while its framework had been approved by Cabinet in advance, it was subject to the political process annually and dependent upon the capacity of government to pass its annual budget. It was subject also to the political pressures within the government. In the first year of its implementation, the Plan reflected the broad scope of the Ten Year Plan, giving attention to both institutional and community located clients, attending to the needs of children and adults, having regard to those with specialised needs as well as those with less acute support needs, and seeking to meet day activity as well as residential needs. As the triennium proceeded however, and the prospects of the election of the government for a further term diminished, the Plan became focussed on the overwhelming requirement to close Caloola Training Centre, an institution which had become symbolic of abuse and neglect within the intellectual disability field. The process of broadly focussed policy and program reform then became, in the end, a narrowly focussed institutional closure program, so that the government might make a significant and lasting impact in a defined area.

There were many implications of the large scale of increased expenditure in the intellectual disability field between 1987 and 1992. It led to a major expansion in service availability both for institutional and community located clients. In its early period, it promoted a high level of creativity in new service design which pushed out the boundaries of thinking about care of the intellectually disabled. The new resources acted as an incentive for more conservative agencies to support reforms. It also created a major administrative problem for the Department responsible for the program. Having appropriated this level of funds, government had an expectation that the funds would be spent in the year they were allocated and in ways which were consistent with its policy intent. While time had been spent on policy development through the early and mid 1980s, little work had been completed on service specifications and administrative guidelines. As a relatively new Department with underdeveloped administrative systems, Community Services Victoria had severe difficulties in spending the funds at all, much less spending them well. These difficulties were aggravated by systemic inefficiencies industrially entrenched inefficiencies and in some cases corruption:

> Our alternative service system, in principle a much better one, was also substantially subverted by management incapacity at program level. We set up costly CRUs for five people, and they nominally had five at all times, but oddly the total number housed across the program did not come close to ten number of CRUs by five. Often there were not more than three there. All the costs were inflated by, say of 60% by permitting the CRU staff to keep their work down by making sure two beds are always vacant. That was the name of the game.

> So you had there an awful lot of people profiting from all the money flowing around. You had a union that had an endless appetite. Theft was endemic. At Caloola, you'll recall, I'm sure Mayday was much the same, you could have a pile of bricks or screenings or fence posts or some bags of cement delivered one night. It wouldn't be there next morning, and it hadn't been ordered for any visible works on site. So everyone was in it. That's where much of the money went.

> (Paterson interview)

The capacity of the Department to adequately account for its expenditure in the program and the perceived sloppiness in its administration, placed it in tension with the growing emphasis upon managerialism and administrative accountability within government, and the developing sense of crisis in the financial management of the state. Significant contributing factors in this process were first, the removal of successive Directors of Disability Services and the installation of a Paterson protégé in that position, and second, a narrowing and focussing of attention upon administrative accountability rather than the reforming goals of an earlier time.

> Terri Whiting left with a great deal of turbulence and significant staff unease. Paul Bartholomew came in and had barely got into the position when John Paterson came down to take on the role. He proceeded to rewrite the history and started to put his stamp on the way he wanted disability to go, and then confirmed and strengthened that by putting his protégé in who then became General Manager Disabilities and proceeded to make substantial changes in head office staffing at a time when regional staff were still stabilising and in fact regions at that stage were still resolving structures.
>
> (Anonymous Respondent I interview)

> We started to move towards a much more economic rationalist type approach. Some of that was undoubtedly necessary: a movement in the direction of being clear about what services were costing and what value we were getting for money, questioning assumptions about service models and stuff like that. But I personally felt it was managed in a way that became too much of the overriding factor and we started to lose some of the issues to do with caring about the people at the end of this day.
>
> (Bartholomew interview)

Politically, the Department became vulnerable because of the difficulty it experienced in delivering on government policy. An early initiative through the IDS Redevelopment budget was referred to as the "children out of Janefield" initiative. This was a response to a government concern that children not be placed in one of Melbourne's largest congregate facilities in the northern suburbs, but be enabled to reside in community settings, preferably close to their families. Two years after the initiative had been funded, the money and not been expended and the children in question were still resident in Janefield.

The political problem contributed to the development within the department of a parallel organisation specifically to meet the major policy goal of the final year of the State Plan, the closure of Caloola Training Centre. An implementation team was established which reported outside Disability Services Division. The administrative problem was addressed, as indicated above, by a narrowing and constraining of the reforming intent of the program. The parallel organisation competed for political attention and for leadership within the field:

> ...it was adequately resourced and the government certainly was prepared to put some money industrially to buy off the unions and they did that. And was

prepared to invest the money in redeveloping. To quieten the outcry from the advocacy groups about people moving from one institution to another there was an investment in providing institutional infrastructure in the community. There was investment in the actual residential support and in the day programs support. That I think enabled the whole process to be saleable to a whole range of groups. There was still some that stood outside it but, they were in the end never going to be influential enough to stop it.

(Dalton interview)

The successful closure of Caloola, which involved the relocation of 440 residents (195 of them to other institutions) the construction of 43 specifically built houses and in a period of twelve months (Brcadmore, 1992), was a logistic triumph, which was celebrated by the then Minister Setches, much to the chagrin of Disability Services Division. When the inevitable change of government occurred in October 1992 however, the achievement was depreciated and all those associated with it were removed from positions of influence.

The Technical System

For the purposes of the study, the technological environment of the organisation will be defined as the dominant mode of service production within the intellectual disability field; the industry within which the organisation existed. It has been noted that the Mayday Hills Training Centre had existed in a largely unchanged state for approximately one hundred and thirty years. Those changes in service technology which had a major effect upon its parent organisation, the Mayday Hills Psychiatric Hospital, the introduction of psychotropic medication, had only peripheral impact upon the Training Centre (see Appendix A, History of Mayday Hills Training Centre), however major changes within the service technology did commence to take place during the 1980s.

The core technology of the intellectual disability services field is concerned with the manner in which care, support and training is provided to the intellectually disabled. Prior to the 1980s in Victoria, this care was principally provided through large congregate care facilities such as existed at Mayday Hills Training Centre. The care itself was largely custodial and sought to provide a protected and secure environment for residents. Care was totally provided at a single location and presumed continuing residence. Few clients progressed to less intensive or more independent environments. The choices available to consumers were usually between total care of an institutional type, and no service at all. No entitlements to services existed within legislation.

The nature of this care was predicated upon assumptions about the client group. Where it was assumed that the intellectually disabled person had few capacities and little ability to learn, the service response was protective and isolating. Because it was assumed that the individual could not acquire and retain skills, it was assumed that he/she would continue to be dependent.

The Legislative and Policy Basis of Care

The Intellectually Disabled Persons Services Act 1986 was the culmination of an era of activism which began with the separation of the Mental Retardation Division from the Mental Health Division of the Health Commission (Department). It was unashamedly a piece of reforming legislation, intended to have a radical impact upon the delivery of services. Section 1 of the Act clearly stated:

> The purpose of this Act is to reform the law relating to services for intellectually disabled persons. (IDPS Act. 1986)

It was the first piece of statute law in Australia to recognise that intellectual disability is not synonymous with mental illness, and sought to address itself to a fragmented, uncoordinated and poorly resourced service delivery system (Health and Community Services, 1993).

The Act in Section 5 outlined fourteen Principles, intended to provide a basis for the provision of services covered by the legislation. These addressed the rights of intellectually disabled people regarding equal access, equal opportunity and normalisation. They made specific reference to the requirement to use the least restrictive option when any restriction to an individual's rights or opportunities was necessary (IDPS Act. s.5). Elsewhere, the legislation set out principles for the way in which services registered under the Act were to be provided (IDPS Act s.23 (3)(a)-(f)).

The aim the legislation was stated as:

> To advance the dignity, worth, human rights and full potential of intellectually disabled persons. (IDPS Act s.6 (1))

Specifically, it detailed 22 objectives intended to realise this. These covered the planning of services (s.6 (2)(a,c,r)), access to generic services (s.6 (2)(b,f,g)), individualised planning (s.6 (2)(d)), service development and regulation (s.6 (2)(c, j, k)), community integration (s.6 (2)(e, f, h)), residential institutions (s.6 (2)(h, i)), staff training (s.6 (2)(b)), advocacy (s.6 (2)(m, n)), and community education (s.6 (2)(o, p, q)).

With respect to residential institutions, the Act included the following specific objectives:

> To ensure that intellectually disabled person in institutions have the opportunity to live in community-based accommodation with the benefit of support services. (s.6 (2)(h))

> To promote a high quality of care and developmental programing for intellectually disabled persons whilst they continue to reside in institutions. (s.6 (2)(i))

An intention of the Act was the separation of service provision for people with an intellectual disability from that of people with a mental illness. To this end, it sought to give definition to intellectual disability, and hence eligibility for service. The definition adopted for "intellectual disability", in the case of a person over five years of age was "a significant sub-average general intellectual functioning existing concurrently with deficits in adaptive behaviour and manifested during the developmental period". The lack of clarity in the definition of the individual words in this definition was ultimately to lead to legal challenges concerning eligibility (Health and Community Services, 1993). While meeting these three criteria was not a guarantee of service, failure to meet them resulted in exclusion from services. A further problem arose with respect to confusion about what was guaranteed by eligibility, in that s. (94) indicated that "a declaration of eligibility entitles the eligible person to receive services under the Act". This was interpreted by some as guaranteeing service availability, rather than specifying the pre-requisites for service access, as the government ultimately argued.

An important aspect of the application of the Act with respect to eligibility was the specification that clients who were receiving services prior to the implementation of the Act would be eligible for the preparation of a general service plan (s.11(4)). These provisions were intended to be transitional but effectively conferred eligibility status on a large number of long term residents of institutions, without the capacity to review their registration as intellectually disabled. The Act thus brought a number of people within its ambit whose diagnosis was uncertain. This was particularly significant in the joint facilities of Mayday Hills and Aradale which had a number of residents with a dual psychiatric and intellectual disability diagnosis.

The Act established the requirements for case planning. A General Service Plan (GSP) was defined in the Act as specifying the major areas of life activity in which support was required and the strategies to be carried out to provide that support. All eligible clients including pre-Act clients (those utilising registered services prior to proclamation of the Act) were entitled to have a GSP (s.9-10). Review of these plans was an entitlement every five years for community based clients and every year for clients in residential institutions. GSPs were viewed as a case planning mechanism, to coordinate and monitor service provision to people with an intellectual disability. Prior to the Act there had been no consistent and comprehensive mechanism in Victoria for case coordination. GSPs were envisaged as having a broad planning function, with representatives from appropriate human services organisations attending planning meetings to encourage inter-agency cooperation.

The Act also established a mechanism for the review of official decisions through the Intellectual Disability Review Panel (IDRP), (ss.27-35 and 51-82) and the monitoring of the quality of care in residential facilities by community visitors. In recognition that the Department was in the position to make decisions that would substantially and sometimes irrevocably affect the lives of clients, a number of those decisions were to be reviewable by the Intellectual Disability Review Panel (IDRP, ss.27-35 and Schedules 1-2). Reviewable decisions as outlined in s.51 of the Act included:

- eligibility for services;
- content of a General Service Plan;
- amendment or review of a General Service Plan;
- admission to a residential institution;
- detention or care of a security resident; and
- use of Restraint, Seclusion or Aversive Therapy.

The IDRP was empowered to make recommendations to the Director General or Minister, and was able "to advise the Minister or the Secretary on any matter referred to it by the Minister or the Secretary" (s.28(c)). An example of this occurred in 1991 when the panel was requested by the Minister for Community Services to review and develop guidelines on the administration of menstrual suppressants to women with an intellectual disability residing in residential institutions and registered services.

The reference within the powers of the IDRP of reviewable decisions in relation to the use of Restraint, Seclusion and Aversive Therapy (s.51) was particularly important for the disability institutions where these practices were most prevalent. The powers recognised that the provision of services to people with an intellectual disability required at times access to powers beyond those available under common law. The legislation permitted the use of physical and chemical restraint, seclusion and the use of aversive therapy, but restricted these to circumstances in which less restrictive strategies had been unsuccessful or where the individual was at risk of serious injury to themselves or others, or was involved in persistent damage to property. The IDRP was empowered to monitor and review the use of these powers, which it, in practice, pursued energetically. The use of restraint (particularly chemical) was a feature of institutional care, as was the restriction of movement and punishment by seclusion (Menzie interview). The insistence by the Review Panel of monthly returns on the use of these practices by residential facilities, the investigation of patterns of excessive use, and the reporting of rates of use, had the effect of bringing to public attention the ways in which client behaviour was controlled within the institutions, and the potential for abuse.

Community Visitors were intended in the legislation as a means of providing quality assurance. They replaced the Official Visitors appointed under the Mental Health Act, and had a statutory mandate in relation to people in services covered by the IDPS Act. Community Visitors were appointed to particular regions to inspect residential institutions and Community Residential Units. Their powers, as detailed in s.54 of the Act, were to:

- ascertain the appropriateness and standard of accommodation, physical wellbeing and welfare of the residents;
- inquire about the adequacy of opportunities and facilities for the recreation, occupation, education and training of residents;
- determine whether services are being provided in accordance with the Principles of the Act (s.5);
- inquire into the use of restraint, seclusion and aversive therapy;
- access client's Individual Program Plans to determine whether they have been complied with;
- determine any failure to comply with the provisions of the Act; and
- respond to and inquire into any complaint made to a Community Visitor by a resident.

(IDPS Act, s.54(a)-(q))

Annual reporting mechanisms were established in statute, with a requirement that an Annual Community Visitors Report be forwarded to the Minister before the end of September each year and tabled in Parliament within fourteen sitting days thereafter.

A further provision of the Act which had major implications for the institutions was that regulating admission to residential institutions (s.18(1)-(4)). This section of the Act provided an extremely limited basis upon which registered eligible persons might be admitted to an institution. These were that: (a) admission would provide the best possible choice of services for enhancing the person's independence and self-sufficiency and is least likely to produce regression, loss of skills or other harm; (b) admission is the alternative which in the circumstances in the least restrictive of the person's freedom of decision and action; or (c) unless the person is admitted to a residential institution the person or any person with whom he or she resides will suffer serious physical or emotional harm. The impact of these provisions was to reduce to a very small number, those who could be legitimately admitted to an institution. Conditions (a) and (c) could be met by few if any potential residents, while admission under (b) relied heavily upon the interpretation of the words "in the circumstances".

The Act marked the beginning of a new era of codification and consolidation of the casework services component of intellectual disability services and the development of a defined services system which was non-institutional in conception. Bridging as it did two distinct periods in the development of intellectual disability services, the Act entailed tensions between the assertion of rights for the disabled, and the requirements of administration and regulation. These tensions were not immediately apparent at the time of its enactment in October 1986 and proclamation in October 1987, but were, during the later part of the decade, to become of critical concern for the development of services.

Principal amongst these was the tension between narrowing and defining the role of the State with respect to intellectually disabled persons on one hand, and on the other hand, seeking to broaden the basis of statutory support and resource commitment to them.

An underlying intent of the legislation was to create a data base and rationale for service provision which would commit government to a greatly expanded role. Intellectually disabled people would cease to be an ill-defined client group, the majority of whom received no statutory support. All users of services would be required to be assessed for eligibility, and if appropriate, registered. Their General Service Plan (GSP) would identify and classify their support needs. These, in turn, could be utilised to develop a comprehensive overview of service requirements across the state. This overview, combined with the moral weight of the Act's principles, would place pressure upon government to increase the level of services available.

However, in defining for the first time a role for the State with respect to individual intellectually disabled people, the Act placed government (and the Department) on an inevitable path towards individualised statutory casework, which was at once more extensive and more particular than the broad planning and resourcing function outlined above. The legislation as a vehicle for both functions was a flawed one, and ultimately was unable to perform either well.

As a tool to facilitate comprehensive planning and leverage upon resources, the Act was not effective because the systems did not exist to either collect the data, or to aggregate and analyse them. The data collection systems which were ultimately sought were properly reliant upon client services or casework staff since the data was predicated upon a case planning framework. These staff became the point at which the tensions between services planning and individualised services had to be resolved. Predictably the contest was resolved in favour of the client, and the quality of data collected were poor. The information systems which were to have made possible the aggregation of data were slow in developing and cumbersome to utilise. They were poorly integrated with work practices and so tended to be neglected by operational staff. After attempting over five years to build discrete Intellectual Disability Services information systems predicated upon the planning functions, the Department abandoned the effort in late 1991 in favour of a system which was integrated with the other client services functions of the Department, and was seen essentially as a support to the casework function.

The legislation played an important role in public education, leading public opinion and generating public support for the rights of intellectually disabled people. Nevertheless there was a tension between this important role, and that of providing a basis for governmental administrative action. There was confusion, for instance, about the status and impact of the Principles annunciated in the legislation (IDPS Act s.5). It was intended that these would confer general rights upon all persons with an intellectual disability. The principles however had no intrinsic connection with the responsibilities of the Department and funded services outlined in the legislation. In fact the only enforceable individual rights contained within the legislation were an entitlement to a general service plan, and if appropriate, an individual program plan.

> We didn't really know how to bring the ideology and operational knowledge into a legislative framework. Generally the provisions [of the Act] have applied and worked. IPPs and GSPs were important, but they had a downside in that they could become meaningless and minimalist. The legislation certainly set some very clear expectations and arrangements that could be perpetuated. It

was important to state principles, entitlements and review procedures. The legislation was great, but the implementation was difficult.

(Scovell interview)

The Act placed considerable emphasis upon ensuring access by intellectually disabled people, to generic services, and this must be considered one of its fundamental objectives. In practice however, this was more effective as a statement of intent or ideology, since the discrepancy between the actions it required of the administering department, and the actual powers of that department, was such that little effective action could be taken. For example, s.6(2)(b) committed the Department to **ensuring** access for people with an intellectual disability to a range of listed generic services such as education or legal services, which were clearly beyond the department's sphere of influence.

A significant impact of the Act upon the institutional disability sector was through the establishment of the intellectual Disability Review Panel and the appointment of community visitors. These, frequently in close association with the Office of the Public Advocate, had the effect of opening to public scrutiny the conditions, the ethos, and the decisions taken within institutions, which had previously been contained within these organisations. It was the report of the Community Visitors to Caloola in 1987 which highlighted the impoverishment of that institution and which provided the initial impetus towards its closure. It was the community visitors to Aradale who first drew attention to the abuses which were occurring there and with the Public Advocate, succeeded in bringing about an official inquiry into that institution. The IDRP, while it made few friends within the Department and especially within the institutions, made a significant impression through its focus upon individual reviewable decisions concerning residents.

The legislation presumed a political environment which could not be sustained through progressively tighter budget cycles. While budget outlays for intellectual disability services were steadily increased through the period 1988 - 1991, they did so in response to public disquiet at the poverty of some institutional environments, and as a product of the State Plan for Intellectual Disability Services. They did not increase as a consequence of the rational comprehensive planning envisaged by the Act's originators. Furthermore, budget outlays in the community services sector as a whole diminished during this time, and the strong growth in funding for intellectual disability services was sustained only by an increasingly narrow focus upon specific projects rather than system wide change or expansion. In the 1991/92 budget year, the resource commitment was made specifically in relation to the Caloola closure project.

It was in the framework that it provided for casework services that the Act came to be most criticised however. As noted above, the legislation provided a mandated basis for statutory involvement in the lives of intellectually disabled people. It did so by prescribing an eligibility assessment and case planning process. In consequence of the planning process, clients were guaranteed nothing additional in the form of services.

The legal framework provided by the legislation was different in critical respects from the United States legislation upon which it was based, despite their surface similarities. It sought to guarantee for registered clients, a General Service Plan (GSP) which would specify agreed broad casework goals, and an Individual Program Plan (IPP), which would translate these into operational programs. The United States legislation however was able to rely upon Federal Constitutional legislation which could guarantee access to care by the least restrictive alternative, and a right to habilitation. While successive legal challenges have rendered this constitutional position weaker, tending now to define minimal rather than optimal requirements, the definition of rights of disabled people constitutionally has had a potent effect (Griffin, 1986, 58).

The Victorian legislation had no constitutional reference and so sought to establish client rights by administrative means i.e., the right to General Service Plans and the reviewability of decisions concerning the usage of restraint, seclusion or aversive therapy. It sought to establish more generalisable "rights" for the intellectually disabled through the assertion of "principles" which prefixed the legislation. These were without legal force.

The Ten Year Plan for Intellectual Disability Services 1988

The policy framework which underpinned the deinstitutionalisation of Victoria's Intellectual Disability Services in the late 1980s, was built upon the ideological and intellectual traditions which had informed the *Intellectually Disabled Persons Services Act*. It was made explicit in a major policy development exercise conducted between 1986 and 1988; the Ten Year Plan for the Redevelopment of Intellectual Disability Services (Community Services Victoria, 1988). This plan was the culmination of two years of research and consultation by Neilson Associates Pty Ltd., a firm of management consultants. It was commissioned by Community Services Victoria with the object of having in place a plan for the complete closure of the State's nine congregate care institutions within a ten year period. As such it was a dramatic gesture by the then recently appointed Deputy Director General responsible for the Office of Intellectual Disability Services (OIDS), Mr Brian Butterworth. The plan as it was finally submitted to Government however, had a broader focus, and represented an attempt to operationalise the principles expressed in the *Intellectually Disabled Persons Services Act.*

An Interim Report, released in June 1987 outlined broad directions for service development within the field, including: efforts to reduce the incidence of intellectual disability in the population; development of effective family and child support systems for families with a disabled dependant; integration within mainstream education; the development of alternatives to congregate care; the expansion of housing opportunities; more flexible funding arrangements; affirmative action in employment; a program of possible closure of major State Training Centres; an expansion and redefinition of the department's regional staff role; community education concerning disability issues; and expanded access to generic services.

The report was widely circulated between July and October 1987 and subjected to consultations organised through the Department's Regional Consultative Councils (RCCs). The Redevelopment of Intellectual Disability Services Consultation Report released by the Minister in January 1988 indicated that while the consultation provided strong support to the underlying philosophy of the Interim Report and the proposed service directions, there was significant community scepticism of the intention of government and the bureaucracy to respond in the way indicated. There was resistance from the families of residents of Training Centres to their relocation based upon concern about the adequacy of available support services, and fear that some residents of Training Centres would be unable to cope in community settings.

The final report was presented to the Minister on 8 August 1988. This report reflected the directions of the interim report, while being more specific in proposed services development for leisure services, criminal justice services, behaviour management and staff training. Importantly, the final report proposed for the first time the redevelopment of programs and services within the institutions to improve the quality of life of residents; and the introduction of case management as a central activity of the Department at the regional level "in order to ensure that every client has a personal and direct contact with a member of staff whose primary concern is to assist clients to gain access to appropriate services, and to maintain contact with clients and their families" (Community Services Victoria, 1988, 70).

The Ten Year Plan addressed itself to the future of Mayday Hills and Aradale Hospitals in the context of dealing with clients living in Psychiatric Hospitals (Community Services Victoria, 1988, 38). The strategy for these facilities was not one which focussed upon their immediate closure, but rather one which would have a waiting list established for relocation when vacancies in other residential support services arose. By these means the plan proposed that all clients could be relocated by 1997 and the facilities would revert entirely to the use of the Health Department. The plan proposed that a choice be offered to staff such that they could opt for employment by the Health Department or could choose to transfer to CSV for employment in what were described as Local Residential Service Teams.

The Ten Year Plan provided a critical framework by which the IDPS Act may have been operationalised. In particular it attempted to give the Act practical effect in the means by which:

- It ended the defacto isolation and neglect of Training Centres, and their residents; in particular, by attempting to define a future for specific facilities, and by proposing the provision of day programs for institutional residents.
- It proposed the integration of intellectual disability teams within a broader regional structure of CSV services, and attention to access by intellectually disabled clients to other community services.
- It identified and sought to define the case management function required within the community service delivery system and to distinguish between this and the consultancy function, previously performed by intellectual disability teams.
- It advocated the utilisation of generic services for intellectually disabled clients particularly in home based care.
- Many of the new service developments outlined within the Final Report were the underpinning of the important service initiatives in the subsequent four years. These included the Singleton Equity Scheme, the Behaviour Intervention Support Teams, and Community Living Support Schemes.

The difficulties facing its implementation however were substantial and went beyond that posed by the time period over which it would require a consistent policy focus. This in itself was sufficient to require that a more modest version be established which could be tailored to the three/four year terms of a Government.

The plan was comprehensive in nature, and could not readily take account of the poverty of the available information systems for planning purposes, nor the relative immaturity of case work systems for the intellectually disabled within Victoria.

Conceptually, the plan envisaged a service system with multiple providing agencies, which would be planned for, using comprehensive information gathered from the client services planning mechanisms proposed under the Act. The system then would be accessed by clients supported through a developed case management service. The reality was that individualised casework services, the underpinning of such a system, were underdeveloped in the extreme. The requirement for such a system had not existed prior to the proclamation of the IDPS Act, and staff until that time saw themselves as consultants. They provided advice but lacked responsibility for cases. The proclamation of the Act, for the first time created a statutory responsibility, even if the responsibility at law went no further than to assess eligibility for service and to provide a General Service Plan. Increasingly, following proclamation, community expectations and the demands of client interactions forced the development of a case work service, but in 1988 no models of practice existed, few resources were available for a client services function, and the role of departmental officers in supporting clients in accessing services was ill-defined.

Further, the information systems which might have supported both the client services and the planning functions outlined in the Final Report, were undeveloped. When they were in fact developed in 1990 they were largely unreliable because they required that staff engage in a set of additional tasks associated with data collection, and failed to integrate those tasks within their existing work tasks. A comprehensive client services information system was finally being implemented in 1992 with its intellectual disability services module scheduled for completion in 1994. At the time of writing (1997), the system had not yet been developed.

The success of the Plan may be measured by the extent of its implementation. Intellectual Disability Service Teams were integrated within the central and regional operations of CSV, and institutional management arrangements, with varying levels of success were integrated with regional management systems. Attempts were made through 1990 and 1991 to establish an IDS case management system, and this was at least conceptualised in 1992 when CSV adopted a corporate case management system.

Through all this however, the critical requirement of reducing the segregation of service development for intellectually disabled clients was largely not met. The Department did not actively pursue the utilisation of generic services for client support, even in the home-based care area which had been most explicitly enunciated in the report. The Ministry of Housing and equity housing arrangements proposed in the report, while already established, had a poor take up rate across the State. The Community Living Support Programs which were established tended to have limited outreach capacity, and over time began to look more and more like the institutional community residential unit programs which the report criticised (Community Services Victoria, 1988, 23).

Importantly, the comprehensiveness of the Report's focus was progressively lost in the implementation of the subsequent State Plan. As the implementation became increasingly captured by the political imperatives of closing Caloola Training Centre, it became more narrow. Ultimately, the goal became not the redevelopment of a services system in order to increase the integration of intellectually disabled people into general community life but more the relocation of a particular group of clients from an institutional setting. In consequence many of the settings chosen for their relocation were either actually institutions or institutional in nature.

In summary, the IDPS Act captured the ideological enthusiasm of the activists. In doing so, it was able to marshal considerable early support. Its ideological nature however meant that it became less relevant as administrators sought to translate it into purposive action. The Hon Michael John, Opposition spokesperson on community services from 1990 to 1992, and Minister from 1992 to 1996 expressed his view about the practical application of the Act:

> ... so you had the new philosophy and all of that "dignity of risk". Complete rejection of paternalism or protection of people for their own good, yet we still continued the practice of such places like Kew where we lock you up for the night, to stop them wandering down to Kew junction. So, we were saying one thing but still practising, in pockets, the other... So, I don't know that I pay a lot of attention to the Act.
>
> (John interview)

The Ten Year Plan for the Redevelopment of Intellectual Disability Services, enabled a comprehensive vision of the development of the service system. Its very comprehensiveness, which for implementation required a consistency and completeness of policy commitment, meant that it was difficult to sustain. It was abandoned almost as it was published. The State Plan for Intellectual Disability Services commenced as an attempt at systematic reform as well as an attempt to ameliorate some of the worst of the State's disgraces. This too was also a victim of political process, bureaucratic restructure and the very real difficulties of sustaining public initiatives over time. By the third year it was clear that the State Plan was required to change from a focus on systematic reform to one which focussed upon the closure of a single, large facility.

The imperatives established then by the legal and policy environment were in some senses quite clear, directive, and comprehensive. They commenced with bi-partisan political support and were able to command considerable resources. Their potency however diminished over time, as the political and bureaucratic environment changed:

> ... I really felt that there was so much else that wasn't done. There was so much that was not dealt with in terms of broader promotion by the organisation about the place of people with disabilities generally in the community: community education, promotion of the rights and abilities of people with disabilities, issues to do with access, issues to do with information, issues to do with carer support ... We concentrated everything on this reform of funding mechanisms. And that's fine but it shouldn't be at the exclusion of everything else, and it shouldn't be without a context of what it is going to contribute towards an overall objective. Ours is an objective about the fact that we are going to, through a distribution of resources, provide more appropriate arrangements for people, and about how that was going to be achieved. That would at least give it some legitimacy. But I never felt that was clear.
>
> (Bartholomew interview)

The Technology of Care

The IDPS Act required a fundamentally different approach to the care of the intellectually disabled, based upon individualised planning, access to socially valued roles, and the utilisation of generic community services. The reality in 1987 however, was that the larger part of the resources committed to the care of the intellectually disabled was provided to operate segregated services, with very little individualised planning. Most residential services were provided through large scale congregate services, and most day activity programs were provided through Day Training Centres which ran mainly segregated services. Even those residential services which had been established on a community living model were often reproductions on a smaller scale of the institutional model, with rigid staff rostering, and little meaningful community contact on the part of residents. Only amongst the early childhood services, where a very strong parents movement had fought to ensure access to generic children's services, was there any significant integration (Green interview).

Before the goals of the legislation could be met, it was required that the principles of the legislation be translated into realisable service models, that resources be found to develop new services or to convert old services to new models, and that staff be trained to perform new tasks. It was in this area that

David Green, former General Manager, OIDS and later Public Advocate for Victoria, believed that the reform movement failed. In his view, the legislation gave a focus to reform which was not adequately transferred into a technology of care. In his view, the loss of focus in reform did not occur only in the late 1980s, but was there before hand.

> There was a struggle for some kind of sense of integrity about the work that gave it identity. This was not the case in the early 80s when reform got going in our field. Paterson and Cleave gave it sharpness, but it was there before. You didn't know what your reference points were. In Disability the operational centre wasn't there. There was a lot of smoke and fire. It was grandiose, and passionate, but not so much coherence and integrity. This partly relates to there being no strong central profession [for good or ill]. We were responsible for the state of the art, the truth, but there was not the professional infrastructure to carry the promise of the legislation.
>
> (Green interview)

A development of alternative service models was undertaken in part through the Ten Year Plan Consultative process. The extensive surveying of opinion amongst service providers, parents and other interested parties, produced a stocktake of contemporary practice. The Ten Year Plan provided a detailed list of service development alternatives covering the areas of case management, residential support, recreation, health, housing, day activities, education and transport. This work was continued within Disability Services Division under Rassaby's leadership. The State Plan provided the budget vehicle by which these services could be adopted.

A principal difficulty facing program reform was the conservatism of the majority of services. Services were predominately state government operated congregate care facilities which were resistant to change, or part of a small non government sector. The non government sector consisted of Residential Care Associations and Adult Day Training Centres. Residential care associations were community based organisations, which were established by government in the early 1980s to manage the growing number of community houses. They consisted mainly of parents of residents whose principal interest was the secure care of their children. Many were opposed to any changes intended to increase the independence of their dependants, preferring a secure if dependent lifestyle for them. Adult Day Training Centres were established as parents initiatives during the 1950s and 1960s as an alternative to institutional admission. They were similarly dominated by parents of users, and were often opposed to individualised programs as opposed to large groups programs provided at a single centre. These services were usually very dependent upon fundraising and frequently wished to preserve segregated facilities for disabled users, which they felt they had a major part in establishing.

> Then there were parents' interest groups, community visitors, and associated single issue groups, and in their eyes, no matter what you did, it would never be enough. The implicit goal of many of the parents was to have all the resources in the whole program devoted to their own particular child. They were quick to invoke rights, but those were absolute - even another disabled person should be removed from a facility if their behaviour infringed on the 'rights' of their relative. There were no limits, and hence there was no possibility of intellectual rigor or consistency in some of the positions taken by advocates. But to them we were *always* in the wrong - almost the surrogate for the evil spirit that had visited their child's misfortune upon them.
>
> (Paterson interview)

Community Living Support Services (CLSS) were intended to develop as more progressive models of residential care. As has been noted previously however, these largely failed to meet expectations. An alternative model for day programming proposed through the Ten Year Plan was brokerage services. Such services would purchase on behalf of clients individual programs from a broad range of potential providers. This would allow participation in an array of programs, would facilitate access to generic services, and would make possible individuals program choices. It was only in the services developed in North East Victoria and the Goulburn Valley as part of the redevelopment of Mayday Hills Training Centre, that this service model was aggressively pursued.

In 1990 a model of purchase of service for day activity services was introduced in order to rationalise these services and ensure that the department was able to guarantee a rate of service for its financial commitment. That purchasing model however, which was based on the unit costing principles which were in vogue at the time, had the impact of reducing the viability of small, individualised and integrative services which inevitably lost economies of scale. It significantly advantaged larger scale congregate facilities, and so ran counter to the intent of the legislation and of formal policy (Keating, 1995).

The provision of an adequately trained work force was one of the most critical tasks facing reform. The majority of the workforce was engaged in providing services within the institutional sector. These staff were variously mental retardation nurses, state enrolled nurses, or untrained ward assistants. At Mayday Hills Training Centre, a minority of staff were mental retardation nursing trained. Most were either psychiatric nurses, or mental health aides.

Mental retardation nursing was a relatively new profession which had developed as the separation of intellectual disability services from psychiatric services was achieved. The basis of training was in addition to basic nursing, a focus on training strategies for the disabled.

As part of its commitment following the industrial dispute of 1985, the state government undertook to provide training for the workforce. Between 1986 and 1990, the state provided six months training in the form of a vocational education certificate for all the previously designated ward assistants. These staff became known as intellectual disability service officers (IDSOs). Training was progressively moved outside the department and into the Tertiary and Further Education (TAFE) sector. This program was abandoned in 1991 when the newly appointed Director for Disability Services decided that trained staff was an unwarranted expense, and introduced a new category of staff, the Human Services Officer (HSO).

The core skills for the specialist staff (MRNs and IDSOs) were associated with "developmental programming", the partialising of tasks in such a way as to be able to teach intellectually disabled clients through process of repetition and reinforcement. Through these strategies, clients were to be taught to perform tasks such as feeding, dressing and personal hygiene tasks, and also alternatives to self destructive or socially unacceptable behaviours. Developmental programming was central to the service reform task and integrally related to the Act, since it formed the key mechanism with which to implement individual program plans (IPPs). The strategy of the Act involved the development of general service plans (GSPs) covering broad personal goals. These were to be given specificity through IPPs, which would be implemented through individualised programming. The decision to abandon the training strategy was thus an abandonment of what had previously been an essential element of reform.

The provision of a trained workforce was a major logistical achievement, and perhaps the most significant factor in improving the quality of care within services in the later half of the 1980s. The strategy however, was limited in its effect because of the constraints upon staff utilising the skills they had developed.

A major constraint was the fact that the majority of staff worked within institutional services in which they were committed to the care of large numbers of residents. The provision of developmental programs assumed that there was time available after basic nursing tasks had been performed to undertake the development and implementation of programs. This was seldom the case. Further, as the decade progressed, greater and greater economies were required within services, such that in community houses, it was frequently the case that relatively junior staff were required to supervise houses unassisted.

A senior manager responsible for a major institution, commented on the discrepancy between the training of staff and the task they were required to perform:

> ... the content of the course was focused on things like normalisation and kind of set goals in terms of care of people. And one of the big problems was that when people were sent off from [an institution], they came back and resigned, because it was so out of kilter. There was a really big resignation rate with people within only a couple of months coming back, because it was so out of kilter in terms of what people were being trained, how people were being trained for particular work, from what was demanded and expected of them when they got back to institutional services. It was very targeted towards the goals of the new set of values that were coming in.
>
> (Anonymous Respondent II interview)

The strategy assumed that programs would be devised by mental retardation nurses, who had the advantage of a three year training program. Throughout the period however, there was a shortage of trained MRNs. As Conway (1992) points out:

> A related outcome of the move to local service provision is that staff are often not available, and rather than have the most qualified staff working with people with high support needs, the lowest trained staff are frequently the only staff available. (Conway, 1992, 71)

The reliance upon mental retardation nurses assumed also that this group of staff would be able to make the transition from a clinical, to a non clinical setting. They were, however, required to perform very different roles in community services, some of which were not related to individualised services, and so outside their training. The development of case plans for clients and the organisation of case management strategies involved skills in negotiation with other providers, the balancing of competing needs, and operation within a relatively uncontrolled environment outside the institution. Many found this transition difficult, or did not attempt it (Conway, 1992).

> The whole Mental Retardation Nursing thing was actually professionalisation of institutionally based practice. It was better than nothing, and it attracted decent people, but it was about an institutional form of care. It was not about doing the things which integration aides do in the schools, which Riding for the Disabled and the various sporting facilities and clubs for the disabled people

do. It was not what even the local cricket clubs often do - taking a few kids that aren't really going to make it but do it to put something back into the community.

I mean that's the real stuff as far as I'm concerned, that makes a difference. The MRN thing wasn't about any of that. And you couldn't pay for it even if it was, not at their rates. It's got to be done in other ways. Their concept of their work was structured around a cradle to grave, single facility model, where the clients, their meal ticket, were there all day, totally captive and institutionalised. That's the last thing the clients needed in almost every case.

(Paterson interview)

The Ten Year Plan foreshadowed the development of a case management service to ensure adequate case planning and the coordination of services to individuals. As the limitations of reliance upon mental retardation nurses to perform these roles, together with their unwillingness to move to clinical settings became clear, client services teams became progressively multi-disciplinary with a preponderance of social work trained staff. This corresponded however with a change of focus in individualised care by which the department was concerned to limit rather than expand access to services. The intellectual disability case management system which was developed in 1991 gave little assistance in the planning and management of client care, but provided a mechanism whereby the closing of lower priority cases would be possible. (Community Services Victoria, 1990).

Summary

This chapter has described the fundamental changes which took place in the late half of the 1980s and the early 1990s in the State of Victoria. The following chapter will summarise these changes, and will discuss them in terms of the structure of environmental change. It will do so utilising the framework developed within this study for the consideration of environmental contingency. It will then utilise the Emery and Trist typology for the classification of the causal texture of the environment.

5 The Structure of Environmental Change

The period between 1985 and 1992 was one of great change within the intellectual disability field in the State of Victoria. As has been described in the preceding chapter, the period was marked by significant change in the pre-eminent philosophical base and technology of care in the field. Changes in the societal perspective of the intellectually disabled person and of appropriate models of care for them developed out of the emergent sociology of the 1960s and 1970s. These perspectives, which underpinned the normalisation movement, focussed upon the role of social institutions in devaluing individuals. They asserted the importance of socially valued roles for the disabled person, and the importance of education and training as distinct from treatment, as interventions.

These changes can be seen in the enactment in 1986 of a major piece of reformist legislation which by its explicit provisions and the expectations it created, reshaped the basis upon which care could be provided in the State. The legislation separated for the first time the care of the intellectually disabled from that of the mentally ill. It asserted the rights of intellectually disabled people to equal access, equal opportunity and to normalisation. For those residing in institutions, it asserted their right to access to community living and to quality services while in the institution. It regulated the basis upon which admission to an institution might be made. It established a right to case planning and sought to create an environment for effective agency collaboration in the interests of clients. It established external mechanisms for the review of decisions which impacted in a major way upon the lives of clients.

The legislation was not without its problems. It created an expectation of developed casework services without there being practice frameworks or adequate resources to support these. It proposed planning systems which were beyond the administrative capacity of the responsible department to establish. It was premised upon a greatly expanded role of government which while sustained in the short term because of the policy initiatives of the State Plan, ran counter to the prevailing trend towards smaller government. Its reforming goals were ultimately frustrated by the fact that many of the structural reforms it proposed were beyond the powers of its administering department, and required sustained political commitment beyond the life of a single government. Its statements of principle, while powerful in their effect, lacked legal force.

The policy vehicle for these major changes in the technology of care, the Ten Year Plan, was to produce far reaching changes in disability services. Beginning as a very specific plan for the closure of the State's institutions, it was transformed following widespread community consultation to become a broad strategy to address the education, habilitation, housing and employment needs of intellectually disabled people, together with support for their families, and for community education. The Ten Year Plan reincorporated a focus upon the quality of institutional care, gave force to requirements for access to generic services and the integration of the previously segregated disability services system within the broader community services framework that this implied. It created a climate conducive to service innovation for disabled people.

The Ten Year Plan foundered on the difficulties inherent in the legislation. Its comprehensiveness was beyond the administrative capabilities of government. The case work, service delivery and information systems it required were underdeveloped, and it required a political will which could not be sustained.

The period was one of major change within the administrative apparatus of the State. In 1985 the intellectual disability functions of the Health Department were transferred to a newly created community services department. This reflected the strong integrative framework which was to be reflected within the legislation. Those changes however, masked strong tensions in the field between integration and separateness. Successive attempts to resolve these tensions within the department contributed to successive internal reorganisations and movements of key personnel and a sense of administrative chaos within the program. The environment of the "joint facilities" was particularly confused and disputed because of the unclear and divided responsibilities of the Health Department and Community Services Victoria.

The period saw a major expansion in the availability of resources for care of the intellectually disabled in the State. At a time of budget reductions in many other areas of government activity, the program experienced incremental growth over a number of years, and a very substantial growth over four consecutive years. This growth, through the State Plan for intellectual disability services, was targeted towards implementation of the Government policy agenda as expressed in the Ten Year Plan. The scale of that growth however, was to cause severe problems for the administering department because of the absence of operational guidelines, and adequate resource monitoring systems. The direction of service system development was in the end hijacked by the political process, and the broad reform agenda was replaced in the final year of the government by a specific institutional closure agenda.

The period closed with a major shift in the focus of government interest away from substantive policy intent and towards a greater concern with the processes of government itself. This was demonstrated by an increasing procedural and managerialist focus in the management of the disability program, and a diminished impact upon program activities from the strong philosophical traditions which enervated the reforms in the early years of the decade.

The Dimensions of Environmental Contingency

Table 5.1 following, summarises the environmental changes which took place for the intellectual disability field in Victoria during the 1980s. The following section will discuss these changes in a summary way in terms of the dimensions of environmental contingency identified from the literature in Chapter 2 of this study.

Movement

The organisations operating within this field were faced with large scale and in relative terms, rapid changes in their technical, political and cultural environments during this time. In the space of a decade, assumptions about the care of the intellectually disabled, the legislative base of that care, and the policy parameters of the intellectually disability program were fundamentally reformed. The program underwent major changes in its administrative apparatus in moving from a health to a community services auspice, and went from a position of relative paucity of resources, to an embarrassment of riches. There were precursors, and an informed observer may well have predicted these developments. The movement towards favourable consideration of the rights of the disabled was after all, an international development which had taken hold in the United States and Europe prior to Australia. From the perspective of the organisations however, this rate and extent of change was without precedent. In the case of Mayday Hills Training Centre it was largely denied, or if acknowledged, its potential impact upon the institution was denied.

Connectedness

The changes within the environment of organisations in the field, as identified, had a high level of connectedness around the two themes of program

Table 5.1   Environmental Changes Effecting the Intellectual Disability Field

Environmental Organisational System

	Movement	Connectedness	Complexity	Environmental Receptivity
Cultural System • the philosophical basis of care • the model of public administration	• significant and large scale change in the basis upon which care is provided • fundamental and sudden change in the role of government and understanding of administrative responsibilities.	• strong connectedness of changes around principles of client rights and normalisation. • developing discordance between philosophy of care and administrative requirements.	• increased complexity in perspective upon service users. • changing expectations of administering department re: accountability.	• strong community support for rights based approach to care demonstrated by bi-partisan political support. • community anxiety about de-institutionalisation and loss of employment in particular communities
Political System • administrative arrangements • resource availability	• rapid and dramatic change in administrative arrangements • instability of changes leading to administrative uncertainty and changes in personnel • large scale increase in resource commitment associated with new policy development.	• reshaping of administration arrangements tied to policy reform agenda and new budget initiatives. • discordance developed between policy objectives and administrative requirements.	• rate of increase in resource availability creates increased complexity because of absence of developed administrative mechanisms.	• major expansion in resource availability created circumstances where new service development was a possibility
Technical System • legislative and policy basis of care • technology of care	• high rate of change relative to the prior experience of the organisation, in legislative framework and policy • changed practice requirements exceeding skills capacity of existing staff.	• strong connectedness between changes in prevailing technology and policy innovation	• technical changes required significant changes in practices and administration of intellectual disability services. inter-related changes required in approaches to health, education, habilitation, employment and day programs • increased complexity associated with new models of care in non clinical settings.	• initially institutions excluded from new technology and expected to wither over time. • major staff training program producing work force trained in new practice technologies. • diminishing commitment over time to training in new technologies.

reform and administrative reform (Keating, 1997a). These were themselves connected at the time of the 1985 machinery of government changes, when administrative restructure was intended to provide a platform for the refashioning of the program from a health to a community service model. This commenced to change as the managerialist focus of government gathered strength and after the appointment of Paterson in 1989. From this time administration reform took on a life of its own and did not occur principally to facilitate program reform. While the normalisation ideology, its attendant legislative, policy and administrative outworkings, had lost force towards the end of the decade, they had already had a profound effect on the delivery of services. Their strong ideological base and inherent coherency and connectedness was a major factor in achieving this.

Complexity

The extensiveness of the changes which took place in the environment were experienced by the organisations as a marked increase in complexity. In an objective sense they represented just such an increase in complexity. The introduction of a new technology changed the fundamental tasks which were required of staff. It affected their training and the value of their qualifications and experience. New legislation and policy introduced new procedures and compliance requirements. The authorising of external bodies to monitor care introduced a level of accountability which was without precedent. Changes in administrative arrangements introduced a new set of officials with which the organisation had to work, and for the "joint facilities" the additional complexity of multiple reporting lines. Perhaps the most significant factor however was that the new technology, favouring as it did community care over institutional care brought the added complexity of threat. While the extent of changes was denied, the new developments brought an uncertainty and a complexity not previously known in the life of the institution.

Environmental Receptivity

The environment of Mayday Hills Training Centre was both lacking in receptivity to the organisation, and rich with opportunity. The highly connected nature of the cultural and technological changes being experienced meant that there was effectively no longer a continuing market for the products of the organisation. Furthermore, the early policy of its sponsor organisation was to allow the institutions to wither on the vine through lack of access to resources. There was, however, an abundance of new resources available to the field, but the organisation had limited access to these because it was an institution and because it was a Health Department institution. The barriers to environmental receptivity then were not to do with the availability of resources, but policy governing that availability.

The Causal Texture of the Environment

Emery and Trist (1965), described the causal texture of an organisational environment in terms the relationship between the elements of the general environment, assessed in terms of their movement and strength of connectedness. To these dimensions, this study has added the new dimensions of complexity and environmental receptivity, utilising the elaborations of the Emery and Trist framework drawn from the literature. The preceding analysis would suggest a rating on these dimensions for Mayday Hills Training Centre as follows:

- *Movement - **High**;*
  Substantial and rapid changes relative to the experience of the organisation.
- *Connectedness - **High**;*
  Significant interconnectedness of factors associated with program and administrative reform, which were themselves related.
- *Complexity - **High**;*
  Increased complexity in most aspects of the organisations operations.
- *Environmental Receptivity - **Indeterminate**;*
  Resource opportunities available, but with significant policy and political impediment to their utilisation.

This description corresponds in the Emery and Trist typology to a Type iv environment, the **turbulent field**. This is an environment in which the rate of change, and the connectedness of its elements is such that the focal organisation has little influence over the environment. It is one in which the accelerated rate of change exceeds the capacity of the organisation for prediction and control, and in which changes in the organisation are generated by the environment rather than the organisation.

Mayday Hills Training Centre then, was faced with a turbulent environment, in which large scale, rapid change was taking place in a highly connected way. The following chapter will describe in detail the way the organisation responded to the powerful influences within this environment.

6 Responses of the Organisation

Preceding chapters have examined the nature of the change which took place within the environment of the organisation and have analysed the culture, the political organisation and the technology of the institution. The following chapter will describe the responses of the organisation to the changes it experienced in its environment.

Overview of the Redevelopment

In early 1988, Mayday Hills Training Centre for the intellectually disabled operated as a isolated outpost of traditional practices in the care of the intellectually disabled. It provided benign custodial care for 178 residents. It was isolated from the mainstream of developments in care, and was relatively unaffected by the changes which were taking place in the administrative apparatus of the State, which were designed to support those developments.

The Mayday Hills redevelopment entailed the reallocation of $9.2m from the provision of congregate care for intellectually disabled people in Beechworth, to the provision of a range of accommodation supports and day activities across North Eastern Victoria. In order to achieve this, it was necessary to develop alternative management arrangements, design alternative service options, retrain and redeploy the workforce, match and prepare clients for alternative services, and protect the resource base in order to ensure its availability into the future. Most importantly, it was necessary that the organisation develop an approach to clients which assumed their capacity for degrees of independence, and which sought to build upon their abilities rather than only compensate for their disabilities.

At the time of the machinery of government changes of 1985 which transferred responsibility for intellectual disability services from the Health Commission to Community Services Victoria, two institutional services had not been transferred. These were the Mayday Hills Training Centre (Beechworth) and the Aradale Training Centre (Ararat). The reason for this was that these facilities were combined psychiatric and intellectual disability services, or "joint facilities" as they became known.

As a consequence of an industrial agreement at the time of the 1985 transfers, a separate nursing structure for the Training Centres was established, although this did not occur until mid 1988. Regional Directors were appointed to Community Services Victoria regions in September 1987 and carried responsibility for all departmental programs including disability services. In the case of the joint facilities however the nature of this responsibility was unclear since the Health Department retained line responsibility, and Regional Executive Officers for Psychiatric Services were also appointed at this time. These positions provided a management focus for all psychiatric services in the regions, including the joint facilities. Further, the newly established Community Services Victoria regions were only lightly staffed initially in the intellectual disability services program, and for the first twelve months of its operation, the Upper Murray Regional Centre which carried responsibility for Mayday Hills Training Centre, had only two staff.

Nevertheless, utilising the implied authority of the *Intellectually Disabled Persons Services Act*, the Upper Murray Regional Centre sought to influence, firstly the quality of services provided by the Training Centre, and ultimately the redevelopment of the facility itself. In doing so, it had to counter the resistance of its own central office which did not see the joint facilities as a priority, as well as the antagonism of the Training Centre staff.

Cultural change, significant adjustment to the basic assumptions of the organisation, commenced in the institution in mid 1988 with the early exposure of the institution to the prevailing "normalisation" ideology then current within the intellectual disability field. Political change took place through a significant modification of the distribution of power and influence within the institution, and technological change, through the introduction of alternative practices for the care of the intellectually disabled, and the development of a range of alternative service models.

The culture of the institution was modified as its staff became exposed through training and external contact with alternative approaches to care, and came to see their clients exercise increased independence as a result of service changes. They were exposed to alternative futures for themselves, and experienced collaborative approaches to service development.

The politics of the institution were changed as the industrial body which represented the majority of staff declined in its influence, as the management of the facility achieved greater focus, and as the resources available to the institution were redirected. The technology of the institution changed as innovative alternative service models were introduced, which sought to integrate clients within community settings.

Commencing in 1990, and continuing until the eventual closure of the facility, a "future initiatives" committee met to plan and develop alternative services to that provided within the institution. This development grew out of the experience of closing the infamous Myrtle House during 1988 and 1989, which was achieved through a joint working party including interested staff, the regional centre of Community Services Victoria and a representative of the institution's management. This process enabled the closure of Myrtle House and the development of an innovative behaviour management program in a community setting. It established a process whereby staff were engaged with the change process and themselves dealt with the internal impediments to change, particularly from industrial bodies. Between 1990 and 1993 the future initiatives committee took responsibility for developing plans for alternative services and followed these through to the point of establishment.

Prompted by scandals in the management of Pleasant Creek Training Centre, another institution for the intellectually disabled located in Western Victoria, the Department initiated in early 1990 a "facilities" review. This was a formal public service mechanism, which had in fact been a product of the 1985 industrial dispute. While in the view of the Union the purpose of such a review was to upgrade classifications of its members, it was used by management to strengthen accountability and clarify the reporting lines of Unit Managers, the most senior officers in each of the institution's residential units. These staff had hitherto seen themselves as senior nurses, with clinical but not managerial responsibilities. They had previously been deployed on an ad hoc basis across the institution. As unit managers came into place, their role increasingly coalesced with that of the future initiatives committee, and line managers within the institution became for the first time responsible for planning and service development.

On December 1, 1991, following six months of intense negotiation, line management of the institution passed from Health Department Victoria to Community Services Victoria. From this point Community Services Victoria was able to directly manage the processes of change it had established within the institution. A Chief Executive Officer was appointed for the institution, who carried also responsibility for the management of the region's other intellectual disability services. In this way, the institution became formally a part of the network of services from which it had formerly stood apart.

In November 1993 the last of the institution's residents moved to alternative supported accommodation within a community setting. The management infrastructure was integrated within broader regional service delivery systems, and the formal entity, Mayday Hills Training Centre, ceased to exist. Its former residents continued to live within the district, usually with those whom they had previously shared their lives. The staff who had previously cared for them now did so in alternative settings. The resources which had previously been utilised to provide their care, were largely retained, and were utilised in new settings.

Responses of the Cultural System

The artefacts of the culture of Mayday Hills Training Centre were modified during the period 1988-1993 as the type and location of services was changed. The most noticeable change could be seen in the physical location of services. Beginning with the Behavioural Intervention Support Team program, and extending through the townhouses and other projects, increasing numbers of clients were accommodated off campus, and the total population of the institution commenced to fall. Figures 6.1 and 6.2 indicate the rate at which the resident population reduced during this period. The reduced number of people present, both staff and residents, had the effect of creating an expectation of closure within the large and under-occupied facility. The commencement of day programs provided off campus changed the daily rhythms of the institution. There was considerable movement in mornings and at evening when residents went to and returned from their day programs. As training began to take effect, and resources became available, more program activity, and improved amenity became apparent on campus. The elderly and severely disabled residents of Grevillea unit, were no longer seen dressed all day in night attire, and seated on commodes.

The significant changes, however, occurred in the basic assumptions of the facility. Building on the analysis of Chapter 5, these will be discussed in terms of *Assumptions about Clients*, *Assumptions about the Facility* and *Assumptions about the Relationship with Management*.

Assumptions about Clients

An important basic assumption of Mayday Hills Training Centre was that residents of the institution were inevitably and unchangeably dependent and so incapable of self-care or of training. The care provided at the facility was thus custodial and protective. These assumptions were at odds with the prevailing philosophy of care within the broader inter-organisational environment and within the institution's sponsoring organisations, though they continued to receive strong support in parts of the general community. A critical aspect of the redevelopment process was the modification, if not complete eradication of this assumption. The events and factors which led to this included the impact of new procedures and requirements flowing from implementation of the Act, a series of sentinel events or cases which challenged assumptions, and the exposure of staff to working with clients in non-institutional settings.

New procedures required that staff be actively involved in the planning of individualised programs for clients. Many were cynical about this and undertook the General Services Planning task begrudgingly. Steve Menzie, a long term staff member of the institution, described the attitude of staff to those requirements:

> Basically when they introduced it [GSPs and IPPs], there was a fair amount of mockery going around. We actually had people come and say to some of our clients who really couldn't make those sorts of decisions for themselves, "say you can go and buy a house." And they really didn't have an iota so of course staff started talking as though this is all a joke and in a sense it was. The idea of the GSPs and IPPs was great for the individual but because there was very little training, people made a mockery of it, until training started coming through....
>
> (Menzie interview)

The insistence by CSV that the task be undertaken, the provision of training to support it, and the monitoring of standards by external bodies such as the Intellectual Disability Review Panel and the Office of the Public Advocate, brought over time a greater appreciation of their significance. An early instance of the application of increased accountability and review by external parties may be seen in the response to the Rattray Avenue sexual assault cases.

Procedures that Protect Rights: The Rattray Avenue Sexual Assault Cases

An opportunity arose in early 1989 to assert the right and the responsibility of CSV to determine standards of care within the Training Centre. This was created by two incidents of sexual assault of female residents of Mayday Hills off campus residences in Wangaratta. These occurred on 27 February and 10 March, 1989. Each involved persons unconnected with the residence forcing themselves sexually upon middle aged women who were former residents of the Training Centre. In each case, the staff supporting the women dealt sensitively with the personal care of the clients, but failed to report the incidents to management for an extended period, and failed to address the systemic issues associated with the security of residents.

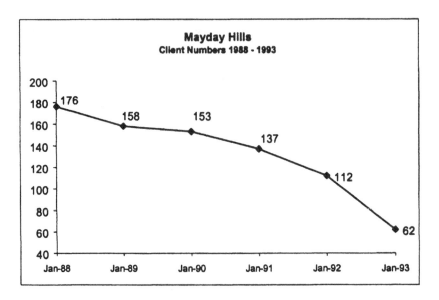

Figure 6.1 Mayday Hills Training Centre: Client Numbers 1988-1993

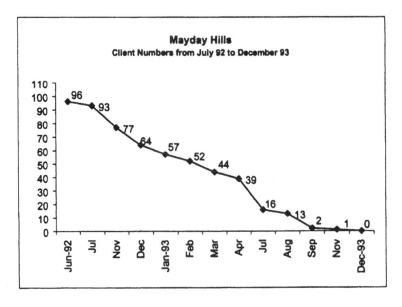

Figure 6.2 Mayday Hills Training Centre: Client Numbers 1992-1993

In response to the incidents, CSV insisted that a panel of review be established to advise the Training Centre Executive on such matters as: required training for staff; staffing levels, the physical security of the residences, the status of discharged clients, health and human relations training for clients, and advice and support to Police dealing with intellectually disabled clients. This Panel consisted of Ms Sheri Brooks, Client Services Team Leader with the CSV Regional Team, Mr Keith McIntosh, Acting Head Nurse from the Training Centre, and Ms Pip Else, Program and Services Coordinator with the North Eastern Residential Care Association, a non-government agency providing residential supports for the intellectually disabled. The Panel reported on 19 May 1989 and made significant recommendations in respect of each of the areas listed above.

The fact of the incidents having occurred had the potential to undermine community living for clients, because it supported the argument that clients needed to be protected. This did not happen but the incidents, the processes of their investigation, and the consequent recommended action, did have far reaching implications for the operation of the Training Centre. CSV's assertion of its role in standards setting, and the acceptance of this by the Training Centre Management set the scene for more significant demands for improvement in standards of care. This was reinforced by the agreement of the Centre management to report incidents of concern to CSV regional management, and in ways consistent with CSV statewide practice.

The utilisation of a Review Panel which drew upon expertise beyond the Training Centre challenged the deeply embedded practices of accountability only within a closed institutional system. Recommendations which required the Training Centre to upgrade the skills of staff in the areas of health and human relationships and to access a broader range of service inputs for client programs, similarly challenged the segregation of the institution, its clients and its staff. Further, it brought the staff into contact with the developing range of services in North East Victoria and challenged them to operate as part of that network.

Sentinel Cases: The Case of Client J

There were significant events and cases which became emblematic of the changes which were taking place in attitudes to clients. These included the movement to independent community living by three behaviourally disturbed residents who had previously been restrained physically and by medication within the institution. The case of one of these clients, who will be referred to as Client J, is illustrative of the impact of such movements.

One of the three clients who was relocated from Myrtle House into the community was client J. He was notorious through the institution for his assaultive behaviour, and was heavily medicated and restrained within the locked ward. The process of J's relocation to a community setting and his success in that setting, was a critical demonstration to the staff of the institution of the possibility of alternative interventions.

J had a "dual diagnosis", that is that he was diagnosed as having both an intellectual disability and a psychiatric illness. His intellectual disability was borderline and so, in common with many in like situations, he had an awareness of the other possibilities which might have been available to him. His frustration lead to frequent violent episodes and the use of both physical and chemical restraint.

Encouraged by a small number of activist staff in the institution, J in February 1989 made an application to the Intellectual Disability Review Panel. In his application, J argued that he wished to leave the institution and to live in a community setting. Because there were serious reservations about his capacity at that time, this application was opposed by the Department. A hearing of the panel ensued at which detailed evidence was taken.

The outcome of the hearing was that J should not be retained in the institution and a recommendation was made by the president of the review panel that his medication be immediately reduced, that he be relocated to a community setting, and that resources be provided to support him in the community. These recommendations raised very difficult issues for the Department, and for the Upper Murray Regional Centre in particular. On the one hand the Regional Centre was a strong advocate of community based care options. On the other hand, it had serious concerns about the appropriateness of immediately discharging a potentially violent client into the community in circumstances where there were not appropriate support services available. It had problems also with the review panel giving a direction that one client should receive support services ahead of others who had been on waiting lists for residential support for some time. The majority of recommendations of the panel were endorsed by the department including those which required a reduction in J's medication regime. Key recommendations concerning community relocation, however, were rejected.

In making its recommendations, the review panel had relied upon Section 18 of the *Intellectually Disabled Persons Services Act*, which required that an institutional placement be utilised only where this was the least restrictive alternative available. The Department may well have argued that there was not a less restrictive alternative *available*. Instead it agreed that he should not be placed in an institution, and indicated that should he choose to leave, no action would be taken to restrain him. It also indicated however, that there was not accommodation or support services available for him at that stage, and that he would leave the institution without these.

This was the first time following the proclamation of the IDPS Act that recommendations of the Review Panel were not accepted in full by the Department. The President of the panel then exercised her right to refer the matter directly to the Minister. At a meeting attended by the then Minister, the review panel president, the then General Manager of the Office of Intellectual Disability Services, and the Regional Director of the Upper Murray region, the Minister indicated that he did not wish to give a directive, but wished the department and the panel to arrive at a mutually acceptable solution in J's interest. J left the institution six months later, after behavioural intervention programs had been put in place for him, and when suitable supported accommodation had been established. He moved to a large provincial centre near to the institution. At the time of writing he has lived with minimal support, modest medication and with continuous employment for more than eight years.

The case of client J was sentinel in a number of critical respects. It demonstrated the efficacy of review procedures, since J's actions in requiring a review of decisions concerning his accommodation were successful in having the Department respond, to the point of Ministerial involvement. It demonstrated that despite its preference for community based care, Community Services Victoria was prepared to take politically unpalatable and potentially embarrassing decisions on the basis of client interests. Most importantly however, J demonstrated to a sceptical institutional staff that one of the most difficult to manage residents could, with appropriate assistance, live successfully in the community.

The Experience of Clients in the Community: The Myrtle House and Grevillea Residents

It was significant that those who were the first to move from the facility were among the most difficult to care for. The Myrtle House redevelopment project targeted the closure of one of the State's most notorious locked wards. Rather than relocate its residents to other institutional units however, it took the three most behaviourally difficult clients in the institution, and placed them with appropriate support within the community. This was a challenge to the view that only the most highly functioning could live within community settings, and that the institution would always be required to provide for the most frail, most aged, or most behaviourally disturbed.

Rob Macdonald described the importance of having focussed on the older and more disabled residents, and creating options for them early:

> ... Myrtle House, and the movement of the Grevillea people, as the first program that was actually approved was for the aged and the disabled people, and yeah because people were expecting us to move the Gatehouse people, because they were easy, or there were a couple of clients who had a bit of money. That would have been an opening just for everyone to say it will happen slowly and just picking out the winners, I suppose... the fact we did it first rather than left it to the end, was one of the best decisions we ever made, I think.
>
> (Macdonald interview)

As further redevelopment occurred, increasing numbers of staff were able to observe formerly extremely dependent clients, exercising new or restored skills. A major factor in the beginning changes in approach by staff towards intellectually disabled people, and the possibility of a future for them, and for their clients outside the institution, was the experience of seeing their clients develop and become more independent outside the institution. Rob Macdonald described what he saw as the important changes:

> For me... it was around people recognising, and it was the move forward. I can remember the first attitudes, that sort of stuff, but I think some of the people began to recognise and value that people with an intellectual disability learnt; they actually had potential to do a lot more than they were doing... it all changed to something more than they were doing... it all changed to something that was supportive of people, looking at trying to develop potential and looking, I suppose, for strengths in everybody.
>
> (Macdonald interview)

Most significantly, as staff relocated to community settings they observed the changed behaviour and more active lives of many of their long term clients. On leaving the institution the majority had active day programs, while previously they had little or none. There were stories of clients who regained speech and who with reduced medication, were able to participate in community life.

For Jim Kesselschmidt, it was the sense of inevitability of the move to community settings for many clients, which enabled many staff to make a transition to a new role. If their clients were to be moving, they would need access to community services, and so there was a need to facilitate this:

...in terms of the actual programming I believe that it got better as time went on, people got more familiar with it and there were a number of factors which made it that way too. ... the reality of yes people knew that people were moving to the community and a requirement was to be providing those sorts of services, and to gear people specifically towards community living was one requirement.

(Kesselschmidt interview)

A major impediment to the development of alternative approaches to clients was the absence of appropriate skills amongst the staff, and an understanding of what was required of them. A senior manager within CSV (in another region) described the difficulty of implementing the new philosophy of care within the institutional environment:

... there were very basic changes where ... people were trying to get the system of care to relate to intellectually disabled people as people first and not as patients you got out of bed, washed, cleaned, put in front of the mirror and so on. That was very powerful in this normalisation, in the fervor... But it was a particular thrust of a particular group of people and my sense was it had absolutely no acceptance or recognition in the institutions. It might as well not have existed, and the management group who were driving that, didn't get that message through.

(Anonymous Respondent II interview)

These difficulties were aggravated at Mayday Hills because it had been isolated from mainstream developments within the intellectual disability field, and because of its history as a psychiatric facility.

... this was a psychiatric culture. Things were done because they were required to be done. Staff didn't internalise and understand why an IPP [an individual program plan] or General Service Plan, or whatever, was required by the Act to be done. They knew it needed to be done, because they were told it needed to be done. But they never internalised, there's a logic and there's a sense to it.

(Kesselschmidt interview)

The progressive availability of staff from the Post Basic Mental Retardation Nursing program, and from the various strategies which were put in place to train Intellectual Disability Services Officers (IDSOs), was a major factor in re-orienting the facility:

... what happened was, you started to get a lot more people coming through who were trained, and therefore the structure was actually filled with people who were trained... There was a different approach in terms of nursing standards and just identifying behaviour rather than illnesses.

(Menzie interview)

There were just five of us that had registration in the intellectual disability area. But then there was this heavy influx of people going through training. First it started off with people going down to Melbourne, then when they brought the training to the actual institution, I believe at first there was some difficulty in recruiting people to do that course, but then they had ample numbers and in fact had to turn people back and had to start scrutinising and setting criteria for people to enter there

(Tai interview)

...by 1990 some of the hard work that had been going on behind the scenes in the previous three years had begun to pay off.. Staff had begun to see that there was a life beyond Mayday. A lot of that was as a consequence of the negotiation for training to occur for staff, to bring them into being ID trained and not psych trained. Where the first unit had closed and the most challenging clients were out there living in the community and that was working to some degree of satisfaction for people... Those who were very strong unionists began to see both their life and the life of the clients was actually going to be better.

(Hind interview)

Assumptions about the Institution

An underlying challenge in redeveloping a major institution, is that of its inertia. Everything about the institutional environment says that change does not happen. This was most particularly the case in institutions located in relatively isolated rural settings.

Employment was continuous, and often generational. Staff had long periods of continued employment; often from the time of school leaving. Many quite young employees had twenty years of employment within the organisation. The absence of alternative employment opportunities, and the relative generosity and security of public sector employment, on rotating shifts which attracted generous penalty rates, militated against frequent changes in personnel. There is thus little opportunity for "new blood" or for the employees to be challenged by colleagues with alterative views.

The nature of institutional employment consistently reinforced the culture of stasis. The tasks traditionally performed by institutional staff were predictable, orderly and locationally consistent. Staff expected to commence work and take up a situation, with the requirement that it would be unchanged when they complete their shift 12 hours later. During the period of their shift they undertook a limited range of activities which are exactly the same as those in which they engaged when last on duty. They worked for two days on an extended shift and then went off duty for two days. In all likelihood, when they returned to duty the environment was exactly as they had left it two days previously.

This is not to say that change does not take place within institutional environments. The resident population reduced at Mayday Hills from approximately 1,000 in 1975 to less than 200 in 1987. What is striking about this, however, was the level of denial amongst the staff of the facility, that any change was taking place. One possible reason for this was that the fundamental tasks for which they were responsible remained unchanged. This and the fact that their exchanges with the broader Intellectual Disability Services field were infrequent and episodic, reinforced for them the essential continuity of their work experience.

Inertia was countered at Mayday Hills by a combination of demonstrated progress and a priority being given to communication. A new Manager of Direct Care, Mr Jim Kesselschmidt was appointed in 1991 who combined a history of employment within institutions, with a thorough understanding of the new technologies of care. He placed considerable emphasis upon internal communication; on spending time with staff explaining changes. This combined with the service development activity which was taking place at the same time, helped to create an environment in which staff were aware of change as it was happening and felt able to participate in it.

Communication within an institutional environment is particularly difficult because of the structure of the working week. Rob Macdonald described some of the frustration associated with trying to communicate with staff:

> ... now if you talk about culture change, one of the things that we really had to come to grips with was "two-on, two-off". We talked to some people and then the whole fucking thing changed and you'd come in the next day and there would be a whole different group of people there, and you'd think "hang on".
> ... and you'd be working with someone for three months and then you wouldn't see them for a month.
>
> (Macdonald interview)

It was important however, that staff knew and understood what was happening. Through 1991, weekly meetings were held with an open agenda, at which both the Regional director and the Chief Executive Officer attended. Meetings were informal and any questions could be asked. Kesselschmidt stressed the importance of communication, and in particular, those weekly meetings:

> ... it was useful for people to attend and ask questions and see their colleagues come back and report what it was like. And with some people there was trust, and with some of those people there was mistrust. So I think it was a bit of a bob each way. I think ... it was often afterwards that people would have questions, and that's when you would be round visiting the units and talking to staff, the things that stimulated discussion and that helped undermine the polarisation of management, the classic opposition of management and union, because it helped communication - the Future Initiatives Group, and certainly when they got well underway, participation in that....
>
> (Kesselschmidt interview)

The changes were difficult for many staff who had been long term employees at the institution. A commitment was given at these briefing sessions that: employment would be available for all who wished to continue to work within disability services; that the new services would be established such that no staff member would have to commute more than forty-five minutes from their home; and that retraining would be available for any staff member who required it. While the union was in decline at this time, it was frequently a tense one, as Kesselschmidt described the situation:

> ... decline doesn't mean it is a straight vertical line, in fact it can be peaks and troughs on the way down... I can remember having to communicate responses to the union on different sorts of things, and staff getting pretty het up about issues at the time, and it required a lot of work, a lot of going down and communicating. I remember one classic when the SPSF was on the scene, and I was doing my night shift, late at night walking into a unit, this was when Paterson had taken over and there was a decree that union meetings had to be authorised or something ridiculous that helped nobody... It was just amazing, at first I thought there was going to be violence, it was pretty hectic at one stage (this is Kurrajong)... the whole issue was the removal of a cleaner when there was one client in the unit... mind you, that was symbolic for a lot of change for the staff, cutting edge stuff. But again it was face to face communication rather than allowing communication to occur in an isolated way.
>
> (Kesselschmidt interview)

Assumptions about the Staff/Management Relationship

The history of management/staff relations at Mayday Hills was not one of cooperative development or of participative management. The hospital operated with rigidly defined hierarchical structures in which medical officers had pre-eminence, nursing staff were organised in graded level representing seniority and paraprofessional staff provide most basic care. While rigidly hierarchical, the structure did not provide for efficient line communication because "two-on, two-off" rosters, and the absence of consistent work unit management, confused accountability and ensured discontinuity of information. A consequence, in part, of these arrangements was an alienated workforce, which was highly industrialised and frustrated with its management.

In 1987/88 management of the facility had effectively been abandoned to the industrial body. No decisions were made without reference to the Union, and even the rosters for units, ie who was on which roster, was approved by the Union. There was a high level of collusion between management and the industrial body in that local management openly admitted that the industrial muscle of the workforce had been successful over a number of years in staving off budget reductions.

Progress in changing the culture of alienation and industrialisation was slow. The possibility of change however was evident from an early stage in the frustration of a number of key staff with the lack of leadership and strategic direction in the hospital. This was expressed in determination of a small group of staff to improve client outcomes through more adventurous program development.

In 1987 these staff had initiated the "Gatehouse Program" as an independent living training program and eventually secured the use of two houses owned by the Hospital in Wangaratta as extensions to the program. While there were limitations in the design of the program it was evidence of the desire of some staff to participate in the development of improved services. These staff were a minority, and were industrially isolated in that they belonged to a socialist left faction of a right wing dominated Union.

A participative process, one which engaged the staff of the institution in the development of a new service option, was adopted in 1989 to deal with the sensitive issue of the Behavioural Management Unit. This was extremely successful in that staff developed a very appropriate community based service model and themselves managed the potentially difficult industrial response to resources moving off the institutional campus. This demonstrated a potential means of continuing the redevelopment. Staff would be invited to participate in the developing of their own futures, through what became known as the "Future Initiatives Committee". This committee involved broad representation from across the Training Centre, and was given a brief to come up with a new service profile for the organisation. As new services were proposed, efforts were made to secure the resources to develop them:

The service development process was based on a sense of local ownership, so there is a sense that the planning, the vision setting, the actual work itself was not something that was being imposed from outside the Region but was clearly being owned within the Region and driven within the Region, and then once CSV was managing the Training Centre then it just became a natural part of it being owned and delivered and driven within the Training Centre as well. Whereas up until then, and even post that, other major redevelopments had been imposed upon Training Centres, this was the only one that really was built up from within the field itself.

(Hind interview)

The process was not an entirely straight forward one however, it had firstly to counter the deeply embedded cynicism within the facility about management good faith.

... there had been a process of strategic planning, you know the hospital performance agreement the year before that David Jones introduced. It was very much a top down thing, and my memory was people participated in that, but no-one expected anything would happen of it, and it didn't. It wasn't going to because it was actually lying to staff that they were going to set the overall strategic direction and everyone knew that wasn't going to happen anyway. That was happening out of 555 Collins Street. When people were invited to participate in something that they could be the influence in, they know something about... they grabbed it because it was real.

(Macdonald interview)

Even among those who were advocates of change in the institution there were reservations about the genuineness of attempts to have staff participate. Jim Kesselschmidt, Manager of Direct Care in the final two years of the Mayday Hills operation expressed his reservations:

Part of me thought it was a bit of a con job, I believed it was necessary for a con job to happen, but part of it was advertising. It was a PR exercise... And part of me wasn't too rapt in the idea in the beginning. I was caught between a loyalty to my staff, and also an understanding that we needed to redevelop. However, later on... I think there was some characters in the last school, there was Steve Menzie and a few others that were quite passionate about deinstitutionalisation... which was useful in order for communication to occur, and that gave an impetus to the Future Initiatives Group.

(Kesselschmidt interview)

Amongst others, particularly in the old administration of the facility there was direct opposition, and an attempt to sabotage the development:

> I can remember standing toe to toe with some of the management that were there and they were, I think as hard to change as the rest of the staff. "X" banned me from going to talk with non-direct care staff, because I had no right to talk to his staff about changing... The crap that went down with those guys, they were just as hard to change, and I think that we had two of the guys that were in the future initiatives who had just come out of post-basic training. There were two or three of them were in post basic training at the time, so they had been stimulated by all these sorts of things and someone turned the light on for them at the end of the tunnel and they raced down at 100 miles per hour.
>
> (Macdonald interview)

> the senior management in the nursing area previously were not supportive of this change, did not agree with the attitudes of the new people into the institution and basically fought it, then there was changes and people started infiltrating the senior management level and started changing those attitudes.
>
> (Tai interview)

For the staff who chose to participate however, it was an opportunity that they had waited for, for a long time. Their experience of having worked within the institutional environment had been one of frustration and powerlessness:

> There was money and resources and interest being turned to the Training Centre for the first time that most of those staff could ever remember and those people who were angry or depressed because there they knew there was a better way to work, and had been depressed by what had been happening under the old regime, saw that CSV and everyone else was taking an interest in what they were doing... I mean the commitment within the Region to even stay dedicated and committed to it even while politically, centrally, perhaps it was going against us. That level of commitment and dedication was just so obvious to the players including the staff in the Training Centre.
>
> (Hind interview)

While talk of redevelopment of the institution was destabilising, the opportunity to plan and to develop the new services, gave them a power in their workplace that they had only been able to exercise vicariously through the union. Steve Menzie, a long term employee, described what he saw as the impetus for the positive attitude to staff participation:

I think that what drove us along was we were never allowed to have a say... I used to stand up to management, but it didn't matter. They said you don't, you don't. That's all there was to it. But here we were all of a sudden making a bit of change and so it was great for blokes like myself and others in similar positions working with Rob and Julie and being able to go in there and say, "Tom said," or "Julie said, and we're doing it!" I think that motivated us a bit... we were having a bit of fun because all of a sudden we were saying well, we were never ever allowed to drive a car up there, let alone make decisions, and all of a sudden, here we were, driving around in cars and people were saying "Its ok, that's what cars are there for." It was pretty simple and basic, but it was giving us a voice.

(Menzie interview)

The committee worked through 1991 and 1992; meeting on a weekly basis; developing concept plans for new services; consulting with the other staff about proposals; identifying potential clients and residents of the new services; and implementing the new services as resources were identified. The first proposals put to the combined Health Department and Community Services Victoria management on 9 May 1990, were for the purchase of a vehicle to support day program activity off campus, and to develop accommodation off campus for six elderly but minimally disabled residents. The proposal provided a detailed analysis of how a vehicle might be fully utilised, and was funded through the Regional centre of CSV. The accommodation facility proposal coincided with the desire to HDV to close down a Drug and Alcohol program which operated from a Mayday Hills owned property outside the institution. Its use for intellectual disability accommodation avoided a difficult political problem for that Department. The Future Initiatives Committee was thus able to achieve success with its first two proposals. Further projects were developed using State Plan or other resources, such that the majority of service development initiatives in the later stage of the redevelopment were initiated by staff themselves. Unlike other like institutional redevelopments, absenteeism and stress related workcover claims in the Training Centre went down, and there were no industrial disputes in relation to the redevelopments. Rob Macdonald described the Future Initiatives Committees process:

I think it is the most stunning change process that I have watched... the Committee worked and I think it was motivated to work and really got going when they actually saw some concrete stuff. We went in, we listened, we acted. For the first time, I think in their experience they had contact where management were interested in what they had to say. Most of the ideas that came out of the future initiatives committee were the staff ideas. And because they were listened to they were empowered and naturally they got the rewards and the positive feedback.

(Macdonald interview)

The Future Initiatives Committee developed a life and a power of its own. The commitment and energy which was brought to the process by Macdonald and the CSV Service Development Team sparked similar responses from key institutional personnel, and combined with the interests of staff in securing their own future. Macdonald's description of the motivation of those involved communicates something of the energy and the zealotry the process acquired:

... we had a vision or a thing in our heads that the IDPS Act was true and correct, and that was the way we were going to go; so we had a mandate and decisions that other people made that were against that, we could actually use the legislation... and we were blinded I suppose by the vision. We used that vision to go ahead and do things and I know there were things that people in finance used to say "sorry you can't do that". "Well, we have! Now what do we do next." We had the passion in our hearts or our heads, around the rights of these people that were in the institution. These guys, the charge nurses, came along because we were on the right ground.... We had that common denominator, I think, between us and the staff, and the other people that weren't on track we didn't care about. They were wrong and we were just going straight ahead... we were going to close the institution, we didn't give a stuff what anyone else said.

(Macdonald interview)

Ruth Tai was a long serving Mental Retardation Nurse, and a Charge Nurse at Mayday Hills Training Centre. She had been amongst the minority of staff who had sought change in the institution over a longer period. She saw the Future Initiatives Committee process as fundamental to the changing attitudes of staff:

It turned them around. And I think also proved a point and that was that the redevelopment was going to occur because the Future Initiatives were a movement I guess that weren't just out in strength to make it happen, but implemented some very formal strategies to incorporate people in it and certainly at the end of the day there were still people who defied it all the way and would not be part of it but that was the nucleus of bringing the majority along.

(Tai interview)

Summary: Responses of the Cultural System

Mayday Hills Training Centre was characterised by a culture based upon assumptions that the intellectually disabled required protective and isolated care, that the institution existed in order to meet the needs of its employees and that it would continue to operate as such into the future. It assumed that the interests of employees and their employer were inevitably antagonistic.

These assumptions were challenged and substantially modified as the institution responded to the changes within its environment. The changes in the philosophical basis of care within the environment were directly antithetical to the assumptions about the capacities of clients. The legislative and procedural requirements which gave expression to that philosophical base, while derided initially, and passively resisted, had the effect of focussing staff energies in ways which enhanced client rights and independence. Similarly, legislatively required external review of decision making, and administratively imposed reporting requirements ensured a level of attention to the formal protections of client rights.

A critical factor in moving the attitudes of staff to clients was the provision of training; involving both the development of skills and confidence in individualised planning and behavioural interventions, and the abandoning of therapeutic techniques appropriate to the psychiatric environment from which the Training Centre had come. In particular the modification of medication regimes was essential in creating space for other interventions to be developed, and enabling clients to be able to respond to alternative approaches.

Changing perceptions of client capacities encouraged an alternative view of the role of the institution. Greater activity by, and in support of residents engaged off-campus introduced a dynamism to the facility which was largely absent previously. Staff who were motivated by a genuine regard for the wellbeing of their clients responded positively to the enhanced quality of life they witnessed. In particular the fact that staff moved with their clients to new services and were able to report to their peers the gains made by individual clients, reinforced a changing view about client capacities, and also about their own futures.

The alienation of staff from management within the facility acted in a perverse way to enhance the prospects of redevelopment. Attention given to communication was welcomed by a staff which felt isolated and uninformed. Access to small amounts of resources to support client programs were powerful incentives for staff who had been denied the most basic program supports. The opportunity to actively participate, and to actually direct service development, gave a sense of exhilaration to those who had been disempowered in a rigidly hierarchial system and who were fearful for their jobs into the future.

The logic of the basic assumptions and their change over time has been represented as figure 6.3.

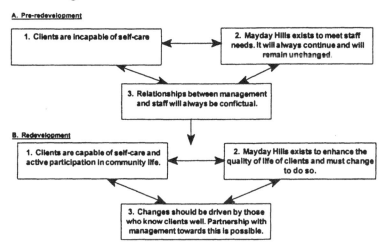

Figure 6.3 The Logic of Cultural Assumptions at Mayday Hills Training Centre

In the same way that pre-redevelopment cultural assumptions were mutually reinforcing, those which developed during the redevelopment period supported and were supported by each other. Because clients were capable of learning and of active participation in community life, they did not require a protective institutional environment, and the organisation must change. The willingness of management to be actively involved with staff in planning a changed role was (1) evidence of a deep belief in client capacities and (2) a commitment to a future for the organisation and its staff, albeit in a changed form.

Responses of the Political System

The political system of the organisation is concerned with the delineation of interests within the focal organisation and the distribution of access to influence and resources by those interests. This section will describe the interests as they existed within the institution and the ways in which their access to influence and resources changed in response to changes within the organisation's environment. These interests will be described in terms of the struggle for power between the health and the community services administrations, between management and the industrial bodies, and between occupational groupings within the institution.

Administrative Power

Determining Influence   The machinery of government changes of October 1985 left unresolved the management of Mayday Hills and of Aradale. One of the concessions by the union was that these two "joint facilities" would remain as a part of the administrative structure of the Health Department, but with provision made within the Community Services Department for resources to be provided for the management of the training centres and for the training of staff. While the Mayday Hills Training Centre was at the time the fourth largest institution for the intellectually disabled in the State, it was the smaller part of the Mayday Hills facility. The history of the institution was firmly within a mental health framework. The loyalties, the traditions and the culture of the organisations were with psychiatric services rather than with community services.

On a broad level however, the environment was being determined from a non health, community services administrative perspective. Government had initiated the machinery of government changes in order to give effect to a social agenda. That agenda reflected a normalisation, access to services perspective. Powerful new legislation was being drafted which again reflected an access to community services, perspective. Resources would be provided in succeeding years for the redevelopment of intellectual disability services, through a community services administration. Highly convergent, powerful changes were taking place within the organisation's political environment which suggested an alignment with the community services administration. The institution at that time however was highly resistant to change, and flush with the recent industrial victory by those opposing change, many believed that the institution could continue as it had previously.

At the time of the transfer of responsibility between the departments, Mayday Hills, as with many other state institutions, was without a permanent management structure. The previous Psychiatrist Superintendent had resigned and had not been replaced. The Office of Psychiatric Services was in the process of considering what its ongoing management arrangements should be, and was later to appoint regional chief executive officers for psychiatric services. At this time however management, such as it was, was being exercised by the administrative services manager and the Director of Nursing, both of whom were longstanding staff members and steeped in the culture of the institution.

The regional office was lacking in staff with a background in intellectual disability services and reliant upon those of the neighbouring Goulburn Region. This was not a situation in which a strong community services perspective could be pursued.

The Regional Director for Community Services however argued that while administrative responsibilities resided with the health administration, authority under the IDPS Act rested with him. As such he would give direction on matters affecting the welfare of clients and programs which should be available to them. In May 1988 he presented a paper to this effect to a joint meeting between the hospital executive and the sub-branch of the Hospital Employees Federation which was accepted by those present, without a strong understanding of its import.

The Health Services Agreement 1988/89

The industrial agreement which governed the transfer of functions between the Departments required that the community services department enter into a contract arrangement with the Health Department for the provision of services. No such contract was entered into for the 1986/87 or 1987/88 years, as the Health Department did not acknowledge the role of Community Services in the joint facilities.

In early 1988 the Office of Psychiatric Services responded to the request by CSV to establish a service agreement concerning the joint facilities with a proposal to prepare a Health Services Agreement concerning Mayday Hills in Beechworth. This was an unusual mechanism in that it was modelled on the service agreements being established between the Health Department and the major providers of health services in Victoria including public hospitals. Use of this mechanism required that the Health Department treat one of its line agencies as though it were an independent entity with which it could negotiate performance measures and resources. The addition of CSV as a party to the agreement added complexity to the mechanisms in that it was to take place without any explicit agreement as to the legal authority of the respective Departments.

The Health Services Agreement of 1988/89 was signed by the Director of the Office of Psychiatric Services, the manager (administration) of Mayday Hills, and the Regional Director, CSV. It was an attempt by the OPS central management to bring the Hospital within the control of the Department centrally through a process of negotiation of both resources and service outputs. In this it was an almost complete failure. The illusion of the hospital as a separate corporation with which the Health Department could negotiate, was perceived by local management (and line staff) to be exactly that. The accepted means of control - industrial power and control over the day to day detail of actual expenditure or information - remained in the hands of the hospital. Irrespective of an agreement, these mechanisms could continue to be used. There were no effective sanctions associated with non-compliance with the agreement which were not available to the Health Department in the absence of an agreement. Those that existed had not been utilised previously and were unlikely to be used following the agreement; and the goals established in the agreement were generally fanciful. In an organisation in which the majority of staff performed routine and predictable tasks, and in which no-one was charged with development or change responsibilities, ambitious and change oriented goals were more likely to generate cynicism than motivation.

The negotiation of the Health Services Agreement, while not fulfilling the Health Department objectives of bringing Mayday Hills under control, did however have some important implications for the ultimate redevelopment of the Training Centre. It acknowledged, albeit imprecisely, the authority of CSV at the Regional level, to establish the strategic directions of the facility. For its part, CSV insisted that it would not sign an Agreement which did not have as a service goal the redevelopment of the accommodation provided in Myrtle House, and which did not include a statement of the resources committed in the Training Centre part of the Hospital. This was the first strong statement of CSV's authority and the first placement of these critical issues on the agenda between the two Departments.

A further Health Services Agreement was attempted during 1989 but aborted at an early stage. It was clear, following a large scale industrial dispute in February 1989 that the critical management tasks were financial and industrial and the elaborate pretences of the service agreement process were unlikely to have an impact upon these. The second Health Services Agreement did not proceed past the first draft stage, but by this point the importance of program direction being provided by CSV for the Training Centre was well established.

Through early 1989 and early 1990, CSV regional staff sought to assert a directive role within the Training Centre. This occurred through the Training Centre Liaison Committee, consisting of the Regional Director CSV, the Regional Chief Executive Officer, Psychiatric Services, the Manager, Intellectual Disability Services and the Director of Nursing for the Training Centre. It occurred through the insistence of CSV procedures for such matters as incident reporting, and in the provision of training opportunities for staff. The most significant opportunity arose with the announcement of the State Plan for the

Redevelopment of Intellectual Disability Services in May 1989. The Region was able to use the possibility of additional resources for service development as an incentive to staff, for change.

Administrative Realignment

A significant point in the process whereby the institution transferred from the formal control of Health Department to CSV was the February 1989 industrial dispute. This is considered in some detail in the section following dealing with industrial power. At this point however, it should be noted as significant in the growing awareness within the Health Department that as it was then constituted, it lacked the capacity to manage an institution for the intellectually disabled. Following the dispute, there was change of emphasis in the relationships between the Office of Psychiatric Services and CSV in the management of the Training Centre. This occurred for a number of reasons.

It provided the first significant opportunity for the recently appointed Regional Chief Executive Officer, Psychiatric Services to become significantly involved in operational issues within the Hospital as a whole, and the Training Centre in particular. It exposed for him the lack of capacity of HDV to manage a major Intellectual Disability Training Centre through a significant dispute, without the support of CSV. This was because the expertise in dealing with intellectually disabled clients was now located within CSV rather than HDV.

CSV for the first time became a significant player in negotiating a matter of major significance within a Joint Facility. This involvement was at the insistence of the union which believed that there was a greater sympathy for its position concerning client care within CSV than within HDV, and that CSV was more likely to be able to negotiate additional resources for intellectual disability services from Government.

The settlement itself gave effect to a number of the emerging concerns of CSV within the Training Centre. While there was no means of ensuring the implementation of additional programs for residents, the agreement which was reached was predicated upon it and additional staffing was provided for this purpose.

The General Manager Resources (CSV) became personally involved in the settlement process and, with the Regional Director, represented the Department in the industrial negotiations. This facilitated his first hand knowledge of the facility, and his commitment to the work of the region in its redevelopment.

As a direct consequence of the dispute, the Regional Chief Executive Officer, Psychiatric Services, wrote to the Regional Director, CSV on 7 February 1989 seeking CSV's ongoing involvement in the industrial relations of the Centre and requesting greater CSV involvement in "the areas of program development, resident service plans and staff education". This involvement had been sought by CSV for more than twelve months and had been actively resisted by the former management of the facility. This letter also raised for the first time in a formal way the future management arrangements for the Centre. It proposed to establish a Operations Executive made up of the two senior officers of the respective departments in the region, together with the Director of Nursing (OPS) and the CSV Intellectual Disability Services Program manager. This mechanism was proposed to "provide a means of formal communication between your office (CSV Regional) and this organisation (OPS Regional) in regard to program resources and development." (correspondence: Regional Chief Executive Officer, OPS, to Regional Director, CSV, 7 February 1989).

Through 1989 and 1990, as CSV progressively developed its alternative services, and as HDV progressively moved to the view that it should mainstream its psychiatric services within the public hospital system, it became clear to all those involved at the regional level that the indirect control of the training centre by the community services administration could not be sustained. The separation of programmatic and administrative authority was unnecessarily cumbersome, it no longer attracted the union opposition which it once did, and it was important that Mayday Hills Training Centre start to see itself as clearly a part of the state intellectual disability services system.

The confusion of responsibilities was increasingly became a matter of concern through 1990 and 1991. The then Acting Public Advocate, Mr John Britton wrote to the acting Director General of CSV on 11 July 1991:

> ... I am writing to seek clarification of the arrangements which apply at "joint" facilities at Beechworth and Ararat. In current circumstances at Aradale in particular, it is crucial that the lines of accountability are clear and that guardians and advocates know to whom they should take any concerns they may have about the well being of either residents at the Training Centre or patients at the Psychiatric Hospital.

> Such is not the case ... the most recent illustration came only yesterday when a distressed and apparently sick Training Centre resident found herself in police cells charged with a quite serious criminal offence. This was no time for debate about whose responsibility she was, who should develop proposals for bail

arrangements to put to Court today and such like ... it was left to her solicitor late in the day to even arrange medical attention....

John Britton, Acting Public Advocate to
Allan Clayton, Acting Director General
CSV, 11 July 1991

The Regional Director CSV and the Regional Executive Officer OPS agreed following the industrial dispute of December 1990 that it was desirable that the training centre transfer to the management of CSV. A meeting took place at Royal Park Psychiatric Hospital in Melbourne in April 1991, attended by the regional directors CSV for both the Grampians and the Upper Murray Regions, and the regional executive officers OPS for both regions. At this meeting, a proposal was formulated whereby responsibility for both Aradale and Mayday Hills Training Centres would pass to CSV. The proposal was put to the General Manager, Disability Services, in CSV and ultimately received endorsement at a Ministerial level. The Regional Director, Upper Murray (now expanded and renamed Hume Region), was given the responsibility for negotiating the transfer of both facilities.

The negotiations were protracted and at times tense, entailing as they did the transfer of resources between the departments. Amongst the contentious issues, were whether CSV should assume responsibility for the Aradale site despite its deteriorating infrastructure and whether one department should purchase administrative support from the other, or absorb the administrative functions of the institution within its regional structure. These issues were eventually resolved and it appeared likely that this transfer of the facilities could proceed quickly, but for the intervention of the disclosure of serious abuse of the intellectually disabled and the Aradale institution operated by the Health Department.

Aradale was located on the hills overlooking Ararat in central western Victoria. It was built at the same time as Mayday Hills and had a similar history. It was located in a similar former gold rush town and had a similar mid-Victorian grandeur to buildings which belied its back-ward squalor and neglect. It was a "joint facility" for the intellectually disabled and psychiatrically ill as was Mayday Hills, but differed in that the intellectually disabled represented the majority of residents. Unlike Mayday Hills however, Aradale had remained isolated from developments within intellectual disability services as a consequence of the decision by the regional director of that region to not take on responsibilities for which his region had not been funded.

In August 1991 the Public Advocate, Mr Ben Bodna received reports of abuses at Aradale which concerned him to the extent that he required of the

Minister for Community Services, urgent investigative action. A formal investigation was undertaken by a team of Health Department investigators. Their damaging report indicated widespread physical, sexual and financial abuse at the institution. This came at the time of similar revelations with respect to Lakeside psychiatric hospital in Ballarat and so compounded political difficulties being experienced by the Health Department. It also came at a time when a state election was imminent, an election at which the incumbent Labour Party government was expected to be unseated. It was a time of great nervousness amongst senior administrators whose positions would be vulnerable with a change of government.

It was expected that a new government would amalgamate the departments of Health and Community Services (this indeed occurred following the victory of Liberal/National Party government in October 1992). The chief executives of the two departments were thus competitors for the leadership of the anticipated new department. The transfer of the joint facilities, in the context of the Aradale scandals became a pawn in that contest.

Dr John Paterson (Community Services) in a strongly worded letter to his counterpart accused the Health Department of failing to protect the interests of his department's clients at Aradale, and refused to assume responsibility for the facility until the Health Department had cleaned up the problems there. In this he relied heavily upon the Governor in Council's order of October 1985 which indicated that the responsibilities of the Health Department would remain unchanged in the joint facilities by the administrative transfers of that year. In reply, Mr Tim Daly (Health) argued that the proclamation of the IDPs Act in 1987 superseded this order and gave the Director General of the Community Services Department clear responsibility for the wellbeing of registered intellectually disabled people. He argued that the problems at Aradale were attributable to the failure of CSV to meet its responsibilities under the Act. The two Departments commissioned contradictory legal advice as to whether authority under the Act could be delegated to another party.

In the event, and putting aside the ambitions of the chief executives, the transfer of administrative responsibility took place on 1 December 1991. It did so with a written agreement that the Health Department would continue to take responsibility for any continuing legal or personnel issues associated with the Aradale abusers.

The transfer of administrative responsibility may be seen as simply a formality, and of little consequence to the processes of change within the institution, especially as twelve months later the two departments which had struggled for so long over their relationship in the "joint facilities" were themselves amalgamated. This was not the case however. The transfer of administrative responsibility formalised what had been taking place progressively in practice for some time, i.e. the movement of the training centre into a community services' philosophical and services framework. It was important also because it enabled a formal integration of the community and institutional services management to take responsibility for the implications for staff of the changes taking place in the mode of provision.

Jim Kesselschmidt, Manager of Direct Care, saw separation of the Training Centre as one of the critical factors effecting change:

> Separating the facilities was really significant, hell, because it really told everybody its on, it's for real, there's a new management structure and its happening... Often things didn't change that much in the reality of people's day to day work, but the perceptions, it really did affect people's perception of the place.
>
> (Kesselschmidt interview)

Following the formal transfer of administrative authority, Ms Julie Hind, the Regional Manager of intellectual disability services was also made Chief Executive Officer of the Training Centre. This was a clear decision to integrate to two delivery systems such that it was not possible for changes to be made to one without the implications for other to be assessed. Institutional staff became staff of the Region with the opportunities for redeployment and promotion implicit within that:

> By the 1990s there was no distinction in administrative and management aspects of the Training Centre and the Region. All positions worked across. The Regional Manager was also the CEO. The psychologists were psychologists for the whole of the region including the Training Centre. The service development team people worked across both. The Training Centre staff were seconded into the Region. So there was a sense that the distinction between the Training Centre and the Region, the boundaries were very blurred.
>
> (Hind interview)

Ms Hind was a strong and resourceful manager who had played a major role in every stage of the redevelopment until this time. She directed the final stages of the redevelopment including the ambitious final stage redevelopment plan.

Industrial Power

Early disputes Historically, Mayday Hills was an industrially difficult site for the Health Department. The powerful Hospitality Employees Federation,

Number 2 Branch (HEF2) - later known as the Hospital and Community Services Union (HASCU), was substantially in control of the Hospital throughout the late 1970s and early 1980s. The Victorian Public Service Association (VPSA) also had a presence on campus, but this union was concerned only with the allied health and administrative staff, who were few in number, and who did not carry the industrial clout which came with twenty four hour rostering and the care and safety of very dependent clients.

HEF(2) had industrial coverage of all direct care staff, both in psychiatric services, and intellectual disability services, and also non-direct care staff i.e. artisan and domestic staff, across Victoria. This placed the Union in a powerful position to threaten institutional services across the state which had the potential to place the safety of dependent people at risk. It was accepted within the Office of Psychiatric Services and Community Services Victoria in 1988, that the Government had little capacity to sustain operations in the face of widespread and sustained strikes in the institutional sector.

In addition to its industrial muscle, HEF(2) also had considerable political influence which it could bring to bear in a dispute with either Department. The Union was affiliated with the Australian Labor Party, and by chance, through the period of this research, had factional alignment with the then Minister for Health and other key ministers of government who were relevant to the Health portfolio. Until 1989 the Union was factionally aligned with the Centre Unity faction as were Ministers Roper and White (successive Ministers for Health). At this time, the Centre Unity faction held sway within Cabinet. From 1989, following bitterly contested internal elections, the Union was factionally aligned with the Socialist Left, as were by chance, Ministers Hogg and Lyster (Health) and Minister Setches (Community Services).

> Just after I started at CSV the HEF2 swung from right to left when the right wing leadership was defeated. The union then immediately assumed at least as much importance to the ALP left as it had previously in the right, and that meant that the left, who were so talkative about "social justice" and looking after the most vulnerable, were also sponsoring a union that harbored criminal elements. The HEF2 was solemnly consulted on everything, even though, we gradually discovered, they were actually running and conniving at many of the most sordid rackets. Some of their institutional branches, such as at Janefield and Caloolla, were run by the leading thieves and bashers. This meant always having baddies in the camp when we "consulted" about disability matters.
>
> (Paterson interview)

Major industrial action had been taken by the HEF(2) in October 1985 at the time of the transfer of Intellectual Disability Services from the then Health Commission to Community Services Victoria. This took the form of a statewide strike which lasted for ten days and took all staff out of every intellectual disability institution in the State. This strike resulted in what became known as the "32 point agreement", which detailed the industrial conditions under which the transfer would take place. The effect of the agreement was to provide substantial benefits for HEF(2) members over the subsequent years in such areas as training and certification, classification structure and remuneration.

The "32 point agreement" had particular implications for the Joint Facilities in that it made provision for Mental Retardation Nursing training, (post-basic training referred to above) prescribed the management arrangements which should operate, and specified additional management requirements for their operation. The Post Basic Mental Retardation Nurse training provided for the first time training which was specific to the requirements of intellectual disability services in the facilities which had existed within a framework of psychiatric services and in which all staff were trained in psychiatric nursing.

At the beginning of the research period (January 1988) the sub-branch executive of HEF(2) was firmly in control of the Institution. It was ably led by two experienced registered psychiatric nurses, Jim Reid and Jurgen Hemerling, who were closely associated with the State Secretary of the Union, Peter Bruce and the Assistant Secretary, Peter Cordova. The hospital had been without a Psychiatrist Superintendent for two years, and was nominally managed by a group of officers including the manager (administration), the Director of Nursing, and a consultant psychiatrist. The Hospital consistently exceeded its budget, and successive attempts to bring about reductions in expenditure were resisted industrially by the sub-branch of the Union. It was the belief of some senior officers of the Office of Psychiatric Services, that there was collusion between local management and the Union in this regard (Jones interview).

During 1988, the Office of Psychiatric Services (OPS) attempted to wrest control of the hospital back from the union and to exercise some financial control. Towards the end of the 1987/88 financial year, the hospital had increased its salary expenditure by 40 effective full-time staff (EFT) and in consequence ran significantly over budget. It was believed by the Assistant Director of the Office of Psychiatric Services, that this was done in order to create an increased budget expectation for the forthcoming financial year. OPS responded by reducing the hospital budget for the 1988/89 financial year by the over-expenditure. A Chief Executive Officer for psychiatric services, Mr David Jones, was appointed in September 1988. This position was responsible for all psychiatric services in the Goulburn/North East Health Department region, but was located at Mayday Hills in recognition of its status as the major provider of services in the region, and the major problems it represented for the Health Department.

Jones responded to the severe budget problems of the hospital by imposing expenditure restraint and by commencing an evaluation of hospital operations, to be conducted by a review team. That team consisted of three management representatives and three union representatives. The review went about its analysis of possible efficiency measures between October 1988 and January 1989 at which point it was suspended as a result of union opposition. Amongst other inefficiencies, the review identified that the catering centre had 53 full time staff who prepared only 70 meals each day, most of which were staff meals. Resident meals were prepared by the Ovens and Murray Hospital for the Aged, which provided regothermic meals. These were then plated and heated by food and domestic assistants within the units.

Sub-branch dissatisfaction with the directions taken by the review were aggravated by the experience of staff on the units during the winter period of 1988. An influenza epidemic at that time had struck the institution, and on a daily basis it was impossible for nursing administration to fill sick leave vacancies. The recruitment restraints imposed by Jones added to the view that management was unsympathetic to the staff providing care, and led to a strike of all staff in February 1989.

The negotiation of the February 1989 industrial dispute was undertaken on the part of CSV by the General Manager Resources, the Regional Director Upper Murray Region, and the Assistant Adviser Nursing Services. The Office of Psychiatric Services (OPS) was represented by the Acting Director of that Office, and Acting Assistant Director, and the Nursing Services Adviser of that Office. The Union was represented by its Assistant State Secretary and representatives of the Mayday Hills sub-branch. The negotiations continued for four days from 24 February until 28 February, during which time the entire HACSU covered staffing of the hospital were on strike. This included all direct care staff, artisans and non-direct care staff. Negotiation sessions, chaired by an Industrial Liaison Officer from the Department of Labour began at 10.00 am and proceeded to 2.00 am the next morning. As these things proceed, much of this time was taken with the parties considering the positions put to them by the other party.

The dispute had been prompted by the experience of under staffing during the winter of 1988 when a severe flu epidemic made the maintenance of minimum staffing agreements difficult, and attempts at expenditure restraint towards the end of that year. The matters under negotiation however were not proposed staff reductions, but a claim by the Union for additional staffing numbers. This was widely viewed within the hospital as an assertion of authority by the sub-branch in the face of an attempt by management to take control of the budget process. It also took place against a backdrop of an impending state ballot for control of the Union. In this the then union leadership was anxious to demonstrate its potency to the membership at Mayday Hills which had been one of the mainstays of its support.

According to the procedures then established by the State Government for the conduct of industrial disputes, the two Government Departments firstly met with the Department of Labour and the Department of Management and Budget. They subsequently met with representatives of the Cabinet sub-committee on industrial relations which placed a budgetary limit on the settlement which could be entered into following negotiation. This limit for the Training Centre was 22 EFT. The Departments were then free to negotiate a settlement which met the requirements. They did so however in the knowledge that their political masters were prepared to fund a purchase of industrial peace, and that the other party, through the agency of the "impartial" chairperson of the negotiations, in all probability knew the limits which had been applied.

The negotiations revolved in the first instance around the facts of rostering practices at Mayday Hills. Years of unofficial union control of management of the centre had produced myriad minimum staffing agreements which committed the Departments. These were not endorsed by HDV, but had been signed by local management. The situation was further confused by the pragmatics of rostering which involved the matching of insufficient trained personnel to work sites on a day to day basis. In consequence there was no agreement between the Departments and the Union as to what constituted the staffing of the facility.

Having finally agreed the current staffing of the facility, negotiations focussed upon areas of dispute concerning additional staffing sought by the Union. For the Training Centre this was for separate staffing of Carinya Unit which had previously been monitored from Myrtle House. The residents of this Unit were largely independent and had not required staffing support. Also additional staffing was sought for Myrtle House and Grevillea Units on the grounds that the demanding clients in these units required additional support. A separate night roster was sought on the grounds of improving safety for residents and staff. The matters of more symbolic and substantive disagreement related to the non-direct care areas, particularly catering services. These were important precisely because they were the areas of most dramatic overstaffing.

The settlement reached represented a complete abandonment of the government position. With only minor amendment, the demands of the union were met. In the case of the Training Centre, CSV did not have major objection to the provision of additional resources for Myrtle and Grevillea Houses. The additional staffing of Carinya and night supervision were simply unnecessary.

The Department was most concerned however that the additional resources be applied in such a way as to improve the quality of life and availability of programs for residents. To this end, the final settlement included the following statement of intent:

> CSV considers that the principal benefit associated with the provision of the proposed additional positions should be the delivery of a much greater level of active therapeutic and developmental programs for residents. It may be necessary therefore at times to deploy staff in accordance with established practice to adequately support programmatic initiatives for residents. (Memorandum of Agreement, Department of Labour, Feb 1989)

The intent of this statement was to facilitate the appointment of staff for the purposes of individual program provision and to make possible flexible deployment across the Units, rather than to increase basic nursing care. In practice neither was possible, and the additional positions were absorbed on to rosters. The settlement cost the Government $641,000 for the Training Centre alone. This was slightly in excess of the limit applied by the Cabinet sub-committee, but utilising the higher salary figure of HDV as opposed to that of CSV, it could be represented as 19.2 EFT; well below the nominal limit given, and hence a success.

The dispute became of a symbol of management impotence. It was not without the positive side however. Julie Hind, later CEO of the facility described the gains from the CSV perspective of the dispute:

> The 1989 (strike) was easier to handle from my perspective, because ultimately Health was responsible for dealing with it, even though CSV were in there advising the Health Department about what to do with it, and the CSV Regional Director was heavily involved. The gains that the Union was going for, we could claim very strongly were gains for the Training Centre as well, and so from a resources point of view, it was actually good for the Training Centre, because it put new resources in. I suppose that set something up with respect to the redevelopment for us later.
>
> (Hind interview)

At Mayday Hills, following the announcement of the settlement, a celebratory barbeque was held by the Union, with the food being provided by management from the catering centre which had been the source of the dispute.

In July 1989 HEF2 notified a further dispute concerning the profile of paraprofessional staff at Mayday Hills Hospital. In this dispute the Union sought the permanent appointment of specified positions to the Mental Health Aide (2) level, and the payment of higher duties allowances on a shift basis. The position of the Government as represented by HDV management was consistent with the February agreement, to support the creation of Level 2 positions, but in the intellectual disability services officer (IDSO) rather than mental health aid (MHA) range. The Department was also not prepared to have higher duties allowances paid on a shift basis as this would create a precedent with potential impacts across the entire public service, where higher duties allowances required a period of at least five days assignment.

The positions of the parties and the outcomes of the dispute are instructive as to their perspectives concerning the joint facilities at that time. From the perspective of HDV and CSV it was preferable to have the senior classification within the IDSO category. This was a cheaper option in that CSV had negotiated a lower profile for these staff within its institutions; that is, if the facility was staffed according to the CSV IDSO profile, there would have been a lower number of level 2 positions. More importantly, such a move would more clearly place the Training Centre within CSV's program responsibility and carry with it the requirement that staff at this more senior level would be required to have some training in the care of the intellectually disabled.

HEF2 took the view that its members were best served by maintaining employment within the Health category. This maximised their options for assignment and appointment to higher level positions across both the psychiatric and intellectual disability sections of the hospital. It also, as indicated above, ensured that a larger number of Level 2 positions were created.

At issue then, was the capacity of management to determine the profile of staff and the training requirements to ensure the adequacy of client care. The outcome of the dispute, which did not go to industrial action, was to abandon these principles. HDV was not prepared to risk statewide industrial action because of an in principle stand in two facilities, and where the costs were being met from consolidated revenue rather than from productivity improvements within the budget of the agency. Also, the degree of government support for a strong stand being taken was, as demonstrated by the February dispute, poor. The settlement entailed the creation of the positions at the higher number, and in the MHA category, with vague codicils concerning review within the processes of "structural efficiency" negotiations (Department of Labour, 26 July 1989).

The Decline of Union Power

In the 1989/90 financial year, Mayday Hills management, having seen a significant addition of resources through the February settlement, was faced with a major budget reduction. Until this time, while reductions were proposed, they were not seriously pursued. Those which had been proposed in 1988/89 had led to a major dispute and were not sought.

In August 1989, on the instructions of OPS Central, local management sought to introduce a staff ceiling of 604 EFT. The salary expenditure of the Hospital had been 640 EFT at 30 June and in August was 628 EFT. It was the view of the HDV and CSV regional management that it was possible to reduce to 614 EFT without breaching industrial agreements, although this was expected to be challenged by the union.

It was at this time that the central leadership of HEF(2) changed in a traumatic contested election. The State Executive Committee which had been built around State Secretary Peter Bruce was defeated in a landslide result which was not anticipated by either HDV or CSV, or by a large number of members of the Union. The new leadership came to power with a stated objective of moving the Union's focus away from the institutions which had traditionally been its support base, improving representation of artisan and non-direct care staff, and improving access to training for all staff (Memorandum: Principal Nursing Adviser to General Manager OIDS, 15 September 1989). An immediate impact of the election result was the resignation of the entire sub-branch executive of Mayday Hills Hospital, and the replacement of its group of sophisticated and industrially experienced members with a relatively inexperienced group. The new leadership which was factionally aligned with the Socialist Left faction of the Victorian Labour Party government was less concerned about the minutiae of issues at Mayday Hills, which had as a worksite been aligned to the outgoing Centre Unity faction. The disruption caused by the election, the relative lack of sophistication in the incoming sub-branch executive, and the diminishing pre-eminence of Beechworth as a worksite for the Union, allowed local management room to introduce reductions in expenditure which had been impossible six months earlier.

Despite this, the management approach taken at this time was an unsophisticated one, reflecting the absence of a strategic view of the future of the facility, and the absence of financial systems which may have allowed management to have control of the budget process. The Office of Psychiatric Services centrally was concerned principally with high priority metropolitan projects - the decommissioning of Wilsmere Hospital and the development of Heatherton Hospital. Its strategic view of the development of Mayday Hills Hospital was limited to a view that HDV, as an agency, was overcommitted in the north east of the State and that reductions should be achieved. A more sophisticated view of the future of the Hospital, linked to the main streaming of psychiatric services within the framework of general health services did not emerge for another twelve months.

The absence of adequate financial monitoring systems, and the limitations imposed by recently negotiated industrial agreements, rather than a strategic redevelopment focus, determined the manner in which savings were made. An immediate embargo was placed upon the employment of staff against positions not covered by the February agreements. This meant that savings were made principally in the VPSA covered areas of administration and in allied health positions. The non-filling of allied health positions was to have an immediate impact upon the quality of care within the Training Centre. In particular vacant positions in the social work and occupational therapy areas were determined to be no longer on the establishment of the Hospital (Minutes, Allied Health Meeting, August 1989).

These reductions, of course, as well as undermining client care within the facility had a negative impact upon the strategic redevelopment of the facility. The very positions deemed to be non-existent were those required to prepare clients for alternative living arrangements.

The Regional Director of CSV put strongly the Department's view that in effecting budget savings in a memorandum to the CEO of the hospital. He insisted that:

- the 1985 transfers agreement requiring maintenance of effort be adhered to;
- the February industrial agreement to which CSV was a signatory be adhered to;
- Training Centre client care not be prejudiced by budgetary decisions;
- Settlement of any dispute not create flow-on issues for CSV institutions elsewhere; and
- In the event of industrial action being taken, adequate care be available for training centre residents (Memorandum: Regional Director CSU to General Manager OIDS, 2 August 1989).

CSV was however in a dependent position, having limited actual power to effect decisions and poor budgetary information upon which to base its interventions. What may have been a strategic opportunity to effect change without some industrial constraints was lost, and the impact of budget reductions was essentially negative.

The changes in the leadership of the sub-branch on campus did have an immediate impact upon the negotiations with management however. Many matters which had previously been negotiated were reopened, and the new sub-branch executive lacked an understanding of the history of prior negotiations. This was an initial source of frustration for local management, but ultimately strengthened its hand in dealing with disputed matters. The new sub-branch executive lacked the clear strategic stance of the former executive and also its charismatic leadership. The issues of minimum staffing agreements which the former executive had used to maintain employment levels and defy earlier cost cutting attempts were allowed to lapse in favour of one-off disputes concerning rostering practices.

Under the new central leadership, Beechworth was of less significance than under the previous regime. The Union had commenced to shift its focus to community based rather than institution based care, and the increasing focus upon issues of union amalgamation and restructure which forced a Federal focus to its energies, diminished the importance of rural institutions. Additionally the fact that the Mayday Hills workforce had supported the rival faction in the election did not endear it to the new leadership.

The relationship was further strained when at the behest of sub-branch executive, the Assistant State Secretary wrote to the General Manager, Resources, of Community Services Victoria, complaining that there had been insufficient consultation with the union by CSV regional management. He raised two specific issues:

- moves to discharge Mayday Hills Training Centre clients and place them on a community register; and
- establishing of a Working Party to look at the restructuring of the Training Centre section of Mayday Hills Hospital (Correspondence: P. N. Nuzem to General Manager Resources, 26 January 1992).

Neither of these had been raised with the union prior to being enacted, he said. The Department was able to respond by pointing out that the clients under discussion in (1) were in fact already resident in the community and that the recommendations dealt only with their status. These recommendations had emerged from a review set in train following the incidents of alleged sexual assault at the Ratray Avenue residence in Wangaratta. The working party referred to in (2) was established to implement the recommendations of the Behaviour Intervention Program Review and was not looking at the restructuring of the Training Centre as such. Both working parties had union representation and progress reports had been reported to the local industrial consultative committee meeting. The Department was able to demonstrate this with reference to the minutes of these meetings (Correspondence: Regional Director, Upper Murray Region to Assistant State Secretary HEF2, 14 February 1990). The central executive was embarrassed by the clumsy intervention and from this point until the final negotiations concerning separation of the Training Centre and the Psychiatric Hospital, paid little regard to the events in the Training Centre at Mayday Hills.

Without a clear strategic focus, the sub-branch executive became fragmented in the early months of 1990. Two groups were to emerge; a grouping based upon traditional industrial concerns of terms and conditions of employment, and an emerging group who were principally motivated by a concern about client care. The first of these groups held formal power within the sub-branch, but tended to act in an uncoordinated and ad hoc manner. It had been used to a regime in which the union effectively managed the facility and in which benefits such as Departmental support for full time union activity at the hospital's expense accrued to sub-branch executive positions. It had difficulty dealing with the changed management arrangements and did not know how to arrest the decline in its power. This was particularly the case as a consequence of its loss of central support from the union. As the power of the first group waned, the second increased, and the coalition established between it and CSV regional management became a critical factor in the further redevelopment of the facility.

By May 1990 the tension between the sub-branch executive and the Central Executive of the Union was such that the entire sub-branch executive resigned. All positions were then filled on a temporary basis by Trevor Lancaster, a mental retardation nurse and unit manager who was both a member of the central Committee of Management of the Union and a leader of those staff who were increasingly becoming concerned to further client care in the facility.

Staff Power

Beginning in December 1989, Regional management commenced a series of briefings for all staff on the future of the facility. The message which was given at the forum of 21 December 1989 and repeated at every available opportunity by the Regional Director and other senior staff, was that change was inevitable. The ageing population of the facility, the non-admission policy, and the fact that institutional care was not a preferred model of care, taken together meant inevitable closure at some point for the facility. Staff were invited to take some responsibility for their own future, and to participate in developing new service options for their clients. In doing so they would create new careers for themselves.

The message was greeted with initial cynicism and denial. As redevelopment progressed however, and staff saw colleagues taking up new positions in community settings, with guaranteed futures, they joined in increasing numbers in the opportunities for redevelopment. Industrial disputes diminished, as did absenteeism and workcare claims.

In December 1990 the unions for the first time found themselves dealing in a dispute with a government which was confronting major financial shortfalls and not inclined to back down in the face of industrial pressure. IIEF(2), following meetings with its institutional members, advised CSV and HDV that industrial bans would be instituted and that members would not report for duty until 10.00am every alternate day. The union took its position on the basis that "nurses professional rates and integration of psychiatric services is the thin edge of the wedge" leading to a loss of separate psychiatric and intellectual disability services and loss of the specialisation of psychiatric and intellectual disability nursing" (Memorandum: Director, Industrial Relations CSV to General Managers CSV, 12 December 1990).

The Government took the view that this constituted strike action and applied the "no work as directed no pay" provisions of the industrial award. As a result, the majority of direct care staff of psychiatric institutions in the State and most Intellectual Disability Training Centres were stood down and from 13 December until 21 December the facilities were staffed by management and volunteers. The government reaction was unanticipated as the Union had not previously had a statewide strike brought on in this way, nor had the Government previously been steadfastly unwilling to compromise. Faced with the prospect of its members being on strike and without funds over Christmas, and the beginning collapse of rank and file support for the action, the union allowed an ACTU face saving initiative to proceed, and effectively backed down.

At Mayday Hills more than a dozen registered nurses had indicated their intention to return to work, and the industrial action had little support from the members who did not see its immediate relevance to them. The strike was a significant step in the disintegration of union support on campus.

Julie Hind described her experience of the dispute, and its significance for the Mayday redevelopment:

> The 1990 strike was a statewide one and I found it much more difficult because we were responsible for the Training Centre. I found it more difficult in the sense of the personal tension that one bought from being responsible for the Training Centre, and going for eight or nine days. Having to do for the first time

the sorts of things that we had advocated for many years to actually get rid of, like chemical restraint and so on. Towards the end of that period [we were] going around and instructing the medicos to medicate a whole lot of clients because we had so few volunteer staff and the clients were so distraught. But in some ways it was the turning point from an industrial point of view because at a local level things began to become much more attuned with the change management way of the Region. As CSV became managers of the Training Centre, the local sub-branch began to see some sense in working with us rather than against us.

(Hind interview)

A high priority for the newly elected leadership of HEF2 was the non-direct care workforce. This group had been alienated by recent developments within the service. They had seen nursing staff obtain higher wages and improved conditions as a consequence of a Nursing and Direct Care Review, with the expectation of further improvement in wages when the payment of professional rates was approved. They had seen major improvement in training opportunities for direct care staff. Their own positions however were tenuous. Limited to employment within institutions they were well aware of Government commitment to reducing institutional care. The increasing focus upon purchase of support services from outside rather than of direct employment by Government held out the prospect of their positions ultimately disappearing.

Soon after achieving control of the Union, the new central Management Committee Group lodged a log of claims with the Public Service Board for salary increases for this group under the structural efficiency principle. This provided for salary increases as a consequence of award variations and work practice changes which could be demonstrated to improve productivity. The first stage of this application (providing a 3% salary increase) was granted by the Public Service Board on 19 December 1989 in return for the Union agreeing to discuss means of improving productivity. A further 3% was available on the basis of actual efficiencies being negotiated. Negotiations on this second 3% stalled in June 1990 principally because of CSV's and HDV's insistence that actual efficiencies be identified (Correspondence, A/Director of Industrial Relations, CSV to Chief Executive Officer of Institutions, 20 June 1990). Following negotiations and threatened statewide industrial action, the revised positions of the Departments became that "work practice changes would only be required for the trialing and implementation of the new structure".

The agreement involved the provision of increased wages in return for the broad banding of categories of non-direct care staff into trades and domestic groupings. It allowed for the creation of some senior classifications of domestic services workers on the basis of their being able to be deployed across work units. Thus within an institution it would be possible to redeploy a cleaner from one unit in which cleaning work was completed to another in which additional cleaning staff were required, on a day to day basis. Under the restrictive work practices which existed previously, this had not been possible.

The timing of the non-direct care agreement was significant for the Mayday Hills redevelopment project, in that it corresponded with the separation of the Training Centre and also the beginning of a demarcation dispute at the facility. In the jockeying for position in the wake of the Australian Council of Trade Unions support for structural realignment of the union movement to form larger and fewer industrial bodies, HEF(2) had defined its future as part of an amalgamated Health Services Union covering both the public and private health sectors. The Victorian Public Service Union (subsequently, the State Public Service Federation of Victoria - SPSFV) saw itself as being part of a nationwide public sector union. The disputed ground between the two unions as they both sought to guarantee their future, was the public sector health provision through the Office of Psychiatric Services and CSV. Mayday Hills became one of the battlegrounds for the ensuing war between the two unions. This was a consequence of the dissatisfaction of the members with the central executive of HEF(2), the personal allegiance of some staff of the facility to the former Assistant State Secretary of HEF(2) who on his defeat at election became a senior industrial officer with the other union, and the anxiety generated by the organisational changes associated with separation.

Separation took place on 1 December 1991. Following the signing of the non-direct care agreement Regional Directors and Chief Executive Officers of CSV institutions were required to obtain local agreement to a "Part A" schedule, which outlined the existing non-direct care arrangements and a "Part B" agreement which outlined proposed new arrangements. This was to be achieved by 20 December 1991, in order that they could be ratified by the Public Service Board and take effect by beginning January 1992. In the event, the anxiety of the department to achieve the structural reforms and hence the budget savings was not shared by the unions, and no institutional Part B Agreements were endorsed by the Public Service Board before July 1992.

At Mayday Hills, consultative arrangements as proposed in the agreement with HEF(2) were established, but were rapidly brought to a close when the entire sub-branch executive again resigned and this time joined SPSFV. In the subsequent weeks SPSFV signed up all but one of the CSV non-direct care staff and approximately 50% of the direct care staff. The Department was left in the situation of having to implement an agreement entered into by one union which had traditional coverage of the area, but which did not have the membership of the workers affected by the agreement.

The matter came to a head in January when it became clear that SPSFV would not allow discussions to take place with staff concerning workplace changes required to allow nominated non-direct care to attend retraining courses unless this was negotiated through them as the union representing the staff. This required defacto recognition of their right to cover the non-direct care area. The Government, whose dominant Socialist Left faction was aligned with HEF(2) would not allow this unless coverage had been granted by an appropriate industrial relations tribunal, either the Public Service Board or the Industrial Relations Commission.

On 20 January, SPSFV notified a dispute to the Public Service Board concerning the retraining of staff. The Union was concerned to use the dispute to further its position in the demarcation dispute, but risked alienating the staff by an intransigent position which denied them access to retraining. The Public Service Board ruled that it could not hear the matter of training until it had first resolved the question of coverage, and determined to meet to discuss this specifically. CSV in response agreed to release the staff for the retraining without agreeing the necessary cost off-sets. This was on the understanding that local management would effect economies where possible in order to make the savings. When the Public Service Board sought to hear the demarcation dispute however, SPSFV issued a writ to prevent this occurring, and instead made application to the Industrial Relations Commission. It subsequently withdrew the application, ending its attempt to extend its coverage across the entire public service.

The impact of the demarcation dispute was to reinforce the cynicism within the workforce concerning their industrial bodies. When the staff felt betrayed and unsupported by one union, they sought coverage by another. That union was ultimately less concerned about their interests than its own future. The fact that it was a management initiated retraining scheme which offered them the greatest prospects at this time, and a management decision to release staff without the necessary budget offsets, was further evidence to them that they had more to gain by local level participation in decision making than by traditional means of industrial negotiation.

Central and Regional Interests

The final stage of the redevelopment involved the relocation of the remaining 71 residents of the institution. This was a complex management task because it involved ensuring that there was not a large pool of excess staff who could not be transferred to new services. It required also that a balance be maintained between the requirements to resource the remaining parts of the institution, while staffing up the new services, as unlike the other major institutional closure projects of the time, additional funding would not be provided by the central administration to maintain both functions.

It was complex for the additional reason that, the site of difficult negotiations moved from the institution itself to the interface between the Regional Centre and the central administration. Until this point the region had been able to proceed with a progressive institutional redevelopment, if not greatly assisted, then certainly not hampered by the centre. As the approach to management of the program at a state level became more controlling and more concerned with administrative as distinct from programmatic requirements, as Ministers came increasingly to identify the Mayday Hills redevelopment as an exception and so gave it greater prominence, and as the anticipated change of government became more imminent, the centre became less supportive:

> ... they wanted to block it and I think it was basically jealousies. I've looked at that hard and fast over a number of years and I've still not been able to see any other reason other than what they saw happening was out of their immediate control. They weren't going to get the kudos for it. The Region had worked so hard with the Training Centre, you had a skilled workforce that was very committed to change, so it was now being held up by the Office of the Public Advocate, by the Community Visitors and by others as being one of the leading lights. Politicians were, at that point singing the praises of what was happening with minimal dollars but a lot of effort in the Region and the Training Centre. There was a sense that the redevelopment and Mayday belonged to the Region and I don't think our bureaucratic masters liked that.
>
> (Hind interview)

The Regional Centre was required to justify every action it took. The Opposition spokesman at the time, and later Minister, the Hon Michael John was critical of the attitudes he saw expressed from the head office of the Department:

> I detected jealousy and suspicion from some of the main players at head office, and a lack of probably, lack of a team spirit about it, and a lack of ability on the part of some of the leading lights to actually give credit where credit ought to have been given... So we had people like Karen Cleave and John Paterson almost wishing it had been their baby and they could pick up the credit for all the good things that were happening.
>
> (John interview)

John visited the Centre on 15 July 1992. He spoke positively about what he saw in particular the staff support for the redevelopment process. A copy of the media report of his visit is included as Figure 6.4.

There was a growing sense of frustration amongst those working on the ground to redevelop the institution, and the centralising and controlling tendencies at the Centre:

> I think that in the end, the only thing that was going to stuff it up was Head Office. And that was, I think, somebody's personal ego, the fact that they had not gone through to do it... that sort of shit is unbelievable. We just went out there and did it. We actually put a lot of work they did in question and they also thought they had no control, no influence and they weren't going to get the pats on the back for something that some rogues out in the bush got away with.
>
> (Macdonald interview)

> We were able to finish it off, but nonetheless they didn't make it easy. They began taking money out of the Training Centre. They began questioning where the money was, where it was going, they basically disbelieved everything we put to them. They refused to offer any money even when at one stage all we needed was $200,000. They began putting a whole lot of obstructions up.
>
> (Hind interview)

In order to progress the redevelopment, the Regional Centre developed a plan which would see the remaining residents relocated to community settings and alternative services developed. This plan was presented to the relevant General Manager of the Department on 22 July 1992. The centre piece of this plan was a demonstration that with a capital investment of $364K, the remaining residents could be moved to community settings, and a total of $500K in recurrent savings could be achieved. The plan received lukewarm support from within Disability Services Branch, but was strongly supported by other departmental executives. It provided a means by which the Department might give maximum effect to a key government policy, with the minimum expenditure of funds. It was also likely to attract the support of the anticipated future government.

On the initiative of the General Manager, Resources and Deputy Director General, the Department's capital request for the 1992/93 state budget, which had already been submitted to Treasury, were withdrawn and the requested capital incorporated. The proposal was included in the state budget and put before the parliament. In the event, the budget was not passed because it was

● CSV client Ada was one of the people Mr John met during his visit to Mayday Hills.

A model hospital 'but it has to go'

By DAVID CARTER

LARGE psychiatric institutions such as Mayday Hills Hospital at Beechworth would close under a Coalition government, the Victorian Opposition's community services spokesman, Mr Michael John, said at Beechworth yesterday.

"I was very impressed with what I saw at Mayday Hills," he said after his inspection.

"But there is no question of keeping the hospital as it is.

"In five, 10, 15 years, all large institutions will close and there is no long-term future for them under any government."

Mr John's visit to Mayday Hills marked the end of a tour of all the State's community service facilities.

The hospital has both community service clients and psychiatric patients under the care of the Health Department.

It was a joint facility until late last year when Community Services Victoria took over its clients with the plan to move them into community housing.

Mr John supports the move but wants a more flexible approach to community housing.

"We do not want to be tied to an ideological model that there should be five or six CSV clients to a house.

"Their numbers could vary or they could live in flats.

"We want to allow most of the Mayday Hills clients to settle in the Beechworth area where we have the people to look after them.

"The Opposition is conscious of the economy of Beechworth and the concern about jobs."

Mr John said he was impressed with the way the CSV in the North-East and its regional director, Mr Tom Keating, had gone about implementing Government policies.

"It is appalling in the rest of Victoria but Mayday Hills is a model for what should have happened," he said.

"There has been a tremendous commitment and dedication from the CSV staff."

But he did not want to buy into the contentious issue of union representation at Mayday Hills.

Figure 6.4 Press Clipping: 16 July 1992 (*Border Mail*, Albury)

overtaken by the state election on 3 October 1992. The newly elected Liberal/ National Party government passed its own budget, which included significant reductions in recurrent expenditure and a freeze on capital expenditure.

The Director Disability Services wrote on 28 October, following the election of the new government, advising that the redevelopment of Mayday Hills would not proceed:

> As we are aware the 1992/93 Interim-Budget has not provided any opportunities to fund the proposed 1992-93 and 1993-94 redevelopment options for Mayday Hills. Capital funds are not available as the State Plan Year 4 was not funded and recurrent funds remain tight... Additionally, I am not sure of the understanding of Minister John but he does intimate that the centre is on an immediate closure path. We need to inform him that this will not happen.
>
> K. Cleave to B. Spalding
> Director Community Support
> 28 October 1992

She underestimated the level of political support for the redevelopment however. The final redevelopment plan was redrafted and submitted to Disability Services Division on 5 February 1993. The redrafted proposal included no capital requirement from the State government and relied heavily upon resident purchase of equity and use of Ministry of Housing accommodation. With the strong support of the Minister, the project proceeded, with the last residents leaving the institutional site on November 1993:

> The Regional Director had arranged some briefing of the potential in-coming members who would form the government and there was a sense of trying to make sure the Coalition understood what the redevelopment was about and what it stood to lose if a change of government delayed the process. I actually found our political masters much easier to deal with, in the sense of being much more supportive that what our bureaucratic masters were. The reigning Labor Party in the early stages were very supportive, but the change of government actually didn't really make much difference and the Minister was still very committed and so were the local members.
>
> (Hind interview)

Summary - Responses of the Political System

The political system of Mayday Hills underwent a major upheaval in the period between 1988 and 1992 as the institution was forced to come to terms with the shifting of influence and resources in its environment.

Administratively, there was a transfer of authority from the health department to the community services department reflecting the formal transfer which had taken place at the State level. This did not happen easily and was not formally mandated until December 1991 when further machinery of government changes were effected. It had in practice taken place earlier however because community services had access to vital resources in the form of critical knowledge and also financial resources which could be used strategically to encourage new developments. Also, it was useful for the health administration to be able to separate the training centre to some degree in order to reduce the leverage on the hospital as a whole by the union.

The period of shifting administrative power, also coincided with an important decline in union power. The sub-branch of HEF(2) had effectively managed the institution for some time. A change of approach to industrial relations by the State government, prompted by increased financial stringency, internal conflict and subsequent discontinuity within the union, and management determination to reassert control over the organisation combined to create a situation in which one of the major supports for the status quo in the institution lost significance in management and in planning.

Staff, who may have expected little change and relied upon union advice to maintain existing benefits and to avoid changes, progressively became aligned with regional management which it saw as concerned to preserve employment, allow training for new employment, and provide appropriate services for clients.

Responses of the Technical System

Mayday Hills Training Centre operated until the mid 1980s with a practice technology which assumed high levels of dependency and, in fact, fostered dependency through treatment methodologies intended to protect clients. The extensive changes which were taking place within the intellectual disability field during this time have been identified in Chapter 6. These involved a fundamental revaluing of clients as independent actors, entitled to socially valued roles and treatment in age appropriate ways.

In response to the changes in the environment of the organisation associated with development of "normalisation" as the guiding principle of practice, and the specific requirements of the Intellectually Disabled Persons Services Act, the technology of the organisation was forced to undergo fundamental change. This required **reskilling** of staff, the development of **alternative service models**, and ultimately the **redevelopment** of the

service system as it operated in North East Victoria. The changes within the service system were finally to contribute to changes within the environment of the organisation itself.

This section will describe the ways in which the technology of care of the institution progressively adjusted to the expectations of that environment.

Reskilling of Staff

The Intellectually Disabled Persons Services Act Implementation   The first significant challenge to the service technology of the institution came through the implementation of the Intellectually *Disabled Persons Service Act*. The Act has been passed by Parliament in October 1986 and was proclaimed as legislation in October 1987. The Act represented the realisation of the aspirations of the reformers in the intellectual disability field, and it was underpinned by a normalisation philosophy. As well as stating in a charter, principles which should underpin the provision of services in the field, the Act created a number of practice and administrative expectations of service providers, the most significant of which was the Department itself.

The Act required of the Department that it have prepared for each registered client, a General Service Plan (GSP) and by each provider of services, an Individual Program Plan (IPP). The GSP, was required to be in a gazetted format, and to address nine life areas. Goals were required to be developed for each life area including residence, and day activity. As such, the GSP may be considered to be a highly structured case plan, produced in a prescribed format. The IPP translated these life area goals into specific service initiatives, indicating the ways in which the goals would be met.

In proclaiming the legislation, provision was made by the government for resources for its implementation. This included the development of client service teams in each of the then nine Health Department regions. Client service workers were case managers who would take responsibility for developing GSPs for clients and managing the coordination of their service usage. Resources were also provided for each of the state's then nine major institutions. This provided staff whose responsibility it was to develop plans for clients located in those institutions. In the case of the institutions which were operated directly by the Department of Community Services these additional staff were provided early in 1987. In the case of the two joint facilities, Aradale and Mayday Hills, while the resources provided by government were available from the time the Act was proclaimed, unease about resources being provided to another government department delayed any effective action to implement the Act until mid 1988. The difficulties were exacerbated in the case of Mayday Hills, because of the fledgling state of the regional team, which had only just been established from the former Goulburn/North East Health Department team, and had only two members. By contrast the regional team servicing the Central Highlands Region and Aradale was longstanding and so able to move more quickly on this new function.

A meeting of senior officers the Central Highlands and Upper Murray regions took place in January 1988 at which the management of the two joint facilities, and the implementation of the Act were discussed. At this point, it was clear that the work was much more advanced at Aradale where planning had taken place for a significant number of clients. The Regional Director of the Central Highlands Region however, was strongly of the view that the Health Department was responsible for the management of that facility and that he had been given the resources and responsibility only for the implementation of the Act. He intended to take no further action on the institution despite having major concerns about the standard of care available there. This was a decision which was to have major implications for the Department at a later stage, when allegations of serious abuses at Aradale came to the fore.

A decision was taken by the Upper Murray Regional Centre that the additional staffing positions should be part of the staffing complement of the regional team rather than the institution itself. Also, the staff would be used, not to prepare GSPs and IPPs for the clients of the institution, but to train the staff of the institution to do these tasks. Appointments of these training officers were made in February 1989.

As might be anticipated, the increased presence of the regional team at the institution was not welcomed by either the management or staff of the facility. They were identified as outsiders who did not have an appreciation of the difficulties or the complexities of institutional life. One of the training officers, Marie Lindley, described the response of the institutional staff to them:

> We were apparently referred to as the high heeled brigade. At that stage, I don't think I owned a pair of high heels. But it was a perception ... It was also that, you know, we will humour them while they were here talking to us but at the end of the day, we were the ones having to deal with the day to day issues; cleaning up the messes on behalf of [our clients]. They don't really know, they've never actually done it.   (Lindley interview)

More significantly, the very presence of the training officers was a challenge to basic assumptions within the institutions. The premises of the Act, and indeed its specific principles, assumed that clients were able to learn skills which could enhance their independence. The prevailing world view of the institution was that clients were unable to learn and would always be dependent.

In consequence, while the training officers were able to establish personal rapport with institution staff, they felt that their training was having little effect. In Lindley's view however, despite a lack of comprehension of the impact of the legislation, there was a beginning change in staff attitudes:

> ... staff's understanding of their role in relation to the people they were working with was pretty basic. I think there was possibly an emerging understanding that people should be doing something with the people they were working with. But they didn't really know how to go about it and they certainly didn't have the skills to be able to move from, yes we understand that this is a good idea, people should be doing things with these days, there should be things for people to do, to putting out some sort of cohesive plan for individuals.
>
> (Lindley interview)

The extent of the failure to meet the spirit of the legislation as well as its forms became clear in September 1988 when a review of General Service Plans of four elderly clients of Mayday Hills was required by the Intellectual Disability Review Panel (IDRP). The IDRP was a tribunal establishment under the Act, with the power to review the plans and the treatment of registered clients. In particular, it was charged with responsibility to monitor the use of restraint, seclusion and aversive therapy, whose frequency of use was required to be reported on in monthly returns from all registered residential facilities. In monitoring the returns from Mayday Hills, the panel noted that it and Aradale registered the highest continuing use of chemical restraint of all institutions and also abnormally high usage of seclusion (the locking of clients within single rooms).

When the panel called for the GSPs of a sample of clients who were reported as being secluded, it noted that the GSPs and IPPs for all four clients were identical and could well have been photocopies of the one document with only the name of the client changed. The panel after reviewing each case, ordered that seclusion be discontinued in each case, following the introduction of programs designed to address the behaviour which caused the seclusion to be instigated. The review process itself was a harrowing one for the institutional staff concerned and indicated, perhaps for the first time, that the institution was no longer a world unto itself.

The early introduction of training commenced a process of skills development which was important for the subsequent change process. Progress was slow however, and despite concentrated effort through 1989 and early 1990, Lindley believed that little had been achieved:

> ... Jenny and I started there in '89 and the Act had been passed in '87. It seemed to me that there had been this Act around for two years and all the lead up to it as well before it was actually passed and it hadn't really had much impact at all and there was very little development in that two year period and I think even the next 15-18 months that Jenny and I were up there it was also very slow. People were understanding that there was a general service planning processes that came out of the Act and individual planning for clients was mandatory. I am not sure that they had progressed in terms of how to go about doing that.
>
> (Lindley interview)

Post Basic Nurse Education

As Mayday Hills Training Centre had been administered as a mental health facility before January 1988, and continued to be managed by a mental health authority until December 1991, the qualifications required of its staff were those of mental health employees. This meant that professional staff were registered psychiatric nurses, and para-professional staff were mental health aides. A small number of staff were trained Mental Retardation nurses, or had dual qualifications. Registered psychiatric nurses usually had three years specialist psychiatric nursing training, which for many had been provided on campus. Mental health aides, required certificates as state enrolled nurses with six months supervised practicum. These staff did not have training specific to care of the developmentally disabled, and in particular, did not have training in developmental programming (the techniques of skills training for the intellectually disabled).

This lack of training and expertise had serious consequences. Very little training or skills development for residents took place within the facility; reinforcing the perspective that residents were not able to learn or to care for themselves. The treatment regimes were those which might have been appropriate to psychiatric patients, but were generally not appropriate for the intellectually disabled. As indicated above, investigation by the Intellectual Disability Review Panel indicated that the highest incidence of chemical restraint of institutional residents in Victoria occurred at Mayday Hills and Aradale, the two facilities managed and staffed by the Office of Psychiatric Services (IDRP

Annual Report 1988/89).

One of the elements of the industrial settlement following the statewide strike of October 1985 was the agreement by the government to provide post-basic training for Mental Retardation Nurses at Mayday Hills and at Aradale. In the case of both the institutions schools operated for the training of psychiatric nurses, but hitherto few staff were trained or qualified in mental retardation nursing. The few staff who were appropriately trained were those who had transferred at some stage from another institution, or who had been recruited from overseas.

The industrial agreement provided for this to change, with the training of eight students each year as mental retardation nurses. They were required to have a general nursing or psychiatric nursing qualification, and funding was provided to back-fill these positions, on rosters within the institution.

Their training was important in that it provided them with the skills of the "new technology". The curriculum included a substantial focus upon developmental programing; the partialising of tasks and the training of the developmentally disabled in these tasks. It also allowed them to move out of the all encompassing environment of the institution, and to be exposed to a range of alternative practice methodologies. It required that they undertake a practicum outside their usual workplace, most often in a community setting:

> ...getting staff who had only ever done psych training into ID training and having them through that, becoming aware of the changes in the ID field and the different practices that were occurring elsewhere, I think began to open some eyes to other ways of dealing with the client group than what they had been part of. Most of them did their placements on the regional team so they began being aware of the sort of lives that people with an ID out living in the community lived and the sort of work people were doing with those people in the community... to have all of these people come through on the regional team and see the other professions, like mine and the psychs and the social workers spend time with the nurses to a point where we began to appreciate the skills of the other.

> (Hind interview)

The post basic training program operated over a four year period from 1989 to 1992, and during that period provided training for thirty two staff. Its impact was slow and the early staff trained through the program felt isolated and to some extent ostracised within the institution. Over the period however, the number of staff who were trained in mental retardation nursing practice increased and the impact of the new skills began to be felt across the institution. The training program also provided a vehicle whereby staff were able to choose to have a career in mental retardation nursing as distinct from psychiatric nursing, such that when the training centre was formally separated from the psychiatric facility in December 1991, there was a trained workforce ready to make the transfer.

Para Professional and Artisan Staff Retraining

Provision for the training of staff within Intellectual Disability Services was established in the "32 Point agreement" struck between Government and HASCU following the statewide strike of October 1985, and was reinforced by the Nursing and Direct Care Category Review (1986/87). These arrangements entailed the progressive transfer of on-campus nurse education to tertiary education institutions and the establishment of an Intellectual Disability Services Officer (IDS) category of staff.

The agreement provided for recognition of existing paraprofessional staff following an abbreviated training course, the development of a short training course (14 weeks) following twelve months working experience as a Trainee Intellectual Disability Services Officer (TIDSO), and an eventual movement to pre-service training through Technical and Further Education Colleges.

Mayday Hills and Aradale Training Centre were anomalous in that few of their staff were appropriately trained. They did not have Mental Retardation Nursing training provided on-campus, and they were not covered by the industrial agreement which guaranteed access to conversion training for existing staff. The "32 Point Agreement" did however make provision for the training of Mental Retardation Nurses on-campus by means of "Post Basic Training". The agreement provided for one year full time training for staff with either Psychiatric or General Nursing qualifications.

The training of paraprofessional staff was more difficult to achieve because of the absence of industrial agreements which covered them, and because of the unwillingness of CSV to accept responsibility for the Joint Facilities. In all eighty six Mental Health Aides were employed in the Training Centre in 1988. These positions were filled from a pool of staff which was used to cover the whole of the Hospital. The implementation of the Nursing and Direct Care Review in 1988 saw the commencement of "short course" training for existing staff with more than two years experience through TAFE colleges. Although the Mayday Hills staff were not included in calculations of training costs, it was possible to include twelve food and domestic services assistants (FADSAs) in the initial intakes for the Wangaratta TAFE College. This was possible because the then manager of non-direct care services in the Hospital was sufficiently supportive, to rearrange rosters to allow the staff to attend the course without their positions being backfilled.

This made possible the first Intellectual Disability Services Officer positions on-campus. The positions were anomalous in that although they were the only trained paraprofessional staff on-campus, their qualifications were not accepted by the Health Department, their employer, and for the next two years they could not be deployed in direct care work. Their training was significant in that it emphasised the need for training specific to intellectual disability, and it was the first instance in the state of retraining the workforce from non-direct care to direct care. Its success gave the Regional Centre confidence that this could be replicated with larger numbers of artisan, catering, and domestic staff. In the short term these staff who had retrained were resented by many of the mental health aides in the facility, who, for instance, made the choice of uniform which could be worn by these staff a matter of industrial dispute.

In August 1989 the General Manager, Resources Division, visited Mayday Hills Training Centre. He had recently taken over responsibility for the Upper Murray Region in a Departmental restructure which saw all General Managers assume responsibility for some regional units. He was also responsible for the staff training function within the Department. Regional management put to him the need for staff from Mayday Hills to be able to access the training to be provided for IDSOs, through TAFE. While he initially appeared to agree with this proposal, when it was put to him formally in September of that year, he refused to allow it on the basis that the staff were the employees of the Health Department and that department had the responsibility to provide them with the training they required to perform their duties.

His refusal meant that funds could not be provided for the backfilling of positions while staff received the fourteen weeks training, and taken literally, they could not access the student places which CSV had funded in TAFE colleges in Wangaratta and Wodonga. In order to allow the training to proceed, the regional office negotiated for the staff to be released for training but not backfilled. This was a difficult process and one which added to industrial tensions. It was possible to achieve however because it could be seen as improving the career opportunities of staff. The student positions were taken up and in all twenty four IDSO staff were trained in this way.

The value of doing this was demonstrated at the time of separation of the facility from the Health Department. At that time a limiting factor was the number of trained staff who could be transferred from the Health Department to CSV. The decision was taken to transfer those staff who were doing the duties at the time of transfer irrespective of qualifications, and to train them afterwards. In the case of Aradale Hospital, where a policy of progressive training of paraprofessional staff had not been implemented, the number required to be trained was 63, in the case of Mayday Hills the number was ten. The estimated cost of providing this training should the Department be forced industrially to provide backfill for all positions was $800,000, the bulk of this to be expended on Aradale staff. The Health Department's "ex-gratia" contribution was $50,000. Had the training of Mayday Hills staff not taken place, the final cost would have been in the order of $1.6m.

During 1991 CSV regional management gave attention to the retraining of artisan staff. As the facility was diminishing in size there was a diminishing requirement for non-direct staff. A significant part of the budget however was committed in fixed costs associated with non-direct care staff. Using a working party made up of artisan staff, the Regional Centre floated the possibility that retraining of non-direct care staff to perform direct care duties might be possible under certain conditions. These conditions were that the staff would be agreed between management and the union to be in excess (and so not require to be backfilled) the staff undergoing the training would agree to be redeployed at the end of their training to a location no more than 45 minutes travel from Beechworth; and they would also agree to forego any expenses reimbursements they might otherwise be entitled to during their training.

The response was overwhelming. A maximum of ten places were available; five full-time in Wodonga, and five part-time in Wangaratta. In all, 28 staff applied for the positions, and the Regional Centre allowed 12 to attend the training, under the conditions stipulated. A further three staff opted to undertake the studies in their own time, and were assisted with three (3) hours per week study leave. By this means it was possible to convert resources committed to an area of work of diminishing importance, to resources which could be flexibly applied to an area of increasing demands. It provided an increase in the overall level of skill in the workforce in the direct care of the intellectually disabled, and demonstrated to many staff a commitment to them personally and their careers.

Early Service Development

The Wangaratta Joint Community Living Support Service   Some efforts had been made by an isolated group within the institution to establish alternative services within the community, but these were not strongly supported by the management of the institution. In 1986 a house had been established in Wangaratta, but was understood to be an extension of the institution. Staff were rostered across this and other on-campus units. They worked institutional hours consisting of rotating twelve hour shifts. Also within Wangaratta, there operated a number of houses for the intellectually disabled managed by a community based organisation, the North East Residential Care Association (NERCA). This association, which consisted mainly of parents of intellectually disabled people, operated two such houses in Wangaratta, one of which provided respite services and the other long term accommodation and support. The two providers, NERCA and Mayday Hills had little contact and in fact an antagonism existed between them.

In April 1988 funding was announced for what was described as the intellectual disability services redevelopment budget (1988/9). This budget proceeded the announcement of the State Plan for Intellectual Disability Services (1989-91), and was intended to demonstrate the government's commitment to the sector. Amongst the initiatives announced was the establishment of what were described as community living support schemes. This service model was intended by the department to challenge the inflexible model of residential service which had been developed in the community over the previous decade, which had been referred to as the Community Residential Unit (CRU) program. These units, while being located within the community, were institutional in their style of operation, had rigid staffing models, and were seen as providing a too narrow range of accommodation support options. They, for instance, provided an unvaried level of supervision, irrespective of the support needs of the resident. High functioning resident received the same level of support as the profoundly disabled because of staffing rigidities. They had difficulty responding to the differing interests and capacities of clients with respect to day activities, and they tended to provide a fixed level of support for clients. Few clients "graduated" out of the service and so additional clients could not receive support.

Community living support services were intended to change this. Instead of providing a fixed residential service for a defined number of clients, the service was intended to provide "flexible support hours" according to the needs of the client. Under this model support could be provided in a range of settings including residential units, private houses, flats or family homes. The level of support could be adjusted according to the capacities of the clients. It could vary between clients according to differential capacities, and it could vary for single clients as their needs fluctuated. This service development was intended to provide a major vehicle for the implementation of the principles of the Act. It was seen as a means of breaking down the isolation of community clients in supported accommodation, and of increasing their community integration through a range of support options. In practice the service model had limited impact across the State. In the majority of cases, residential support was provided to people living in traditional community living services.

The prospect of additional resources being available for this new model however, provided an important incentive at this early state in the redevelopment of Mayday Hills. NERCA had sought additional funding to establish additional CRUs for a number of years. Pressure was being experienced within that organisation because of growing waiting lists. It was clear that any additional resources would not be available for traditional CRUs, but for the new CLSS model. Similarly, the institution was facing financial pressures and was unwilling to provide additional resources for community based care. The new service model, with new resources provided was potentially a means of developing further service options, while not having to draw upon the recurrent resources of the institution.

The regional office of the community services department saw the new model as a means of promoting change within both providers. In both cases the providers could potentially be persuaded to become more flexible in their delivery mode. A proposal was put to the central administration of the department, to establish a joint CLSS scheme to be managed by a joint management committee consisting of the two providers. It would draw clients from both the community and the institution and would integrate the existing residential developments with an expanded flexible residential support service. The proposal, because it was seen as innovative and likely to lead to significant systemic change was endorsed centrally and received funding.

The processes of establishing the service were difficult however, because the two organisations had extremely different approaches to service delivery, their respective client groups were different, and because, at this stage, the prospect of additional resources did not represent sufficient incentive for collaborative action. It was important however that the resources had been made available, and despite not being utilised quickly, continued to be available. It was important also that staff from the institution were for the first time required to establish a relationship however strained with another service provider and to enter into discussion as to how services should be provided.

The Behavioural Intervention Support Program (BIST)

The development of the Behaviour Intervention Support Program was the first significant cooperative project linking CSV with the staff of Mayday Hills. The project involved the redevelopment of Myrtle House, the institution's locked unit for behaviourally disturbed clients. The unit was of major concern to the region from the beginning of its involvement with Mayday Hills, in that, it provided the lowest standard of care in the facility.

The development of the Behaviour Intervention Support Team (BIST) was critical in the process of redeveloping Mayday Hills Training Centre. It was important in that it established the joint regional/institutional, and management/staff mode of cooperative planning and service development. It was also critical in demonstrating to both regional and institutional staff that alternative means of providing care could be found for even the most difficult institutional residents.

The BIST Program was developed as a means of closing the notorious Myrtle House unit of the Training Centre. Myrtle House was in 1989 a locked residential unit for nine behaviourally disturbed residents. When in June 1988 the first Health Services Agreement between the Health Department Victoria and Community Services Victoria was being negotiated, the CSV Regional Director refused to sign an agreement which did not include a commitment from the Health Department to provide a more appropriate residential environment for the clients concerned. Between June 1988 and June 1989, the Health Department's management of Mayday Hills sought to avoid taking any action on the unit. The then Manager of Administrative Services, Mr John Green, following the complaints of the CSV Regional Director, spent some time in the unit, and was motivated to develop a capital works submission to improve the physical fabric of Myrtle House. This was to be staffed at an increased level, and when Green left following the industrial dispute of February 1989, the project received no further support.

The matter was brought to a head industrially when the HEF(2) sub-branch notified of health and safety issues in the unit and refused to staff it. Mayday Hills administrative management claimed that the costs associated with refurbishment of Myrtle House were prohibitive and proposed instead that another disused residential unit "Olivene" might be used instead. In the interim, the CSV Regional Director, and the Chief Executive Officer, Psychiatric Services agreed to establish a joint working party to develop a program design for a new behavioural management unit. The Working Party was established in July 1989 and consisted of Ms Sheri Brooks representing CSV, a representative of nursing administration, the charge nurse of Myrtle House, another staff member from the unit, and a representative of the occupational therapy department.

The working party struggled for some months to develop a design for the unit and for a program which could provide a satisfactory service for the three highly functioning residents who had very severe behavioural difficulties as well as the six lower functioning residents who were more dependent and required high levels of support. A turning point in their considerations came with the visit to the facility of CSV's consultant on behavioural management issues, Mr Garry Radler. Radler encouraged the working group to think more broadly than the presenting needs of the current resident group. He challenged it to focus on what it saw as the needs into the future, and requirements for behavioural management within the wider community. With this input, the working party reported that a behavioural management unit should not be established on campus, but that the three highly functioning clients should be supported in a community setting, and the remaining clients be integrated within the other units of the Training Centre, with specialist assistance. The working party, with its proposals supported by the Training Centre Liaison Committee was reconstituted and with industrial representation, formulated implementation plans for the project.

The completion of the program design, coincided with the announcement of the State Plan for Intellectual Disability Services which provided for the establishment in its first year of Behavioural Intervention Support Teams. Because the region had completed detailed planning of its behaviour management program, and was able to offer a significant contribution of resources from the institution, it was able to negotiate to have one of these projects. In July 1990, the first BIST Program was established as a joint initiative between CSV and Mayday Hills Training Centre. Through the program, two mental retardation nurses became part of a regional consultancy team on behavioural management, together with a psychologist provided through the State Plan. The three most difficult to manage clients moved off campus, with residential support provided by redeployed staff who left the institution.

The development of the BIST Program, because of the substantial opposition to change from staff on campus, took two years:

> We had a very strong Union in terms of them objecting to absolutely everything that went on in the last part of the 80s... Some of the early redevelopment actually took two, nearly three years, particularly closing the first unit, Myrtle House. There was always a sense of taking two steps forward and one back because you'd no sooner negotiate part of the redevelopment and it would change at a management level both at a sub-branch level and then centrally. The union was actually very volatile. We would have undertaken negotiations with some players and got agreement only to have that altered three month down the track and you'd be back at the drawing board because they were then not taking any note of the previous sub-branch or the previous agreements that had been reached.   (Hind interview)

This opposition came as much from Nursing Administration as it did from staff within Training Centre units (Brooks interview). The factors in its success were in part the impetus provided by outsiders, Brooks and Radler, who were able to encourage fresh perspectives on the part of the staff concerned. In the case of Brooks, this was facilitated by the fact that she had previously worked at Mayday Hills, and so had some of the credibility of having been an insider.

The BIST program, at the time of its establishment, was not seen by the majority of staff as being positive. The two staff who took up positions on the regional consultancy team were trained overseas, and so not part of the enmeshed Beechworth community. They were able to appreciate alternative means of providing care. Amongst many long term staff, there was considerable resentment towards CSV and the prospect of change taking place with the institution.

The project was seen as resource rich, and beyond that which was deserved by the clients who were moving into community settings. They were difficult to manage and generally disliked. Brooks describes an attitude of "why should they get this", masking a fear that there could be substantial change for clients (Brooks interview). There was resentment also at having to assimilate into the other units of the Centre, clients who had previously been segregated because of their behaviours. There were over the following year, a number of attempts by some staff to re-establish a behaviour management unit (locked ward) on campus; as this was an accustomed way of handling difficult behaviours.

Despite these difficulties at the time of its inception, the BIST Program was a significant first step in new program development. It demonstrated that it was possible to have joint program development between the Regional Team and the institution, no matter how difficult this was. It was demonstrated that this could be achieved despite many hurdles and obstacles (Brooks interview). This important first step made it very much easier for the latter program developments to take place.

The project demonstrated to staff of the facility that there were employment options for them beyond Mayday Hills. Though the anxieties remained, and for many the prospect of working in community settings was frightening. The project was the first time that Mental Retardation Nurses were appointed to positions on the Regional Team and as such, made an important statement to the staff of the institution about their acceptance within that organisation. It also allowed a confronting of the stereotypes of mental retardation nurses held by many regional staff. Their reputation as having few skills and maintaining restrictive work practices, could be confronted within a shared work environment (Brooks interview).

The NERCA Equity Fund

An early opportunity for new service development was provided by funds from another institution. Janefield, an institution located in Melbourne's north eastern suburbs, was one of the state's largest congregate care facilities. In the 1987/88 budget, funds were provided by the state government for the relocation of children from that institution to community settings. As with most institutions, the average age of residents was in excess of 50 years. There were however, in this facility, a number of younger people who were inappropriately placed there. The budget allocation was intended to enable a more appropriate placement for them.

One of these young people had come from north east Victoria and his family were resident there. Progress in achieving the relocation was slow however, and as the end of the financial year approached it seemed likely that the Northern Region which was responsible for Janefield would not have achieved the relocation, and would not have spent the allocation. A proposal was put by the Upper Murray Region in May 1987 that funds be provided to establish a residence in the Upper Murray region to accommodate the young person from the region who was then located at Janefield. This residence would also provide for three other young people who urgently required residential support. One of these who was profoundly disabled had been resident in Wodonga hospital since his birth seven years previous.

A total of $120,000 was provided for this project, and the funds transferred to the North Eastern Residential Care Association prior to the end of the financial year, in order to avoid the embarrassment of under-expenditure and the possible return of the funds to consolidated revenue. Instead of utilising the funds in the way they were approved however, the Region developed an innovative scheme which maximised the use of the resources for residential support. This involved using the funds to provide equity for a larger number of clients by loaning the funds to them. As they repaid the funds, over time a larger number of residences would be created for a larger number of clients. The fund was created, and in addition to the four originally identified clients, another 60 clients were provided with equity loans towards their own homes, including 22 from Mayday Hills.

The project was an important step in the redevelopment of Mayday Hills, for a number of reasons. It established a mode of operation for the region whereby access to scarce resources was negotiated, and innovative means were developed to stretch these resources to have maximum effect. It introduced the idea of creating client equity in these residential options, which was to be an important factor in the redevelopment of the institution. Finally, it was the first instance in the state of the use of equity schemes, and as such established the pattern whereby innovations in service design and administration were pioneered in the Mayday Hills redevelopment before being adopted elsewhere within the intellectual disability system.

The project was also important as an indicator of the sort of tensions which emerged in the later stages of the redevelopment between the region and the central administration of CSV. The new management of the Disability Services Division in 1991 was jealous of the reputation for innovation and progressive development enjoyed by the Upper Murray region. When the General Manager of the division became aware of the project, she sought but could not be provided with a copy of a Ministerial approval for the revised use of the funds. It could be demonstrated that senior officers of the department had been informed of the project and supported it, and that the gains for proceeding in this way were amply demonstrated. Nevertheless, it was used to suggest that the region was behaving in an uncontrolled way.

State Plan Development

The IDS Redevelopment budget (1988/89) provided the opportunity for early service development which linked Mayday Hills Training Centre to the community sector and commenced thinking within the institution about new technologies of care. The state Plan for Intellectual Disability Services and its associated budget allocations provided the opportunity for significant redevelopment of the resources of the institution. The Minister for Community Services announced the Plan with an initial commitment of $10m for the 1989/90 year. The Minister appointed a community committee to oversee the implementation of the plan, and its chairperson, a former state parliamentarian who had recently lost his seat in parliament, Mr Mike Arnold visited the Upper Murray Region, accompanied by the General Manager for Intellectual Disability Services, Mr Allan Rassaby, on 26 July 1989. They attended a meeting of interested people at Mayday Hills that night to discuss the implementation of the State Plan (Upper Murray Regional Consultative Council, 1989). Rassaby and Arnold met with staff of the Upper Murray Regional Centre, and were given details of the proposals from the centre for service expansion, (Upper Murray Regional Centre, plan for State expansion - State Plan Funding, July 1989).

The approach that was advocated by the regional centre was one which linked Mayday Hills Training Centre with the state plan development. Resources from the Training Centre would be combined with new State Plan resources in such a way as to significantly expand service options for both community and institutional clients. This would counter to some extent the need for "hump funding" (double funding of both old and new services during a transition period), enable significant progress to be made, and respond to the community expectation that new resources would be applied to community rather than institutional clients.

From the commencement of the redevelopment, it was critical that community support for community based care be developed. A broad array of community responses was evident in the consultation conducted by the Regional Consultative Council. These included strong support, particularly from those who had disabled family members, through concern about possible dangers from disabled people, to outright opposition. Some of that opposition came from within the town of Beechworth, because of the progressive loss of employment from the town (Upper Murray Regional Consultative Council, 1989).

One area of potential community opposition was from those in the community whose family members were on waiting lists for supported accommodation, and who believed that those in the Training Centre were well cared for, and that any new service should be provided for community clients. With this in mind, an attempt was made to ensure that each new project established for Training Centre residents would also create options for community clients:

> Every one [of the new services], whether they were accommodation or day services, needed to accomplish a service for the client that was coming out of Mayday Hills and in some way needed to expand the opportunities for people where were living in the community. For every part of the redevelopment, the challenge was placed on staff to look at how you can improve the quality of life for this person in the Training Centre... but also how can that add to the resource base for people who are sitting in the community who otherwise won't get anything.
>
> (Hind interview)

This was achieved by utilising innovative rostering arrangements and by stretching the resources provided through the state plan to the greatest possible extent. The chart included as Table 6.5 indicates the level of additional beds created as a consequence of the redevelopment.

**Table 6.5   Additional Community Accommodation Achieved as a
Result of the Mayday Hills Redevelopment**

Target	Actual	Additional Capacity

1988/89
12 x TC Beds
4 x Community Outreach
	12 x TC Beds
	1 x TC Outreach
	10 x Community Outreach
	(51 - 61 hrs pf)
		• 1 x TC Outreach
		• 6 x Community Outreach
		- Increased Outreach
		  hours
		- Better use of pooled
		  hours
		- Challenges to work
		  practice

1989/90
2 x TC Beds
 	
1990/91
6 x TC Beds
	8 x TC Beds
	6 x Community Beds
	
	18 x Community Clients
	Outreach
		• 6 Community Beds
		• 18 Community Outreach
		• Closure of "locked" unit at
		  Mayday Hills
		- Increased staff skill in
		  challenging behaviours
		- Beginning of regional self
		  sufficiency

1991/92 15 x TC Beds	15 x TC Beds 3 x Community Beds	• 3 Community Beds • Outreach to be developed at yet unkown level
Total 35 x TC Beds 4 x Community Outreach	35 x TC Beds 1 x TC Outreach 28 x Community Outreach (plus additional potential)	1 x TC Outreach 24 x Community Outreach (plus additional potential) 9 x Community Beds

Source: (Community Services Victoria, 1992)

It can be seen that from the funds provided from external sources, the number of supported community places created exceeded targets by 24 CLSS outreach (average 51-70 hours/fortnight) and nine community beds.

The proposals put forward by the Regional centre were not accepted in their entirety, but were to provide the foundation for service redevelopment over the following three years:

   • A collaboration was established between the Regional centre and the General Manager, who developed a good understanding of the objectives of the Regional centre, both with respect to development of the service infrastructure of the region, and the redevelopment of the Training Centres. Rassaby gave active support over the subsequent two years to many of the innovative approaches taken by the Regional Centre.

- The proposal based residential development on a combination of CLSS funding for recurrent costs (including both a State Plan funded and Training Centre funded component), and equity housing for capital costs. Equity housing had been piloted within the region in the NERCA Equity Housing fund, and was anticipated to be established across the State through the Singleton Equity Company. When the statewide scheme was established, the Upper Murray (Hume) region became its largest collaborator, taking up sixty-one places, many of which were not utilised by other regions.

- A strategy of over-achieving against State Plan targets was proposed as a means of reducing the size of the institution. This became a critical means by which sufficient resources could be generated from the institution to fund further redevelopment. It was useful also, however, in driving innovation, since more flexible and creative service models were needed in order to generate efficiencies.

- The broad approach which was adopted was not one of institutional closure alone, but was focussed upon the development of an integrated service system covering the North East of the State. The proposal began from a view that the region lacked a service system but did have a small number of isolated, institutional service providers. The task was to refocus and redevelop those services, provide a strong integrative framework, and ensure that services worked together to meet client needs.

- The proposals entailed an approach to the provision of day activities which was entirely integrative and focused on participation of the disabled in mainstream community activities.

The proposals were not funded in their entirely, but were supported through the funding of the BIST Team (part funded from Mayday Hills), a modest expansion of CLSS; such that redevelopment of the institution could commence in a concerted way. Over the following three years eighty seven people were relocated to community settings from Mayday Hills, using a combination of State Plan and Institutional resources. An additional thirty three community clients received residential support over and above those community places which were funded through the State Plan.

For David Green, this was one of the distinguishing features, and most valuable aspects of the Mayday Hills redevelopment:

> ...the more the centre [of the Department] becomes preoccupied with appearances and symbols of things like big institutional closures, the more it creates a false reality. What was distinctive about Mayday and the children's home closures [before it] was that the resources were re-invested in ways compatible with community requirements. This is incompatible with big block buster events.
>
> (Green interview)

Residential Services

A series of residential projects were established which enabled residents to move to Wodonga, Wangaratta, Benalla, Shepparton and into Beechworth township. These were usually staffed from Mayday Hills, by staff who chose to move to a community setting. Residents were selected through a General Service Planning process, with critical factors being whether they had family or social support in the location, or the location of their day activities program if they had one. Rosters were flexible and based up on the assessed support needs of the residents. Flexible rostering reduced down-time during the day when residents were attending day program. It proved extremely effective, and the rosters developed from the Mayday redevelopment community houses came eventually to be adopted across the State.

The housing options were developed with the need of the residents in mind, as well as the requirement that they be based on age appropriate and socially appropriate models. Many of the residents of Mayday Hills were elderly, and so a model of residential support based upon adjoining two bedroom units was developed. This is a familiar housing model for older people in the community, but one which enabled effective care to be spread across a number of residences. Again this model of community care which was developed out of Mayday Hills, came to be reproduced across the State, and was replicated for the later Caloola closure project.

Day Activity, Employment and Social Support Services

The State Plan proposals from the Upper Murray Region pioneered an aggressive approach to integration of disabled people within generic community based day activities:

> People with an intellectual disability in the Upper Murray Region have currently limited access to day activity options and most of this is restricted to segregated

services. There is an excellent network of neighbourhood houses [16 in all], TAFE colleges, centres of adult education and senior citizens' centres throughout the Region that could be accessed if means were made available. (Upper Murray Regional Centre State Plan Proposals, 1989)

As each funded CLSS place included resources for day activities, it was possible to utilise those funds for the development of day activities. As resources were progressively freed up from the institution, the pool of day activity funds could be expanded.

In every case, and counter to the approach adopted in the other regions of the State, the resources were applied to projects which integrated clients within mainstream community education, recreation or other activities:

> In the day services we looked for a more integrative approach than the traditional ATSs and so a number of what were then innovative programs were established around brokering of day services, so that individual packaged services could be designed for clients, rather than put them into a day facility where they sat for the next thirty years doing exactly what they had done the first day they entered it.
>
> (Hind interview)

The first such program was the *Access for Developmental Disability (ADD) program* which was established through the Albury/Wodonga Continuing Education Centre. This program exposed intellectually disabled clients to a range of adult education courses through a "starter" sequence. The client would then select a full program to undertake, which they would do with a volunteer attendant. The program was successful in introducing a large number of intellectually disabled people to adult education. It received a national adult education award in 1993.

The Community Options program was one of the first adult day activity brokerage programs for the intellectually disabled in the state. It operated on the basis of pooling available funds, and purchasing an individualised program from a range of providers of recreational, educational, or employment services. This enabled the activity to be tailored to the needs, interests and abilities of the clients. It also gave flexibility over a working week, as the clients program could vary each day across activities, again depending on interest and ability. These projects were established in both Wodonga and Shepparton.

The North East Leisure Service (NELS) was established to facilitate access to mainstream sport and recreational activity by the intellectually disabled. It was auspiced by the North East Sports Assembly, a community agency concerned with the planning of mainstream leisure activities. *Human Employment Services* and *Goulburn Valley Trainers* were established as community based supported employment agencies. Both had their origins in the attempt to create realistic employment options for some of the residents of Mayday Hills Training Centre. Amongst the employment related programs were the *Wangaratta Bakery project*, and the *North East Agriculture Trainers* (NEAT); both established as commercial enterprises. The NEAT program was particularly successful in training employees for the growing re-afforestation industry in the region. It utilised the facilities of TAFE, while providing employment.

An important social support initiative, the *Volunteer Friends program*, grew out of one of the early industrial disputes at the Training Centre. It was noticed that the residents of the Training Centre were almost entirely without social relationships apart from those involving other residents or staff. The volunteer Friends program was established to create a pool of volunteers who would make a personal commitment to one resident and engage with them on a monthly basis in a social activity. The program attracted significant public support, with activities including movie going, family picnics and bushwalking.

The Family Reunion program developed out of the personal interest in genealogy of a direct care worker, Brenda Fitzgerald. She responded to the wishes of a resident to know who her family was by undertaking a search of family records. She discovered that the client had a brother who was entirely unaware that he had an elderly intellectually disabled sister resident for most of her life in a state institution. Similar searches revealed many other like circumstances. Fitzgerald was taken off line and worked full time for two years on tracing family connections. She was successful in locating the families of more than 30 residents, most of whom were unaware of the existence of their family member, and most of whom welcomed the opportunity for contact. One such family was that of Verna West who had been placed in state care as an infant, having been taken from her single parent mother. She spent 63 years in intellectual disability institutions, despite a questionable diagnosis, much of that time at Mayday Hills. Her sister, the eminent journalist Rosemary West, was located by Brenda Fitzgerald, and commenced to take an active interest in her sister. Verna was reunited with her mother, and her story and Brenda Fitzgerald's work was featured prominently in a feature article in the Melbourne Age. Rosemary West received an international journalism award for this story. The program of family reunion, was eventually established in other state institutions, to give long term residents access to the families they had been denied by their history of care.

These and other projects had the effect of moving the focus of day activities away from segregated congregate activities, to smaller scale, individualised, and integrating activities. They were bitterly opposed by the older style Adult Day Activity providers, who believed that any new resources should be directed to them to expand their campus based programs. Their opposition was increased by the realisation that this was happening in the other regions of the state. Over time, however, they modified their position as they realised that the only way they would get access to new resources was to modify their own programs. In a number of cases, their traditional services entered into collaborations with the new agencies and services, to jointly operate the new programs.

Final Stage Redevelopment

The final state of the institutional redevelopment took place in the twelve months between October 1992 and November 1993. During that period, the remaining ninety six (96) residents moved to alternative accommodation.

The redevelopment plan presented to general managers of the Department in July 1992 provided the basis for these moves. The plan proposed that from the base recurrent funding of the institution, then $7.59m: 71 additional community residential support places would be created; six supported accommodation places; 73 day programs; and case management services for 50 former training centre residents would be established. In addition, a service for dual diagnosis clients, which would be available as a resource for such clients across the state, would be established. These new services, valued at $4.9m, would be additional to the $3.54m already committed to community based services from the Mayday Hills budget as a consequence of the redevelopment activities which had taken place over the preceding years (Community Services Victoria, 1992).

Though the budget proposed was not funded because of the change of government in October 1992, the redevelopment did proceed for the first time as a formal project of the Department. As such, the pace of the client relocations was dramatically increased. While during the four years from 1988 till 1992 a total of 82 residents had left the training centre for alternative accommodation, it was proposed that over the coming 12 months, 96 would do so. This would tax to the limit the capacity of the region and training centre staff, since unlike other institutional closures, this was to be undertaken without additional project staff, and while the staff concerned continued to meet their responsibilities to the other 800 registered intellectually disabled clients within the region.

The strategy developed for the closure consisted of seven parts (Community Services Victoria, 1992):

- the development of client profiles in consultation with clients, their carers, their families where these were known and wished involvement, the Office of the Public Advocate and the Guardianship and Administration Board;
- the development of a staff residency profile to identify the staff's home location and work location preference;
- an assessment of community attributes, including anticipated future need for services, current number of placements and community tolerance of and support for the disabled;
- the development of project proposals through the Future Initiatives Group;
- the utilisation of nine project teams to progress individual developments;
- the development and implementation of exit plans; and
- the "recruitment" of staff for the new services.

As part of the Department's Caloola redevelopment, a detailed process had been developed to ensure client participation in the planning concerning their relocation from the institution. This process, called the C-core process maximised the choices available to individuals. With the Mayday Hills redevelopment, a more limited range of choices would be available. The majority of placements would be within the region, rather than across the state as had been the case with Caloola. All residents would leave the institutional setting while in the case of Caloola, approximately half were relocated to other institutions. Resource limitations required that some grouping of residents on the basis of level of disability or requirement for support was inevitable. To guard against the possibility of abuse however, and to ensure that within these constraints, the choices of clients with respect to day activities, co-residents and location were maximised, the Public Advocate was approached and requested to monitor the decision making process. The Public Advocate, Mr Ben Bodna chose to personally become involved, and chaired GSP review meetings for all clients at which plans for them were formulated. He continued to monitor their placement following relocation:

The techniques around change management for service development were based also on empowering the client group. We had brought [it] in very early in the piece, even when it was with Health. Office of the Public Advocate and the

Guardianship Board and Community Visitors [were involved] so that the people who were there to empower the clients were empowered... the people who were responsible for them, who were their voice, were actively engaged in the Training centre and that was really quite unusual around the state.   Most Training Centres, and most Regional Directors didn't like having any of these people near their Region or anywhere near their facilities, but it was an open door policy. We actively encouraged those people to come and work with the client group, work with staff, and then advocate and push where they could for change.

(Hind interview)

Staff residence profiles were of critical importance in keeping faith with the staff of the facility. They had been assured at the time of separation from the Health Department that were they faced redeployment, the disruption to them and their families would be minimised. This was operationalised as an undertaking that no one would be required to work and at location more than 45 minutes drive from their home. As the workforce at the Training Centre had increasingly over a number of years been drawn from a broader geographic area than the township of Beechworth, this enabled a reasonable spread of potential service locations. It was critical at this stage that the confidence of the staff that management was concerned about their personal wellbeing, be maintained.

Community profiles were critical in assessing the capacity of disparate communities to support relocated residents. The Regional Centre was conscious in planning the location of services that the proposed residents, who for the most part were elderly, would be able to utilise the services for no more than ten to fifteen years. After that time, the services should become resources for the wider community which had disabled members who would require accommodation and support. It was critical that these services be located in areas which were either under-serviced or where needs were anticipated. Community tolerance was also a critical factor, as it was clear to members of the regional team that some local communities were more supportive of disabled people in their midst than others, and also that the relocation of numbers of residents over a period of time had led to a concentration of facilities in some parts of the region. Based on the assessment of these factors, it was decided that new facilities should be developed in Rutherglen (two houses), Benalla and Myrtleford, which previously lacked services, as well as extending provision in Wodonga and Wangaratta.

The Future Initiatives Group had shown itself to be critical in earlier stages of the redevelopment, in the identification of client needs and the development of innovative responses to these. This was based on the staff's intimate knowledge of the clients, through close personal contact over many years. Utilising this knowledge for instance, it was pointed out that there were some residents who prior to coming to the institution had lived on rural properties. At Mayday Hills they had continued to live in an open semi-rural environment. It was of concern that they would find it difficult to cope within a suburban environment. With this in mind, two of the new projects were developed as rural services; one at Tarrawingie, and the other at Chiltern. The Tarrawingie project (Tarra Lodge) was developed in conjunction with the Wangaratta TAFE rural industries training project, in order to facilitate day program access for clients and also to ensure that the rural location did not lead to social isolation.

Nine project teams were allocated responsibility to implement the major projects identified by the Future Initiatives Group. Again these were constituted in the main by staff from the Training Centre, who were, literally creating their own jobs. This ensured that there was a high level of ownership of the new services by the staff, and a commitment to their success. The timing of the movement of clients from each unit was planned to coincide with the closure of residential units on campus. This avoided costly doubling up on staff, and also avoided multiple moves of clients around the campus prior to movement off campus. The logistics of this were complex but generally successful. To facilitate this process, the staff for each new service were identified in the months prior to relocation and rostered into the appropriate ward to enable the development of transition plans for residents and the orientation of both staff and their clients to the new locations. Where possible clients commenced attending their new day programs well in advance of moving, so that the number of changes in their lives at any one time was reduced.

Summary: Responses of the Technical System

Table 6.6 summarises the emergent technology from the redevelopment of Mayday Hills Training Centre and may be compared with Table 3.3 which summarised the pre-redevelopment technology. This technology is based upon a perception of client attributes by which they are understood to be capable of learning and of active participation in their own care. Their needs are understood to change over time, and they are understood individually rather than collectively; having very individualised needs and aspirations. At the heart of the technology is the case planning or General Service Plan methodology. The General Service Plan provides the basis of intervention and of coordination of a range of dispersed activities, which have ceased to be controlled or delivered by a single agency. The technology requires a reduced reliance upon bio-physical interventions, and looks to the provision of "normalised" environments which are challenging and learning techniques based upon developmental programming. The interaction between staff and clients is individual rather than collective and is increasingly reciprocal. Clients, and their advocates, are increasingly powerful in decision making, and mandated authorities are able to review critical decisions.

This configuration was developed in the period 1987-1993 through a combination of processes which included: the exposure of the institution to the externally imposed demands of the new legislation; the provision of training for both Mental Retardation Nurses and Intellectual Disability Services Officers and retraining for non-direct care staff, and the development of new and innovative services. The new service development represented an aggressive application of the normalisation philosophy to the services began developed out of the institution, and also to the developing network of services in the north-east of the State. The service initiatives of the redevelopment became a model for those developed at a State level and to support other institutional redevelopment.

Table 6.6   Summary of Components of Mayday Hills Training Centre Redevelopment Technology (1993)

Client Attributes	Knowledge	Interaction	Client Control	Operations
• clients viewed as capable of training • client needs vary over time • client viewed as individuals rather than collectively • client histories as care plans	• environmental intervention by the provision of stimulating/ challenging circumstances • cognitive intervention through learning strategies	• interpersonal reliant upon staff/client interaction • guidance - cooperation. Client active participants in care • communication between individual staff member and individual client	• control of carers limited by external review processes • clients self-directing where possible • involvement of client advocates	• move away from whole of life care. Life areas addressed by a range of agencies • care coordinated through General Service Plan

Summary of Organisational Responses

This chapter has detailed the responses of the organisation to large scale, discontinuous changes within its environment. These responses have been discussed in terms of modifications to the cultural, political and technological systems of the organisation. The cultural responses have been identified as mutually re-enforcing modifications to basic assumptions: about clients and their capacity for self care; about the institution, its purpose and future; and about the nature of the employer/employee relationship. Political responses have been identified as changes in the relative power and influence of competing interests within the organisation. These changes included shifts in administrative power from a health to a community services administration, a decline in Union power, and the rise of influence by the staff of the institution. Technological changes reflected the influence of new approaches to the care of the intellectually disabled, reflected in training programs, revised procedures which enhanced client rights and new service designs which promoted individualised programs.

The following chapter will analyse those responses in terms of the modified Emery and Trist framework. It will aggregate responses across the organisational systems and classify them in terms of internal, transactional and environmental dependencies. It will then identify patterns within these aggregated responses, in order to answer the research questions.

7 Analysis of Organisational Responses

Analysis of Organisational Responses

The preceding chapter has described the responses of the focal organisation to the changes within its environment. The following chapter will consider these responses in the context of the modified Emery and Trist framework as outlined in Chapter 2.

In summary, that framework identified that organisational responses to environmental change can be considered in terms of internal dependencies, transactional dependencies, and environmental dependencies, where internal dependencies refers to the internal relationships between the constituent components of the organisation, and are entirely contained within the organisation. Transactional dependencies are concerned with the relationships between elements of the focal organisation and its task environment. Environmental dependencies are concerned with the relationships between elements of the general environment of the organisation, and so will in many circumstances be beyond the direct influence of the organisation (Emery and Trist, 1965; Miles, 1980).

Drawing upon the case study data, the major organisational responses are tabulated below (Table 7.1), and classified according to whether they may be considered as **internal, transactional** or **environmental dependencies**.

Internal Dependencies

The components of the organisation can be usefully considered in occupational and functional terms. Occupational disjunctions were between: direct care nursing staff, direct care (non nursing) staff and non-direct care staff. Differentiation on functional grounds can be made between: management, employees, and industrial bodies. Each of these groupings is discussed below.

Direct Care Staff were powerful within the organisation because of the organisation's dependence upon them for the delivery of core functions, and their numerical preponderance. They were however, alienated in that it was a deeply held belief within the organisation that relationships with management were necessarily adversarial, and because of their position of felt inferiority relative to psychiatric services staff. They were increasingly under pressure as their skills were becoming less relevant to contemporary practice in the field of intellectual disability.

Non-direct care staff were less numerous and also less powerful within the institution. They faced less threat because of changes in the technology of care, but progressively greater threat as the impact of government budget reductions came to be felt, and as the institution reduced in size.

Table 7.1   Summary of Organisational Responses

Dependency	Response	
1 Internal	1.1	Increased differentiation between management, employee and industrial functions.
	1.2	Increased levels of integration on critical product development functions, with a corresponding decline in adversarial industrial activity.
	1.3	Increased importance attached to technical competence.
	1.4	High levels of organisational decentralisation; adoption of flat structures which facilitated participative planning and service development.
2 Transactional	2.1	Client access to external review.
	2.2	High levels of innovative product development, impacting upon product choice in the "market".
	2.3	Development of coalitions with other regional service providers and advocacy bodies.
	2.4	Opportunistic resource exploitation; negotiation of domain flexibility by means of generous resource exchanges.
	2.5	Merger within broadly defined community services infrastructure.
3 Environmental	3.1	Engagement with the politico-legal superstructure to negotiate the conditions for continued support of organisational goals.

Direct Care (non-nursing) staff, were the least numerous and traditionally the least powerful amongst the occupational groups. This group consisted of social workers, occupational therapists, and case-aides who worked in limited day activity programs. While they lacked the traditional power of rostered staff, they were well placed because of their flexibility and the breadth of their skills base to respond to the emerging demands of the environment.

Management consisted of senior administrative staff, nursing administration, after September 1988 the regional administration of the Health Department, and the regional administration of the Community Services Department. In the initial stages of the redevelopment, the local administrative management and nursing administration was closely associated with the staff of the institution and was actively involved in a coalition with them to preserve the institution. This changed as central administration demands for greater accountability increased and professional management personnel were appointed.

Industrial bodies consisted of HEF(2) and to a less extent VPSA. These commenced from a position of power in the institution, whereby they provided effective management and in the process created extremely favourable conditions for their members. This underwent a change as the relative power of the union movement was reduced over time, the skill level both centrally and locally within the union reduced, and as employees saw opportunities to further and/or protect their interests by non-industrial means.

Key changes in the relationships between these groupings are set out as items 1.1 to 1.4 in Table 7.1. These involved structural changes as expressed in levels of differentiation and integration, changes in relative power distribution, changes in product choice, and changes in mechanisms of coordination.

Differentiation and Integration

The changes within the internal dependencies of the organisation indicate two distinctive trends with respect to integration and differentiation.

Differentiation within the institutional environment had previously been principally on occupational grounds, reflecting a highly regulated workplace (Mintzberg, 1979) i.e. in circumstances where the activity was principally controlled by factors specific to the tasks to be performed in the workplace and the tools available to perform these. Thus distinctions between occupational groupings reflected a clarity of division of labour reflecting artisan (cooking, cleaning, maintenance) tasks, direct care (health, maintenance, nursing), and individual client programs (non-nursing direct care). The changing environment introduced a degree of externality to the determination of work roles, such that distinctions between occupational groupings became blurred. All direct care staff were expected to be proficient and involved in individual programming, whether they were nursing, para-professional nursing staff or allied health staff, and they were provided with training to facilitate this. As the redevelopment progressed the delineation between direct care and non-direct care staff also became blurred, with many artisans undergoing training, electing for secondment to direct care services providing day programs, and identify that their future lay in having direct relationships with clients rather than in providing artisan services.

Differentiation however, did increase between those staff who were responsible for the management of the facility and those providing services. While management had previously acted simply as an administration which provided services in support of direct care, the imposition of externally supposed budget restraint and increased accountability requirements caused a separate delineation of the management function.

Increased differentiation of function is clearly discernible. As increased pressure for change was experienced, the confusion between management and industrial bodies was resolved. A management function was delineated by the Health Department and management priorities separate from the industrial priorities of the institution's workforce were defined. This included priorities associated with budget reduction and reduction of workforce demarcations. A further clear delineation of the staffing complement of the training centre, which had hitherto been indistinguishable from psychiatric services staff was effected. As the demands of the technological system became more significant, a delineation between trained and untrained staff became noticeable, and the normative judgements attached to these categories were, over time, reversed. Trained staff moved from low to high status within the institution.

The other trend which may be discerned, is in some senses antithetical to this - an integrative movement towards collaborative action between management and the two major industrial groups for the purposes of service development. This activity is significant because of its specificity. Previous attempts at collaborative action, including the joint review of budget activities, and the Hospital Service Agreement process were unsuccessful, although an argument could be made that this was in part related to the political cycle. Nevertheless, this had the impact of increasing cynicism about collaboration. The later collaborative activity associated with the establishment of the future initiatives committees was highly successful in that it was practically relevant to the day to day activity of staff (rather than involving the setting of global objectives) and it met substantive goals of both management (the development of more appropriate service options) and staff (job and location security, and continuing care for vulnerable clients).

Power Relations

The case study indicates a process of considerable change in the internal distribution of power within the organisation during the redevelopment process. In summary, these changes were: the relative increase in the influence of residents over decisions which affected them; the transfer of administrative power from industrial bodies to local management; an increase in influence on the part of those formally trained in intellectual disability and of those able to respond positively to opportunities.

These changes in the internal distribution of power can be seen to mirror the nature of the changes in the environment. The changes in the technology of care enhanced the relative position of those who were trained in this technology, and strengthened the relative position of clients whose rights were protected by that new technology (as expressed in legislation). The political changes, and changes in resource distribution favoured the provision of particular service products over others, and promoted an approach to more accountable management. As such it promoted opportunities for product diversification, and penalised the continued provision of institutional residential services. It enhanced the position of management relative to industrial bodies and encouraged adaptive responses. The cultural changes in the environment enabled the development of a view of change as opportunity rather than threat and a discarding of the defensive denial of the possibility that change could come to the institution. They promoted a view of residents as capable rather than incapacitated, and favoured the development of collaborative rather than adversarial approaches by staff concerned for their continued employment.

An alternative perspective on the changes in the distribution of power within the institution would describe them in terms of the rise and decline of interests within the organisation according to their capacity to exploit the resources available within the changing environment.

Hospital management was transformed in order to be able to capitalise on the legitimacy available within the management environment, ie formal management approaches came during 1987/88 to have a currency they previously lacked. Industrial bodies, able to exploit the weaknesses of the State Government with respect to union power, were able to enhance the positions of their members, but when this weakness declined, the power of HEF(2) correspondingly declined, as did its capacity to secure the loyalty of the staff of the institution. The community services administration was able to exploit the resource environment in a way which was not available to the health administration. Access to the resources of the State Plan made possible some new service developments, but also demonstrated an administrative potency which translated into local political influence. The pre-eminence of the *Intellectually Disabled Persons Services Act* in the late 1980s gave a currency to client rights which was exploited by clients themselves, by activists associated with the Intellectual Disability Review Panel and the Office of the Public Advocate, and by administrative reformers who wished to promote particular service types over others.

A further view of changes in the exercise of power within the institution would focus less on its distribution than upon the manner in which it was exercised. This view is linked to the analysis above of differentiation and integration as it took place in the evolving structure of the organisation and is concerned with whether power is exercised in a centralised or decentralised manner.

The tensions between differentiation and integration within the organisation which have been identified, were reflected in the structure of the organisation and the exercise of authority within it. What can be seen is a greater degree of formalisation of management and administrative functions, and a countervailing decentralisation of authority through product development task groups, which abandoned hierarchy.

The formal organisation was one which became progressively more defined in an hierarchical sense. This entailed the separation of the Training Centre from the Mental Hospital, the appointment of a Manager, Direct Care Services and a separate nursing administration. It included an abandonment of the functional confusion between industrial group leadership and facility administrators. It included the definition of unit managers, as managers rather than as senior nurses. It entailed the organisation becoming more rule driven, placing greater emphasis upon incident reporting, and reporting on client welfare.

The informal structure adopted through the future initiatives groups however, was non hierarchial and influenced not by formal position, but by degree of interest and by the nature of the skills of the participants. Membership was by self-selection and while "guided" by service planning and development staff, was a genuine expression of decentralised power through an organic, "team" structure.

The structure then entailed both a centralisation of management authority and a decentralised exercise of that authority in one time critical function; that of product development. In this view, the adaptive response of the organisation with respect to the distribution of power, was to make possible cohesive political action (i.e. responding to resources availability and to changes in the nuances of policy) while promoting innovative technological development.

Product Choice

In addition to modifying the manner in which it developed services, the changes in the internal dependencies of the organisation were characterised by the exercise of product choice ie the organisation in changing the manner in which it developed service options, also changed both the nature and the type of services it provided.

The type of services was diversified from residential care provided in a congregate setting to a range of integrated service types including residential care in a variety of settings, day activities, social support services and specialist support services. The residential care options included purposely designed aged care units, community care units with variable staffing support according to the assessed needs of residents, support for individuals and small groups in private accommodation, equity housing, and rural households.

Day activity services changed from being a marginal activity on campus provided by a small and isolated staff group, to one which was considered essential to the well-being of clients. While the institution had previously been assessed as having one of the lowest levels of day activity of any residential facility in the State, the replacement services were reviewed as averaging 25 hours per week for all residents (Picton, Cooper and Owen, 1996), a high figure taking into account the age and disability profile of the residents. The replacement services, as well as providing an enhanced level of day activity, were significant in that they were generally provided through services integrated within generic community services such as the continuing education centre, supported employment, and recreation services. The redevelopment pioneered in the State a brokerage model of day activity provision which purchased individualised programs for clients from a wide variety of activity providers, rather than block provision of places at Day Activity Centres. Social Support Services included family reunification support and a volunteer friends program which recruited and supported community volunteers to provide individualised social interaction for residents.

Specialist support services included the Behavioural Intervention Support Service and the Dual Diagnosis Program which were distinctive because of their origins within the institution and their orientation to providing a service for the regional community.

The nature of the replacement services, was as significant however as the diversity of service types. This was characterised by a preference for services which were integrated with mainstream community services rather than segregated intellectual disability services albeit in community settings, high levels of collaboration with community providers, and the inclusion within the new services of residents who had not previously been resident within the institution. Finally, one of the most distinctive features of the new service developments was the fact that all former residents of the institution were accommodated. This may be compared with all other examples of institutional redevelopment in Victoria in the period, in which a proportion of the more severely disabled or behaviourally difficult were relocated to other institutions (Picton, Cooper and Owen, 1996).

The pattern of product development is significant on a number of counts. It betrays a level of flexibility which could not be anticipated from the inertia of the institution's past and its resistance to early attempts at reform. It demonstrates a level of commitment to the new technology and the changed cultural environment in excess of the community services agencies elsewhere in the state where services were frequently developed in a segregated manner. The nature and types of product choices also indicate an astuteness in the development of coalitions of interest with external providers, and with a broader range of local communities which gained by the increased availability of services.

Product choice as demonstrated in this instance may be characterised also as the choice of generalist rather than a specialist model of service provision, and can be seen as a means of exploiting the resource environment more effectively. The provision of a narrow range of residential service options had left the organisation vulnerable to changes within the resource environment. The dominant model of care provided by the organisation was no longer favoured by the environment and resources were being progressively withdrawn from it. The selection of a broader range of product options may be seen as a selection of service products now favoured by the environment, and also as a means of spreading the risk associated with future changes in favoured service types.

Method of Coordination

The nature of the changed expectations of the care of the intellectually disabled during the later part of the 1980s introduced a level of complexity and a rate of variability to the work life of staff within the field which had an inevitable impact upon the coordination of that work.

The institutional regime was distinguishable by its tendency towards inertia and its limitation of opportunities for variability. The lives of both staff and residents were governed by schedules and rosters. Times of meals, activities (such as occurred) and medication were uniform. The majority of services were provided on campus and so the pattern of activity was largely uninterrupted by external events. Residents followed the same daily and weekly timetable regardless of personal preferences or individual care needs.

In these circumstances the mode of coordination of work was a combination of direct supervision and of standardisation of work practices. Direct supervision took place through the agency of "charge nurses" who were responsible for the conduct of each "ward" or unit of the facility. They, in many respects, oversaw the activities that took place in the unit, but fell short of clear management. Until Paterson's facility review reforms in 1990, they tended to be seen as senior nurses who were responsible for nursing care in the units. They were themselves on rostered two on/two off shifts rather than "management hours" and so lacked continuity, and they had no responsibility for the non-direct care resources applied to the units, despite the importance of the interactions of these staff for the lives of residents. Coordination was thus achieved principally through standardisation of work processes.

Activities of staff within the institution were to a significant extent governed by rules, and by established patterns of behaviour. Rules governed the times at which activity took place, what activities were permitted, and who was able to participate in them.

In some cases these rules were established by regulation, for instance, governing who was able to dispense medication. Often however, they were established by industrial agreements. Such agreements determined the staff levels and composition of the staffing of each shift, and the duties which might be performed by each classification of staff. There was, thus, little requirement, or indeed capacity, for independent judgement on the part of employees.

The changes identified within the technology of the field, the distribution of power and in the culture of the institution brought about major changes in the way that work was coordinated within the organisation. These changes related to the locus of accountability, the variability of tasks, and the location of tasks. Taken together, these transformed the nature of work in the organisation and the manner of its coordination.

External accountability was established through the Intellectual Disability Review Panel, the Office of the Public Advocate, and the role assumed by the community services administration in monitoring compliance with the Intellectually Disabled Persons Services Act. For the first time accountability moved off campus and away from local management. This introduced a degree of unpredictability to the provision of care, firstly because the framework for that accountability was the individuality of a client's General Service Plans, and the Individual Service Plans which operationalised it; secondly because there existed authorities which had, and exercised, a capacity to direct that practices either cease or commence, without regard to established pattern.

The development of the alternative services introduced a degree of flexibility and variability into the nature of the work also. From an early point in the redevelopment, the larger number of residents was going off campus for day activities. Which activities they attended was not determined by their unit of residence, but by their GSP. In consequence the routines of units were disrupted by the movement out each day of residents. Staff accompanied residents and found their days determined increasingly by the responses of residents to the external challenges they faced rather than the routines of the facilities. Working increasingly in smaller groups, and with variable daily routines, staff were drawn into individualised relationships with residents.

As residential services became located off campus, the degree of variability and hence, individual worker discretion, was increased as a consequence of the increasing range of activities with which residents and their careers were involved. Providing for smaller numbers in small group care situations, staff became involved in a complexity of individualised care which was not possible or desired within the institution.

Located in dispersed care situations, staff were frequently alone in providing support to residents, with managers supervising clusters of houses rather than individual units. As such they were required to operate with a high level of self direction, for which there could be little standardisation.

In these circumstances, the principal means of the coordination of work activities became the standardisation of work skills. This was achieved through extensive training schemes, which had as their goal, the development of a trained workforce, able to exercise considerable discretion in the resolution of unanticipated problems.

Transactional Dependencies

Transactional dependencies are concerned with the exchange relationships which exist between the focal organisation and elements of its task environment. In this the focus of discussion is the relationships between the organisation and its mandating and resourcing authorities; the health and the community service administrations, its relationships with other service providers, and its relationship with the community within which it operated.

As described above, the transformation of the focal organisation was from one which was essentially self-contained and largely inwardly focussed to one which had a more broadly defined product base, was broadly dispersed rather than centrally located, and was engaged in collaborative service development strategies which were transforming its internal distribution of power. The changes in its transactional dependencies drawn theoretically from the case study, will be discussions in terms of **domain choice**, **collaborative relationships**, and **identity**.

Domain Choice

The organisation, through its choice of products elected to operate in a differently defined service domain. This domain, which has been described above has been characterised as diversified, generalist and exploitative of resource opportunities. This choice it followed was not one which was entirely internal to the organisation. It was transactional in that it required at least the compliance of mandating and resourcing authorities in order to proceed. It was critical that the organisation was permitted the domain flexibility to make choices which enabled its redevelopment.

An examination of the case study indicates the way in which that compliance was significant. In the Neilson Report, the proposed policy direction for the institution was to close by means of depletion of numbers over a considerable period of time. The strategy was to starve it of resources and of clients.

In fact, Mayday Hills was amongst the first of the major institutions to close in the period after the Neilson report; following close on the redevelopment of Caloola, and preceding that of Aradale, Pleasant Creek and Janefield. This was achieved by a mixture of permissiveness (in that freedom to innovate and to create opportunities for redevelopment were allowed) and of resource availability (in that despite the Neilson policy settings, the institution was enabled to access State Plan resources to seed new developments).

The reasons for this are complex and interwoven with the changing political fabric of the time. Early support for initiatives was obtained because the proposals involved the usage of relatively small amounts of resources as a means of "leveraging" out from the institution (and the Health Department) larger amounts of resources (eg BIST). Also, some early projects received the support of policy makers in that they piloted new approaches to care, or new configurations of service providers (institution and community agency). During the Rassaby and Bartholomew periods as General Manager Intellectual Disability, the alignment of the Regional Centre with the central branch on matters of policy and of philosophical approach and the position of leadership in institutional redevelopment it assumed, ensured that support and measured access to resources was available. During the final redevelopment period, while the central branch was antagonistic, the continuing support of Ministers of differing political persuasion enabled the redevelopment to proceed. The financial return that could be offered by the organisation for being allowed to continue with redevelopment was such as to attract support from other sources of power within the mandating authority.

In these terms, it may be said that one of the distinguishing features of the transactional dependencies of the organisation was the high level of domain choice that it was able to negotiate with its mandating authorities. This was made possible by the availability of resources in the environment which could be exploited, the willingness of successive central administrations and Ministers to allow the organisation to choose an alternative domain, and the capacity of the organisation to deal flexibly with the prevailing currency of transactions, whether this be resources, ideology, legitimacy or political capital.

Collaboration

The redevelopment of the institution moved it from a position of self-sufficiency to one of mutual dependence with other organisations within its task environment. At its most simple, this collaboration entailed the simple exchange of client services. Residential clients from the institution were able to access the day activity programs of the Murray Valley Day Activity Centre, without which their residential placement may not have been viable. In return, the Murray Valley Day Activity Centre was able to obtain access to residential support for some of its community clients which would not have been possible without the institutional redevelopment. But relationships were more complex than that. The presence of the larger number of ex-institutional clients in the community stimulated other service developments such as the brokerage schemes, volunteer friends and continuing education programs, which were accessed by other agencies and their clients. Service collaborations such as the NERCA equity scheme, and CLSS were initiatives which could only have been developed as a collaboration of the institution and a non-government agency.

Perhaps the most important manner and effect of collaboration however, was in the impact of service innovations upon cultural underpinning of services for intellectually disabled in North East Victoria. The case study has described an underdeveloped services network which consisted mainly of segregated and segregating services. The predominant model of service provision was the stand alone adult day activity centre. The regional residential association provided largely institutional small group care options. The imposition of the institution in the process of developing innovative integrative service options, frequently in collaboration with those other agencies, radically altered the way in which those agencies themselves operated.

Identity

Changes in the transactional dependencies of the organisation in addition to effecting the nature of its relationships with elements of its task environment, producing as it did significant collaborations, also went to the identity of the organisation.

It has been seen that prior to the redevelopment of the institution, it had a high level of integrity of function. It provided whole of life care for its residents, and had a continuity of staff and of residents. The institution was viewed from both the outside and the inside as monolithic. The identity of the organisation was defined in terms of its historic continuity, but also in terms of its contrast with the external environment. The staff of Mayday Hills, in resisting the incursion of external reformers, were asserting in a performative manner the identity of the organisation.

The early attempts at reform were resisted as being contrary to the established practices of the facility, were seen as antagonistic towards the interests of staff and were genuinely believed by many to be contrary to the interests of residents. Where clients are understood to be unable to learn to care from themselves, it follows that attempts to promote their independence, must be seen as antagonistic to their well-being. Their attempts at change, while expected to fail, ran counter also to the deeply held belief in the immutability of the institution.

The ultimately successful attempts at change represented a revision of the identity of the organisation. That revised identity was expressed technologically through the adoption of an alternative practice methodology and service dimensions, and culturally through the, at times, strident adoption of a client's rights ideology. This was a cultural change in that it assigned value in terms of client interests rather than employee or local community economic interests. In a political sense, the change in identity was most dramatic, in that it took the form of a merger of the institution with a critical element of its task environment; the regional community services administration.

The formal political processes of this merger were marked by: the transfer in 1985 of responsibility for intellectual disability from the Health Department to the newly created Community Services Victoria; the separation of the Training Centre from the Psychiatric Hospital in November 1991; the appointment of a chief executive officer with responsibility for the training centre and for other intellectual disability services in the region; and finally the complete absorption of staff and residents within community based services in November 1992.

The processes of merger however, owed as much to less formalised developments, amongst the milestones of which were: the assertion of the regional director of authority over program directions in the Training Centre; the establishment of BIST Program; the emergence of Community Services leadership in industrial disputes within the training centre; and the leadership shown by Mayday Hills unit managers during training following the 1990 facility review. These events and trends demonstrated a progressive and evolutionary rather than dramatic or planned merging of the institution with the Department.

The process of remaking the identity of the institution has been described as a merger rather than an absorption or a take-over, because in the process, the department in the region, and to some extent within the State, itself underwent important changes. As indicated above, the transfer of significant additional resources, staff and clients into the community system modified that system. Similarly, the importing into the department of these additional elements, changed the department. An indication of the extent of that change may be seen in the changed reception that institutional staff received on transfer into community based services.

The prevailing view within the regional administration in the early stages had been that the staff themselves had been institutionalised and would not be able to make the transition to community care. A watershed was reached with the appointment of Ruth Tai to a senior management position within the region, and the progressive acceptance of larger numbers of ex-institutional staff into responsible positions. The future initiatives committees, which were essential to the redevelopment, had as their impetus, a recognition of the skills and commitment of the institutional staff and a valuing of their knowledge of residents and their needs.

A final, and perhaps ironic aspect of the fashioning of a new identity was that within the redeveloped service system identity came also to be defined in opposition to an "outside" interest. The central administration of the department's disability services division, was increasingly being viewed at the regional level as out of sympathy with the reform movement in intellectual disability services which had driven service change in the field for the previous decade, and which had been a major environmental influence on the redevelopment of Mayday Hills.

Environmental Dependencies

The relationship between the organisation and its general environment, which is captured in the Emery and Trist framework as **environmental**

dependencies may be considered in terms of reciprocal influences upon the technology of care, the exercise of administrative power, and cultural attitudes to disability.

Environmental dependencies are by definition those relationships which are relatively impervious to organisational influence and so potentially most powerful in determining organisational behaviour. The reciprocity in relationships is less obvious than the influence upon the actions of the organisations by the general environment. It is nevertheless significant.

The changes in the general environment had a clear and powerful impact upon the institution. Cultural changes in community perceptions of intellectually disabled people, combined with newly developing treatment modalities, and the election of a reformist government prepared to make a priority of social expenditure combined to provide the impetus for change in the intellectual disability field, and in institutions in particular. These powerful influences, mediated through a newly created administrative department, strong legislation, and policy and budget commitments, created the circumstances in which the redevelopment of the institution would take place.

The case study however, does identify a number of respects in which the redevelopment of Mayday Hills may be seen to have influenced the general as well as the task environment, at least to the point of reinforcing the direction of change. By the piloting of new service types, and the initiation of others, and in particular in the aggressive assertion of integrated service delivery models, the redevelopment gave practical expression to the normalisation policy being pursued. It was not alone in this, but was one of the stronger service development sites in the State in its pursuit. To an extent, the redevelopment of Mayday Hills was responsible for restoring to the overall reform picture, the role of institutions. It asserted that institutions could be reformed, and from within, rather than always from without, either by attack or by neglect. Again it was not alone in this, but amongst the more prominent exponents.

The redevelopment project played an important part in the continuing process of institutional redevelopment also in the modelling of a process of financial management which enabled the progressive freeing up of resources while limiting the overall costs of redevelopment. The approach developed in relation to Mayday Hills was significant in managing the cash flow of the much larger Caloola redevelopment.

Politically, the redevelopment played a role in the maintenance of the political commitment of successive Ministers to institutional redevelopment. Minister Matthews was deeply affected by his visit to the institution in the early stages. Ministers Setches and John took a particular interest in the change process, frequently using it as an example of what could and should be achieved.

Summary

Mayday Hills training centre was during the period 1988-1993 faced with high levels of environmental change which in consequence of its rate, complexity, and connectedness may be defined as turbulent. Further, those changes emanated to a significant extent from the general environment of the organisation. As such, they were largely impervious to influence from the organisation itself. Utilising the languages of the literature, the organisation faced an environment of high causal texture.

The rate and extensiveness of externally induced change created for the organisation a technological problem in that its practice technology was no longer valued or required by the environment. It faced a political allocation problem in that demands for increased accountability and fiscal restraint challenged the established pattern of benefits and of authority within the institution. It faced a cultural problem in that the values of benign containment which had underpinned its operations for more than a century were at odds with those mandated by legislation and supported by regulatory bodies.

The organisation sought to solve its technological problems by processes of skills acquisition and service modelling. It resolved its political allocation problem by a radical re-ordering of the political economy of the organisation whereby coalitions were established between occupational groups and management in order to secure service redevelopment and continuity of employment. It resolved its cultural problem through the development of values coherency around principles of clients' rights.

In the process of resolving these core organisational problems, the organisation underwent a major re-ordering of its internal relationships and its relationships with both the task and general environment. These changes revolved around a simultaneous differentiation of management and service delivery functions, and an integration of these around the tasks of service design and implementation. Professional skills related to care of the intellectually disabled came to be valued both for their contribution to client well-being and to the continuing employment prospects of staff. The organisation developed a radically decentralised internal decision making structure which empowered multi-disciplinary and multi functional teams to design and implement new service initiatives.

The relationship between the organisation and elements of its task environment was similarly radically transformed. The organisation moved from a stance of disengagement from policy and program initiatives within the disability field, to one of active participation and even exchange. The organisation came to pilot important state initiatives, including behavioural intervention support services, and community living support services, and to initiate a number of service developments including the townhouses program, the client equity program, dual diagnosis program, the volunteer friends program and the family reunion program, all of which were subsequently adopted elsewhere. The organisation became a disproportionate user of the Singleton Equity program. Importantly, the organisation entered into an exchange relationship with the funding body which dominated its task environment whereby resources became "unfixed" from its core operating functions and were utilised for flexible program development in exchange for access to new resources. While there was a nil sum of total resources available, this exchange relationship created a degree of resource flexibility without which the redevelopment could not have taken place.

The relationships between the organisation and its general environment was of fundamental importance for the way the organisation behaved and developed. As might be anticipated however, the relationship was not one which involved a high level of exchange. The general environment is by definition, that part of the environment which is less amenable to influence by the focal organisation. The elements within this general environment have been identified as high level legal, political and economic factors.

The case study indicates a determinative influence by those factors, related to the prevalence of the normalisation model of care for the intellectually disabled, and the changing model of public administration. It can be seen however that in the course of the redevelopment the organisation moved to a more radical enunciation of the principles of normalisation than became the case for the mandating agency of the state. The model of administration which required an increasing emphasis upon performance criteria and fiscal reporting, to the exclusion of practice goals, forced a change of emphasis in the later stages of the redevelopment, but here also, there was some reciprocal influence in that the financial modelling undertaken for the final stage redevelopment underpinned in part the model adopted for other institutional redevelopments.

The contribution that the redevelopment made to the broader political environment, while small, was significant. It demonstrated, and was frequently cited as evidence, that institutional redevelopments could be achieved on an economic basis, without the requirement to transfer residents to other institutions, and without large scale industrial disharmony. In announcing the closure of the institution to the Victorian Parliament on 17 November 1993, the then Minister for Community Services, the Hon Michael John, described it as "among the most successful examples of deinstitutionalisation in the country" (Hansard, 17 Nov. 1993, 1884).

8 Implications for Organisational Theory

This study has provided a narrative overview of the processes of redevelopment of one of the State of Victoria's major institutions for the care of the intellectually disabled. It has proceeded to utilise the framework developed within the theory of organisational responses to environmental change to develop a theoretical perspective on those changes which took place. This final chapter will discuss the findings of the study in terms of their implications for the study of organisations. In doing so it will consider the implications of the findings of this study in terms of the major approaches to the organisation/environment relationship identified in Chapter 2. Finally, it will place the discussion in the context of the two major theoretical frameworks identified in the literature: the organisational adaptation approach and the population ecology approach. With respect to the first of these, the findings of the study will be broadened to more generalised hypotheses which might be examined in later studies. With respect to the second, it is acknowledged that the case study does not provide a basis upon which generalisation may be made about populations of organisations. This section is thus discursive in nature, and intended to identify factors relevant to the survival of the institutional organisational form.

Key Findings

The case study identified a range of responses by the focal organisation to changes within its environment. These have been discussed in the preceding chapter in terms of internal dependencies, transactional dependencies, and environmental dependencies and were tabulated as Table 8.1. For the purpose of consideration of their theoretical implications, these responses on the part of the organisation may be aggregated to identify five key findings. These, are summarised as follows:

213

Table 8.1 Major Findings and Their Relationship to Organisational Responses

Finding		Organisational Response
1	The organisation increased its domain flexibility through the adoption of alternative practice technologies, innovative product design, opportunistic resource utilisation, and generalist product diversification.	Increased levels of integration on critical product development functions with a corresponding decline in adversarial industrial activity. Increased importance attached to technical competence.
2	The organisation enhanced its political alignment and access to information by increasing its internal differentiation according to management function.	Increased differentiation between management, staff, and industrial functions.
3	The organisation enhanced its innovativeness through decentralisation of decision making and internal integration associated with its product development function.	Increased levels of integration on critical product development functions, with a corresponding decline in adversarial industrial activity. High levels of organisational decentralisation, adoption of flat structures which facilitated participative planning and service development.
4	The organisation enhanced its exploitation of the resources in the environment and consolidated its political support by merger with critical parts of its task environment.	Development of coalitions with other regional service providers and advocacy bodies. Opportunistic resource exploitation; negotiation of domain flexibility by means of generous resource exchanges. Merger within broadly defined community services infrastructure. Engagement with the political superstructure to negotiate the conditions for continued support of organisational goals.
5	The organisation sought to achieve cultural alignment with key elements of the environment by the promotion of values coherency.	Increased importance attached to technical competence. Client access to external review. Engagement with the political superstructure to negotiate the conditions for continued support of organisational goals.

The implications of each of these major findings for the theory of organisational change, will be considered under the summary headings of: 1) **domain flexibility**; 2) **political alignment and differentiation**; 3) **decentralisation and integration**; 4) **resource exploitation** and 5) **values coherence**.

Domain Flexibility

Domain flexibility has been identified within the literature largely as a quality of the environment (Miles, 1980), that is, whether the environment is sufficiently permissive to allow the organisation to translate its activities from one sphere to another. In this case study, this was certainly true of the environment. Resources were available within the environment to effect change, and at least in the early stages, a combination of permissiveness and benign neglect allowed the organisation sufficient room to move to modify its essential activities. An important aspect of the exercise of domain flexibility in this instance however, was the capacity of the organisation to respond to that flexibility. The organisation was not a passive recipient of the largesse of the environment, but actively utilised resource opportunities and political opportunities as they presented themselves. This was not without difficulties and false starts, as can be seen with the introduction of alternative practice technologies. Of particular use to it however, was the creativity it was able to employ in the design of new service types. These convey a level of flexibility and responsiveness to environmental cues which would not be anticipated in an organisation with the conservative history of this institution.

It is not immediately apparent how the organisation came to exercise the flexibility that it did. Among the factors which would appear to be important however, were: the impact of training specific to the field of intellectual disability; the threat posed by external forces; and the encouragement and creative spirit engendered by the community services staff who worked with the future initiatives committees.

The domain choice exercised represented a transformation from a specialist (i.e. congregate residential care service), to a generalist services framework (i.e. multi-service type network of highly dispersed elements). This choice of service domain represented a move from a product which was out of favour with the environment, to a range of products which was likely to receive support. The choice was also of a model which left the organisation less vulnerable to changes within the environment. Hannan and Freeman (1989) have noted that the choice between a specialist and generalist model of organisation is a key one with respect to organisations seeking isomorphism. A generalist model entails a decision to maximise exploitation of the environment, over a narrow range of activities. It is a powerful position, but one which leaves the organisation vulnerable to changes in the environment, should its chosen field become less favoured. A generalist model offers less capacity to dominate a resource environment, but reduces organisational vulnerability since the decline in acceptability of one product can be compensated by growth elsewhere.

Political Alignment and Differentiation

Lawrence and Lorsch (1986) have identified differentiation as a key dimension on which organisations vary, contingent upon the level of turbulence within their environments. They found that successful organisations faced with a complex and rapidly changing environment tended towards high levels of internal differentiation of function, reflecting the differential rates of change and variability within their environments. Thus, such organisation may be expected to differentiate divisionally between, for instance, research and development, production, and marketing functions, which require differential responses to aspects of the environment.

This case reflects similar process of increased differentiation in response to increased environmental complexity and rapidity of change. It varies from the Lawrence and Lorsch model however, in that the increased differentiation was not in the direction of a divisionalised form (Mintzberg, 1979), but entailed a greater differentiation of management, service delivery, and industrial advocacy functions.

Prior to the redevelopment period, the organisation had differentiated principally by occupational category and by division of labour. Organisational divisions reflected disjunctions between medical, direct care and artisan staff. Management as a function was identified but was largely undifferentiated. The nature of the environmental changes experienced, in particular those relating to the changed accountability requirements of government, necessitated the development of a clearly differentiated management function. The organisation was required to be able to analyse its own performance, plan future action, and negotiate change with its workforce. In order to be able to effect change it needed to break the collusive relationships which existed between its management and industrial bodies. It needed also to be able to distinguish between the needs of the organisation and those of its staff.

Decentralisation and Integration

Lawrence and Lorsch (1986) have also identified that successful organisations which develop highly differentiated structures in order to deal with complex and rapidly changing environments require the development of integrative mechanisms which bring together the differentiated elements. This function was performed by a participative service development mechanism; the "future initiatives committees". In this instance the integrative mechanism was not an established position which spanned the divisions of the organisation, as identified by Lawrence and Lorsch, but a fluid organisational structure. It could be argued however, that the role of "integrator" as identified by Lawrence and Lorsch was in fact performed by the staff of the service planning and development team which was responsible for servicing and supporting the future initiatives committees.

The study supports the key elements of the contingency model of organisational responses developed by Mintzberg (1979) and reported in Chapter 2 of this study. That model identified that as the environment of organisations become more complex and more dynamic, those organisations may be expected to decentralise power, to develop organic as distinct from bureaucratic structures and to coordinate work by means of mutual adjustment rather than by standardisation.

Decentralisation in this case needs to be understood in relation to decisions about service design, not decisions about strategic direction. As has been noted above, the organisation simultaneously strengthened its management focus, while devolving and dispersing its product development function. Having said that, it should be noted that the decision making power which was decentralised was of a genuine sort. Employee initiated service development proposals were acted upon and organisational resources were deployed according to these decisions. This was viewed by staff as potent and relevant where earlier paper exercises of participation in planning were viewed cynically. While the management structures of the organisation remained hierarchial and bureaucratic, the future initiatives committees represented an adoption of organic structures in which members of the organisation participated without reference to rank within the organisation and outside their usual position description. Their work was collaborative and coordinated by mutual agreement rather than by direction. Because the work was innovative and outside the previous experience of the organisation, it defied standardisation.

Resource Exploitation

Continuing survival and prosperity of formal organisations is related to their capacity to exploit resources from the environment. Within this case study the strategies employed by the organisation to exploited resources took four forms: opportunistic exploitation of "new" resources which were made available to the field; the development of coalitions with elements of the inter-organisational field in order to maximise the total resource base for new service development; the conversion of committed organisational resources from other activities to allow new activities; and the "purchase" of resource security by the meeting of the political goals of its sponsor organisation.

While resource dependence is acknowledged within the literature as a critical aspect of organisational adaptation, the complexity of these resource utilisation strategies is not identified. The case study would suggest that in order to ensure that an organisation has continuing access to resources required to sustain its operations it may be expected to engage in a complex array of resource acquisition and utilisation strategies of the sort identified.

Values Coherency

Emery and Trist (1965) have noted that a turbulent environment is one which allows an organisation very little capacity for adaptive response. Major changes in the environment are generated from the general environment and as such they are largely outside the influence of the organisation. There is a high level of convergence within the environment and so little capacity for tactical activity to reduce uncertainty. They conclude that in order to restore a level of predictability to the environment, organisations may seek to achieve consensus with key elements of the environment on value grounds.

In the case study of the redevelopment of Mayday Hills Training Centre, there is evidence of values coherence being sought through a process of cultural alignment.

At the commencement of the redevelopment process, the case study notes the discordance between the basic assumptions of the organisation and those of the environment. The organisation held assumptions about the capacities of intellectually disabled people and the nature of the service which should be provided to them which were antithetical to those being promoted by major agencies within the environment, including its sponsor organisation. The organisational processes associated with the achievement of cultural alignment included staff training, the adoption of client rights procedures, the development of new service models based upon community integration, and the espousal within statewide forums of a strong normalisation position.

These changes within the cultural stance of the organisation were achieved over time; were strongly resisted within parts of the organisation; and were never endorsed by every part of the organisation. They nevertheless became the dominant cultural values of the organisation and an essential factor in the organisation being able to achieve coordinated action in responding to its environment. Convergence with the dominant cultural values made possible collaborative action with other agencies within the inter-organisational field, and enabled the flow of new resources from the sponsor organisation. This would have been unlikely had the organisation continued to be culturally misaligned.

Summary - The Adaptation Perspective

The case study identifies then a number of simultaneous adaptive responses by the organisation which tended to enhance its capacity to survive and continue to produce services in the face of a turbulent environment. These were internal adaptations including an increase differentiation of management and service delivery functions, together with increased integration across these functions through the development of participative mechanisms; transactional adaptations including the optimising of resource utilisation, and the occupation of a relatively resource rich service domain; and environmental adaptations, focused upon the generation of values consensus.

The study supports the theoretical perspective which stresses the intrinsic relationship between the technical design problem, the political allocation problem and the cultural problem faced by organisations adapting to change, while accepting the distinctive nature of these (Tichy, 1993). The study identifies the complex inter-relationships between the technological, political and cultural variables in the environment, and within the responses of the organisation.

The study, further, supports the contingency perspective upon the organisational/environment relationship, and, in particular, the structural responses to environmental variables identified by Mintzberg (1979). The study demonstrates that the movement from a relatively simple and stable environment to one which was comparatively complex and dynamic, was accompanied by a movement towards a more organic and decentralised organisational structure. The study notes however, that this movement was focussed upon the product development function of the organisation, and that, with respect to the strategic planning and management functions, the organisation became more hierarchial and more centralised. The study supports with some modification, the contingency account of Lawrence and Lorsh (1986), in that while it identifies processes of differentiation and integration, it does not do so with respect to the cognitive and emotional orientation among managers of different functional departments. It identifies differentiation of the management function as such and identifies integration in terms of a temporary structural arrangement. The differentiated management function may be seen as responding to one specific of the political environment; the requirement for increased fiscal and political accountability.

The study identifies a range of strategies utilised by the organisation to reduce its vulnerability to change within the environment. These were essentially cooperative strategies (Hasenfeld, 1983) reflecting the highly dependent nature of public sector agencies. They included elements of **compliance**, as in the adoption of clients' rights procedures, elements of **coalition** as in the relationships established with other organisations within the task environment, and also elements of **co-optation**, as in the joint service development projects which tied the sponsoring organisation to the focal organisation. It has been argued that a principal means of sustaining the organisation and generating greater certainty in the environment was a strategy of **convergence**, whereby goal or value coherence was established across the field. This may be compared with the **disruptive** strategies evidenced in the early stages by the industrial body (Hasenfeld, 1983; Resnick and Patti, 1980; Motamedi, 1976), which despite their early success, proved to have limited utility. The level of homogeneity of the elements of the environment was such that resistance was futile.

The study utilises a modified version of the Emery and Trist (1965) framework for analysis of the organisation/environment relationship and while it cannot be said to test that framework, does demonstrate its utility. The framework enabled the sorting of data according to **internal, transactional** and **environmental** dependencies and demonstrated the diminishing degree of influence over environmental variables along this continuum. It provided for a classification of the environment according to dimensions which have a high level of consensus within the literature. In this respect, this study proposed a crucial modification to the framework drawn from the literature, by the inclusion of **environmental receptivity** as a critical dimension on which environments may vary (Miles, 1980).

The study however, would suggest that environmental receptivity should not be thought of only in terms of the willingness of the environment to supply resources to, accept the products of, and allow flexibility of product choice, to the focal organisation. Environmental receptivity is negotiated between the environment and the organisation, and includes both the flexibility allowed by the environment and that which the organisation is capable of exercising.

Summary - The Population Ecology Perspective

One of the critical issues raised by the Mayday Hills case study is concerned with organisational survival. The question may be asked as to whether the organisation did survive, or whether its transformation and merger with elements of its task environment was such as to constitute complete dissolution of the organisation. This is largely a matter of definition which cannot be satisfactorily resolved. The researcher would take the view that there is sufficient continuity of mission, function, client group and personnel to sustain an argument for continuity, although there can be little doubt that the organisational form, as expressed in structure and strategy was greatly changed. The discussion then, is largely about the maintenance of organisational forms.

Whettan notes that the dominant theoretical orientation in the area of organisational decline is the natural selection model (Whettan, 1980). The principle components of this orientation are the ecological processes of variation, selection and retention. In a population of organisations, variations in member's characteristics occur as a result of both planned and unplanned changes. In consequence, the model does not require the assumption of rationality or intentionality (Whettan, 1980, 347). Selection reflects a differential rate of survival within a population, as a consequence of differential reinforcement from the environment. Retention signifies that certain valued characteristics are preserved, duplicated or reproduced in the population. This model assumes that change within a population of organisations occurs slowly, over generations of organisations.

The model is powerful in dealing with the seeming irrationality of the reality of the failure of some organisations and the survival of others. Kaufman asks why some organisations adhere to practices which cause others to die? Why the world is not filled with old organisations? Why organisations with the smartest people do not always survive longest? (Kaufman, 1975). It is less useful however in explaining the persistence of an organisational model for an extensive period of time, and its relatively sudden demise as a dominant mode of production of services of a particular sort.

There is considerable debate within the literature as to what characteristics of organisations may lead them to survive dramatic changes within their environment. Some have argued that large size and old age are liabilities under turbulent environmental conditions; larger and older organisations being more bureaucratic and inefficient and hence less able to change and adapt quickly (Bennis and Slater, 1968). Alternatively, it has been argued that younger organisations are more vulnerable as a consequence of inexperience and lack of resources. The consequences of bad decisions and sudden environmental changes are intensified, and the negative consequences of interpersonal conflict are more difficult to contain (Boswell, 1973). Similarly, considerable disagreement exists over the relative advantages and disadvantages of decentralisation (Porter and Olsen, 1976; Yarmolisky, 1975).

This study has not concerned itself with the ethical or practice debates concerning deinstitutionalisation. Its focus has been upon organisational change of which deinstitutionalisation, within a particular setting, is one example. Consideration of a population ecology perspective however, leads to a consideration of the prevalence of institutional care as an organisational form.

The transformation of Mayday Hills Training Centre from a congregate care institution to a dispersed supported accommodation system with a focus upon the integration of residents into mainstream community activity, is but one example of the major change in the organisational mechanisms of care in the State of Victoria in the period between 1970 and 1995. In the specific field of intellectual disability, the numbers receiving care in institutional settings decreased from approximately 4,000 to a little over 1,500. This is one facet of the transformation from large scale institutional mechanism of care to smaller scale "community based" care.

Across the fields of intellectual disability, psychiatric care, aged care, welfare services, and juvenile justice, a parallel development has taken place. In every case, institutional bed numbers have fallen dramatically, and to some extent, provision has been transferred to an alternative mode of care.

Nor can the decline in institutional numbers be described in terms of the political orientation of governments. The periods reflected in these figures involved the governance of both Labor (reformist) and Liberal (conservative) government at both the Commonwealth and State levels. The Kennett Liberal government on its election in October 1992 committed itself to policy of institutional reductions essentially similar to that of its predecessors.

What should be made of this? Does the analysis of the processes of the redevelopment of Mayday Hills contribute to our understanding of the more general social processes involved in institutional closure?

This study would suggest a perspective which is concerned with the prevalence of organisational forms within the contemporary environment. The redevelopment of Mayday Hills can be understood in the context of the complex responses of the organisation to changes within its technical, resources and cultural environment. The closure of Mayday Hills Training Centre, when placed in the context of the contemporaneous closures of St Nicholas Hospital, Caloola and Aradale, in the intellectual disability field; the large scale reduction in psychiatric services beds across the State, the closure of the majority of Children's Homes, and reduced level of nursing home beds as a proportion of the elderly population of organisational forms represented by the institution. In Astley and Van der Ven's terms, while organisational adaptation perspectives and population ecology perspectives are in a prima facie sense in tension, it is possible to broaden the view from the adaptations of a single organisation to the fate of populations of organisations (Astley and Van De Ven,1983).

The questions to be addressed concern firstly the reasons for the decline of institutions as the dominant model of care, and secondly, whether this should be viewed as a sustainable direction in the ecology of organisations. The two are clearly linked, since examination of the reasons for the decline of the organisational forms would also identify whether the environmental conditions which prompt it are inexorable and whether the organisational responses are inevitable or simply evidence of sub-optimal adaptive responses.

Hannan and Freeman (1989), have identified the essential elements of organisational form as consisting of: the formal structural arrangements; the operating rules; and the normative assumptions of the organisation. On the basis of the case study of the redevelopment of Mayday Hills Training Centre, the characteristic properties of the organisation and what might be assumed to be the environmentally preferred properties may be summarised as follows:

Table 8.2 Comparison of Institutional and Environmentally Preferred Organisational Blueprint

	Institutional Blueprint	Environmentally Preferred Blueprint
Structure	• specialist service framework • stand alone facility/self contained • hierarchical management • rigidity in divisions of labour	• generalist service framework • geographically dispersed service delivery • organic, participative service planning structures • multi skilled staff, reduced demarcation by occupation
Operating Rules	• whole of life care • majority of activities take place on campus • highly patterned activity/rule driven	• care dispersed over multiple agencies • care integrated within mainstream community services • individually determined case plans
Normative Assumptions	• residents to be protected • residents unable to learn/be trained	• client self directed • client can be trained, and can learn to provide self care to some degree

The Mayday Hills case study does not provide an empirical basis from which to draw conclusions about the selection of a preferred organisational model by the environment. It does however, allow the hypothesis of an organisational blueprint which might be isomorphic. The case for such generalisabilty relies in part upon a view of whether the pattern of organisation observed within Mayday Hills is essentially the case for the institutional organisational form, and also on a view as to whether the process of selection as hypothesised in this case, might be extended to other cases which fitted the model.

Implications for Policy, Practice and Education

The case study of the redevelopment of Mayday Hills Training Centre has implications for the understand of the ways in which public sector agencies respond to the complexity of change within their environments. Their implications are relevant to policy, to practice, and to education.

Policy

Social policy is concerned with the possible options for official action which are available to the community in meeting its social goals (Emy, 1976, 31). The implementation of those choices however, must take place within a context of a prevailing and a required technology, a range of political and resource choices, and a context of values and social attitudes. Key delivery agencies form part of that context.

The capacity to deliver major reform in the intellectual, disability field in Victoria in the late 1980s was supported by a concerted attempt by government to redefine through legislation and through policy initiative, a framework for the provision of care. The capacity to deliver the sort of fundamental change which was envisaged however, was inevitably influenced by the broader policy context of the day; in particular, policy concerning the reform of government business. This included the restructure of public activity, increases in accountability requirements, reductions overall in government outlays and the de-emphasis of professional expertise as opposed to managerial expertise.

The introduction of major policy reform takes place also within a context of technology. There are established ways of doing things. Policy innovations must account for the development of new technologies and also the means of their dissemination. The societal context, represented by the basic assumptions within the community, and, more particularly, those individuals and organisation immediately affected by policy reform form a critical contextual variable.

Within this general framework of inter-related technological, political and cultural elements, established program delivery institutions have a particular importance. Such organisations, in this instance congregate care institutions, are the embodiment of old ways of meeting social goals. They are preservers of old technology, they represent earlier policy decisions and resource commitments, and they are the carriers of cultural values. Organisational change within institutions of this sort is essential to policy reform within the public sector. An understanding then of the ways in which these organisations respond to changing cues within their environments is critical to the reform process.

Among the findings of this study, of significance for the policy reform process is the importance of the development of domain choice for such organisations. Earlier attempts to change the delivery system for intellectual disability services by allowing the institutions to wither failed because of a political reaction to the neglect of the workforce and because of public reaction to the abuse that resulted from neglect. It is irresponsible and politically dangerous to ignore the contribution of important, if outdated, delivery systems.

An understanding of the complex relationship between elements of the political and policy system, the technological and the cultural systems within the environment is critical for the implementation of major policy reform.

Established organisational delivery systems as the embodiment of former policy choices, old technology and of cultural values are an important focus for policy reform. An understanding of the ways in which these organisations respond to environmental change is critical to the reform process.

In particular, this study emphasises the importance of **domain choice** being available to such organisations. The resources and expertise within established delivery systems can be invaluable in establishing new systems. This case study suggests reason for confidence that the resources of these organisations can be utilised in this way.

Practice

The case study suggests a number of strategies which may usefully be employed by managers seeking to redevelop established organisations. These strategies include; the **exploitation** of **resource opportunities**, the **establishment of coalitions** within elements of the task environment, and effective **negotiation with the politico-legal super-structure** for the protection of change initiatives during periods of vulnerability.

Critically important however, for the practice of management of organisational change in response to environmental change, are strategies for the **engagement of staff** of the organisation. The case study identifies a mechanism which was particularly useful in this instance, in harnessing the energies of staff to support the change process. The essential elements of that mechanism were that; it was **relevant** in that it impacted directly upon the work of the staff and could draw upon their expertise; it was **significant**, in that its recommendations were acted upon and these were the means by which the organisation reshaped its activity, and it was **honest**, in that it did not purport to be something that it was not. The strategic development role remained clearly with management and was not represented otherwise.

The case study suggests important lessons for the management of change within the institutional sector. These include the importance of effective resource exploitation, coalition development and political negotiation. In particular it suggests **the importance of internal structures which promote positive responses to change amongst staff by meaningful engagement with the demands of the environment.**

Above all, the case study emphasises the importance for social work practice of the management of change within formal organisations, and the development of the practice skills required to implement strategies of the sort developed in this case.

Education

The world of practice is being transformed by changes in understanding of the role of government in the securing of social goals, by changes in models of communication, information processing, and models of administration. The case study highlights some of the impacts of these changes, and at a defined point of time, upon one area of practice; the institutional disability sector. As such it highlights a number of areas for attention in the training of professionals.

Within the disability field, it draws attention to need to train practitioners in practice technologies which are implicit in individualised training based interventions. The reform of the disability sector assumed a level of skill which was largely absent within the field. Such training must address itself to interventions with individuals, and with service delivery systems.

The case study also identifies a range of generic skills and knowledge in organisational change which are critical for practitioners in a time of rapid environmental change. These relate to **organisational analysis**; in particular the mapping of relationships between an organisation and elements of its task and general environments, and an understanding of the complexity of the relationships between technological, political and cultural variables. They relate also to the **internal management of change**, particularly strategies for the engagement of key internal stakeholders in the change process.

The case study identifies some areas for attention within practitioner education particularly in relation to effective practice technologies, and the capacity to respond to change. It identifies the importance of knowledge and skills in the generic areas of organisational analysis and the internal management of change.

Further research

The case study method has been utilised in this research as a means of providing a detailed description of a single instance of organisational change in response to a changing environment. It has been noted that the method allows generalisation to a theoretical framework, in this instance, the theory of organisational change and adaptation. The findings of the study address themselves to this general theory.

Further research might address itself to the confirmation of the findings of this study through the testing of hypotheses constructed from the findings. Some hypotheses which may be tested through further case study or alternative qualitative methods are as follows:

- In order to enhance political alignment, organisations will adopt structures which facilitate the processing of information about the environment and enable effective decision making.
- In a turbulent environment, domain flexibility is critical for organisational survival. This requires an availability of resources and alternative roles within the environment, and a capacity on the part of the organisation to exploit these.
- Flexible structures which enable decentralised decision making and participative planning are likely to lead to innovative problem solving, and a capacity to maintain organisational commitment during implementation. This activity is best focussed upon product development activity which is both meaningful for line staff and amenable to problem solving approaches.
- In order to enhance predictability within the environment, to reduce competition for scarce resources, and to enhance political alignment, organisations in turbulent environments will seek to achieve consensus with key elements of their environment concerning fundamental values.

Conclusion

The redevelopment of Mayday Hills Training Centre for Intellectually Disabled was one of the largest and most significant institutional redevelopment projects undertaken during a period of major change in the mechanisms for the public provision of services to disabled people within the State of Victoria. The project had major implications for the residents of the centre and for other disabled people in the north-east of the state who were the ultimate recipients of its redeveloped services. It had major implications also for the staff of the centre who had to develop new careers in a dramatically altered service structure. It had implications for the community within which the institution had operated for 130 years and which had come to expect that it would always be there, and would always provide employment.

This study has argued however, that this major organisational change should be understood in the context of the complex technological, political and cultural changes taking place within the intellectual disability field and in the

State of Victoria at the time, and the interplay between the organisation and elements of its task and general environment.

The study has detailed the adaptive responses of the organisation to changes within its environment, and has analysed these responses thematically in terms of changes in the organisation's internal dependencies, transactional dependencies and environmental dependencies. It has used these findings to confirm some elements of the theory concerning the organisation/environment relationship and suggest some modification to other elements. Finally, on the basis of these findings, it has proposed a number of hypotheses which may be tested through further research.

The social, political and technological environments of organisations will continue to change, and it has been observed that the rate of that change is increasing over time. Successful organisations will continue to adapt to those changes and in doing so, will transform the way in which services for the vulnerable and the disadvantaged are provided. As that process continues, it will be critical that the social work profession and those responsible for the management of human services organisations monitor the processes of change, and seek to understand the underlying principles of organisational responses to changing environments.

The Case Study of Mayday Hills Training Centre is in part the story of how a range of people; residents, staff, administrators (both central and regional), and social reformers; and the organisations of which they were a part, were forced by the turbulent changes in their environment, to undergo significant cultural, technological and political change. That they were able to do so is a story of hope, in that it demonstrates that such transitions can be made, and a tribute to their courage and resilience.

Appendix A

Schedule of Interviewees

Respondent I   (Anonymous)
Respondent II   (Anonymous)

Mr Paul Bartholemew   Deputy Director General, Community Services Victoria, (1988-1990)
General Manager, Intellectual Disability Services, (1990-1991)

Ms Sheri Brooks   Psychologist, Mayday Hills Hospital, (1983-1985)
Psychologist, Upper Murray IDS Team, (1987-1990)
Manager, Behaviour Intervention Support Team, (1990-1992)

Mr Doug Dalton   Assistant Director, Office of Intellectual Disability Services, (1986-1987)
Regional Director, North West Region, (1987-1990)
Chief Executive Officer, Caloola Training Centre, (1990-1992)

Mr David Green   General Manager, Office of Intellectual Disability Services, (1987-1989)
Director Office of Older Persons, (1989-1992)
Assistant Director, Aged Care Division, Department of Human Services, (1992-1995)
Public Advocate, (1995-to present)

Ms Julie Hind

Team Leader, Intellectual Disability Program, Goulburn, North East Region, (1986-1988)
Regional Coordinator, Intellectual Disability Services, Upper Murray Region, (1988-1991)
Chief Executive Officer, Mayday Hills Training Centre and Area Manager, Hume Region, (1991-1993)

The Hon Michael John

Opposition Spokesperson on Community Services, (1990-1992)
Minister for Community Services, (1992-1996)

Mr David Jones

Assistant Regional Director, Health Department, (1986-1988)
Regional Chief Executive Officer, Psychiatric Services, (1988-1992)

Mr Jim Kesselshmidt

Director of Nursing/Manager, Direct Care, Mayday Hills Training Centre, (1991-1993)
Manager, Residential Services, Hume Region, (1993 - 1995)

Ms Marie Lindley

Skills Development Officer, Mayday Hills Training Centre, (1989-1990)

Mr Rob Macdonald

Program Advisor, Community Services Victoria
Manager, Service Planning and Development Hume Region

Mr Steve Menzie

Staff Member, Mayday Hills Training Centre (25 years)
Unit Manager, Mayday Hills Training Centre

Dr John Paterson

Director General, Community Services Victoria, (1989-1992)
Secretary, Department of Health and Community Services, (1992-1996)

Ms Heather Scovell

Regional Coordinator, Intellectual Disability Services, Loddon- Mallee Region, (1980-1986)
Assistant Director, Office of Intellectual Disability Services, (1986-1987)
Regional Director, Community Services Victoria, North West/North Eastern Region, (1987-1990)

Ms Ruth Tai

Mental Retardation Nurse, and Unit Charge Nurse, Mayday Hills Training Centre, (1981-1990)
Manager, Residential Services, Hume Region, (1990-1991)

Appendix B

Historical Background to Mayday Hills Training Centre[1]

Mayday Hills Training Centre, or Mayday Hills Hospital, as it was known through most of its history, had its origins in the overcrowding, poor classification and inappropriate accommodation for the mentally ill, which was evident from the earliest days in the settlement of the Port Phillip District. These were brought to the notice of successive Government inquiries before becoming a major focus for the "Barry Commission" in 1862, whose task it was to report on aspects of the running of "Yarra Bend"; at that time the principal location for the provision of institutional care to the mentally ill. At that time, and in practice for the next 70 years, little distinction was drawn between the mentally ill and the intellectually disabled.

The Barry Commission reported to Parliament on 8 December 1862:

> That a new asylum to contain 500 patients be erected near Melbourne, and that two district asylums to contain 250 patients each, be erected in eligible places in the interior of the colony. (Hansard, 8 December, 1862).

The Commission proceeded to gain the opinion of "competent persons" throughout the colony to guide them in selecting sites for the two provincial asylums. Circulars were sent to Police Magistrates, Judges of mining districts and the Medical Officers of country hospitals. The Commission further reported that:

> After careful examination of the information thus obtained, we have consequently decided to recommend that these asylums be erected on suitable sites [to be selected after personal inspection] within the districts of Ararat and Beechworth.

> We are led to the selection by a wish to provide for cases of lunacy occurring in districts where the means of railway and other communication are not available for their transport to the metropolis.

[1]This section draws heavily upon the original research of Mr Doug Craig, former Manager, Mayday Hills Hospital.

232

Figure AB.1   **Photo: Mayday Hills Hospital 1867**

It is significant that both recommended sites, were also the location of major gaols which would appear to have been providing care for numbers of mentally ill who were awaiting placement at Yarra Bend; placements which seldom materialised because of overcrowding in that Institution.

An Institution for the care of the mentally ill was built at Beechworth according to the recommendation of the Commission and opened on 24 October 1967. The imposing Victorian architecture and expansive grounds were to become home to many thousands of ill, distressed and disabled people for more than a hundred years.

Simultaneous with the opening of the new facilities, the first statutes were enacted referring specifically to the care of the mentally ill. The "1867 Statutes" were modelled on British and Canadian regulations and prescribed attention to the care, rights and humane treatment of patients. They were premised however upon institutional models which stressed the need for physical isolation, large scale, and farming enterprises in order to minimise the cost to Government. Accordingly the Beechworth asylum developed an insular environment, and a tendency towards self-sufficiency.

Apart from relatively minor changes in legislation, and the steady expansion of the physical accommodation of patients at the asylum, very little change took place between 1867 and the early 1950s. Throughout that period, the institution operated as a world unto itself. Patients worked the 200 acre farm, which provided produce to the institution. All patients' needs were met by the staff of the facility, which included tailors, seamstresses and bootmakers.

In the early hours of 12 August 1951, fire raced through the male wing of the hospital almost destroying the whole section. In consequence, many patients were relocated to Melbourne, and ultimately, in 1959, six "temporary" buildings were erected to accommodate the increasing numbers of residents. These buildings were based upon the design of the Victorian Education Department buildings which were being erected across the State as schools expanded to provide an education for the post-war baby-boom generation. What in schools were classrooms became dormitories in which up to 50 beds were lined up one after another.

The central hallway which ran the length of these buildings enabled the supervision of the sleeping arrangements through glass partitions - a modern panopticon. The buildings concerned had a thirty-year life, and although provided for "temporary purposes", two were still in operation in 1992 as residences for the intellectually disabled residents. In 1959 the number of residents exceeded 1,000 for the first time, a figure which was maintained until the mid 1970s.

The more significant changes which occurred during the 1950s however related to the legislative and practice changes in the care of the mentally ill which accompanied the establishment in 1952 of the Mental Health Authority. The Asylum became the Beechworth Mental Hospital and the perimeter wall which shielded the hospital and its residents from the outside world, and even the immediate community of Beechworth, was demolished. The proliferation of new psychotropic medication enabled the abandonment of many of the physical restraints which had previously been used to control patients. In 1954 the Hospital's first therapy unit was constructed, and some early moves were made to establish linkages with the community through the establishment of the Country Women's Association's "Homecraft Unit" in 1958.

The developments of the 1950s were continued in the subsequent decade, with progressively greater attention being paid to the rights and needs of individual patients. Pensions and benefits were made available to residents making possible for the first time the purchase of individual clothing, and a lessening of the uniformity of dress. Old habits die hard however, and it was 1990 before residents were assured of their own clothing, and underwear ceased to be communal. The 1960s also saw the beginning of new divisions of labour and the emergence of the nursing (initially psychiatric only) profession which was to dominate the facility and the service system generally over the ensuing decades.

From the perspective of the intellectually disabled, the most significant development was to occur in 1980 when the Mental Retardation Division was separated from the Mental Health Authority. Although still within an overall Health Department, and continuing to be dominated by psychiatrists, this division began a process of focussing at a State level on the distinctive requirements of the intellectually disabled, as opposed to the mentally ill. Ironically, it was the first two rural institutions, and now the oldest institutions in the State, Beechworth and Ararat which gained least from this development. Both these facilities together with Brierly Hospital in Warrnambool had, unlike most institutions, large numbers of intellectually disabled residents as well as psychiatric patients. They became termed as "joint facilities", and continued to be managed in effect as psychiatric facilities. A Psychiatrist Superintendent was then appointed as the manager of the facility and the gradual emergence of intellectual disability as a distinctive discipline and branch of public administration which took place elsewhere in the State failed to take effect in these facilities. The isolation of the "joint facilities" from the mainstream of intellectual disability services was to be cited 30 years later by the Committee of Inquiry into Aradale Hospital, as a major factor in the perpetuation of abuse of client rights in that facility (Health Department, Victoria, 1991).

The 1970s was for the newly renamed Mayday Hills Hospital a period of physical change. The hospital was so renamed at centenary celebration (1967), by the Governor of Victoria, Sir Rohan Delecombe. The name derived from the original name of Beechworth, "May Day Hills", modified to echo the international signal for distress. Remaining perimeter walls were demolished and a number of ancient buildings replaced with geriatric psychiatry wards. A new Early Treatment Unit (psychiatry) was constructed (1977). These developments were for psychiatric clients only, and contributed to the pervading sense within the intellectual disability "Training Centre", of being the "poor cousin". Also built in this period (1980) were new catering complexes for both Mayday Hills and the neighbouring Ovens and Murray Hospital for the Aged. In testimony to the growing power of the union which at that time had coverage of all direct care (nursing) and non-direct care (artisan and domestic) staff, the resident meals were prepared by the Ovens and Murray Hospital using cook-chill processes and transported to Mayday Hills. The Mayday Hills catering centre, from the time of its opening, provided meals principally for staff. This was to become a major point of industrial contention during 1988/89.

While progress had been made during the 1960s in treatment regimes and attendance to client rights, not all development had been positive. The self-sufficiency which had been the mark of Victorian-age institutions and which had continued throughout the first half of the twentieth century became a victim of cheaper commodities, and greater competition in the supply of food. Vegetable gardens became no longer viable, followed by dairying and piggeries. With the discontinuation of these farming activities ended meaningful day activities for most residents. Because of the activities had been seen as primarily economic rather than therapeutic or training related they could not be sustained in a changed economic environment.

At the same time, the growing power of the Hospital Employees Federation No 2 Branch (HEF 2), saw a more rigid delineation of work tasks and the multiplication of categories of non-direct care staff, each of which had defined tasks which could not be undertaken by others. By this means, resident involvement in domestic activity was also discouraged.

The first significant reduction in resident numbers occurred in 1974 with the regionalisation of admissions to the Institution. This meant that admissions were not accepted for either psychiatric and intellectual disability services from outside the Goulburn Valley and North Eastern Victoria areas. The long history of transfers from metropolitan facilities to Beechworth ceased from this point. In consequence, resident numbers fell to 718 in 1974. In 1980 the numbers had reduced to 519 and in 1988 were 357, 178 of whom were intellectually disabled.

Such reductions were desperately required as many of the buildings which were more than a century old were deteriorating rapidly, and many were severely overcrowded. Turquoise Ward (psychiatric) in 1975 provided accommodation for 78 residents, and Myrtle House (intellectually disability) accommodated 60. By 1988 these numbers had reduced to 28 and 14 respectively.

The overall reduction of resident numbers allowed, through the 1970s and 1980s a refocussing of parts of the psychiatric service upon community psychiatric services rather than institutional services; a development which was not reflected to any significant degree in intellectual disability services. Community psychiatric nursing services were established in Wodonga in 1977 and Wangaratta in 1980. An alcohol rehabilitation program which commenced on campus with a view to assisting residents, transferred to a property in the Beechworth township in 1986, and became a resource to the wider community.

The development of a community focus within the Training Centre for the intellectually disabled was more sporadic and less substantial. In 1979 the Health Commission had determined that there should be a separate resourcing of mental retardation services, but the Mental Retardation Division continued to be administered by the Mental Health Division until February 1981 when a Director was appointed to administer the service separately. The Mental Retardation Division under the leadership of Errol Cox, a prominent reformer in the intellectual disability field was aggressively committed to alternatives to institutional care. The regional Intellectual Disability Team which was established in 1981, saw itself as being principally responsible for clients located outside the institution, and had little impact upon the Training Centre at Beechworth. Exceptions to this were the establishment of Community Residential Units in Wangaratta and Wodonga which provided alternative accommodation for eight former residents of Mayday Hills, and the accessing of Day Training Centre places in Wodonga and Wangaratta by eight residents of the institution.

Following the transfer of the Mental Retardation Division to the new Department of Community Services in October 1985, the Mayday Hills Training Centre continued to be focussed internally and to be essentially institutional in its service. As a "joint facility", the budget and management of which was entirely with the Health Department, it was largely isolated from administrative and programmatic development in the field of intellectual disability.

In consequence two of the largest Institutions in the State, Aradale at Ararat, and Mayday Hills at Beechworth were isolated, backward looking in the programs they provided, and at the mercy of the budgetary decisions of another agency.

In October 1987, Community Services Victoria consolidated the regional management of all its program operations under 18 Regional Directors. For the first time, this meant that institutional services for the intellectually disabled were under the same local management as services for non-institutional clients. At this point there began a major redevelopment of the Mayday Hills Training Centre, which was to see the number of on-campus residents reduce from 188 to nil over a six year period, and see the service system for the intellectually disabled in North East Victoria transformed.

Appendix C

Schedule of Unpublished Official Documents

Disability Services Division (1993). Accommodation Support Data.

Health and Community Services (1993). Preliminary Proposals for Amendment to the IDPS Act 1986.

Deusburys Chartered Accountants (1992). *Report on Singleton Equity Housing Limited,* Melbourne.

Community Services Victoria (1992). Final Redevelopment Plan, Mayday Hills Training Centre.

Memorandum, Regional Director, Upper Murray Region to General Manager, Office of Intellectual disabilities, 2 October 1992, re: Behavioural Management Services, Mayday Hills Training Centre.

Caloola Closure Project (1992). Total End Cost (TEC), Financial Analysis, June.

Hume Region, (1992). Mayday Hills Redevelopment Plan.

Personnel Management Branch (1992). Mayday Hills Workforce profile as at 2 April 1992, Community Services Victoria.

Hume Region (1992) Proposal for the re-development of Grevillea House, Mayday Hills, Hume Region, April.

Ministerial Briefing, Deputation to Minister for Health and Minister for Community Services Victoria by Beechworth Shire Council regarding Mayday Hills Hospital, Regional Director, Hume Region, 27 March 1992.

Matters arising from the Aradale investigations, Regional Director, Hume Region, February 1992.

Memorandum: To A/General Manager Disability Services Division, from Regional Director, Hume Region: Handover Report: Joint Facilities Transfer, November 1991.

Ministerial Briefing, Minister for Community Services, Joint Intellectual Disability/Psychiatric Services Facilities, 2 October 1991.

Ministerial Briefing, Minister for Community Services, Minister for Health, Future Management Arrangements for Joint Facilities, 8 August 1991.

Funding and Services Agreement, between Community Services Victoria and Health Department Victoria, concerning Mayday Hills Training Centre for the Intellectually Disabled, June 1991.

Wodonga Townhouse Project Proposal, 28 April 1991.

Client Consultation Proposal, Mayday Hills Training Centre, Community Services Victoria, 21 January 1991.

Minutes, Industrial Consultation Forum (HEF(2)) - 1988 - 1991.

Minutes, Training Centre Liaison Committee - 1988 - 1991.

Briefing: Director, Disability Planning and Review to General Manager, Community Services Victoria, 10 November 1990 re: Joint Facilities.

Putting the Client First, Information Kit (1989), Guidelines for institutional management following the Wallace inquiry into Pleasant Creek Training Centre.

Office of Intellectual Disability Services, Allocation of State Plan Resources to Regions, November 1989.

Staff Handbook, Mayday Hills Psychiatric Hospital and Intellectual Disability Centre Beechworth, July 1989.

Office of Psychiatric Services. (1989). *Data Base, Training Centre, Mayday Hills Hospital.* Davidson, S. June.

Services Agreement (1988) between Community Services Victoria and Mayday Hills Hospital concerning the Behavioural Intervention Support Team.

Regional Coordination Strategy Team (1987). Current Roles and Function in CSV Programs and Transfer Plans, August.

Department of Labour, Head of Agreement, Mayday Hills Hospital Industrial Dispute. 24 February 1987.

Public Service Board (1986). Review of Management Structures of Aradale and Mayday Hills Joint Facilities.

Public Service Board (1985). Transfer of Intellectual Disability Services to the Department of Community Services, October.

Administrative Arrangements Order (1985). Governor in Council. October.

Office of Psychiatric Services (1980) Budget information.

Bibliography

Aldrich, H. E. (1972). "An Organisation and Environment Perspective on Cooperation and Conflict between Organisations and Manpower Training Systems", in Amant, R. Wegandhi (ed). *Conflict and Power in Complex Organisations, An Inter-Institutional Perspective.* Comparative Administration Research Institute, Kent State University, Kent, Ohio,

Aldrich, H. E. (1986). "A Population Perspective on Organisational Strategy", in Aldrich, H. E., Auster, H. E., Staber, U.H. and Zimmer, C. (eds). *Population Perspectives on Organisations.* Acta Universitatis Upsaliensis, Uppsala.

Alford, J., O'Neill, D., McGuire, L., Considine, M., Muetzelfeldt, M. and Ernst, J. (1994). "The Contract State", in Alford, J. and O'Neill, D. (eds). *The Contract State.* Centre for Applied Social Research, Deakin University Press, Melbourne.

Alford, J. and O'Neill, D. (eds) (1994). *The Contract State.* Centre for Applied Social Research, Deakin University Press, Melbourne.

Ansoff, H. I. (1977). "Managing Surprise and Discontinuity : Strategic Response to Weak Signals", in Thorelli, Hans B. (ed). *Strategy & Structure - Performance.* Indiana University Press, Bloomington & London.

Astley, W. G. and Van de Ven, A. H. (1983). "Central Perspectives and Debates in Organisation Theory", *Administrative Science Quarterly.* Vol 28, 245-273.

Beilharz, P., Considine, M. and Watts, R. (1992). *Arguing About the Welfare State.* Allen & Unwin, Sydney.

Belchers, J. R. (1991). "Moving into Homelessness after Psychiatric Hospitalisation", *Journal of Social Service Research,* Vol. 14 (3/4).

Bennis, W. G. and Slater, P. E. (1968). *The Temporary Society.* Harper and Row, New York.

Bennis, W. G., Benne, K. D. and Chin, R. (1976). *The Planning of Change,* (4th ed). Holt, Rinehart and Winston, Inc, Fort Worth, USA.

Benson, J. K. (1977). "Organisations: A Dialectical View", *Administrative Science Quarterly,* Vol 22, 1-21.

Blau, P. M. and Meyer, M. W. (1987). *Bureaucracy in Modern Society (3rd ed).* McGraw-Hill, New York.

Boswell, J. (1973). *The Rise and Decline of Small Firms.* Allen & Unwin, London.

Breadmore, P. (1992). Presentation Notes, "Proceedings", *Moving with the Times, Caloola Closure Conference.* Melbourne.

Brown, H. and Smith, H. (1992a). *Normalisation; A Reader for the Nineties.* Tavistock/Routledge, London and New York.

Brown, H. and Smith, H. (1992b). "Defending Community Care: Can Normalisation do the Job?". *British Journal of Social Work,* 22(6), 685-693.

Brunninks, R. H. Meyers, E. C. Sigford, B. B. and Larkin, K. C. (1981). *Deinstitutionalisation and Community Adjustment of Mentally Retarded People.* Monograph No 4. American Association on Mental Deficiency. Washington.

Bryson, L. (1989). "A New Iron Cage? A View from Within", *Canberra Bulletin of Public Administration.* 16, No. 4, 255-67.

Bryson, L. (1992). *Welfare and the State.* Macmillan Press, UK.

Bryson, L. (1994). "Directions and Development in the Australian Welfare State; A Challenge for Educators", *Australian Social Work.* Dec. Vol. 47. No. 4, 3-10.

Burns, T. and Stalker, G. M. (1961). *The Management of Innovation.* Tavistock, London.

Campbell, D. T. (1979). "Degrees of Freedom and the case study", in Cook, V. and Reichardt, C. S. (eds). *Qualitative and Quantitative Methods in Education Research.* Sage Publications, Beverly Hills, CA.

Carlson, R. O. (1964). "Environmental Constraints and Organisational Consequences: The Public School and its Clients", in Griffiths D. B. (ed). *Behavioural Science and Educational Administration,* National Society for the Study of Education. Chicago.

Castellani, P. J. (1987). *The Political Economy of Developmental Disabilities,* Paul. H. Brookes Publishing Co., Baltimore.

Clegg, S. (1981). "Organisation and Control", *Administrative Science Quarterly,* 26, 545-562.

Clegg, S. (1990). *Modern Organsiations: Organisation Studies in the Postmodern World.* Sage, London.

Cohen, S. and Scull, A. (eds) (1983). *Social Control and the State; Comparative and Historical Essays.* Martin Robertson, Oxford.

Cohen, S. (1985). *Visions of Social Control.* Polity Press, Cambridge.

Community Services Victoria (1987a). *Survey of the Utilisation of Chemical Restraint within Intellectual Disability Institutions.* Melbourne.

Community Services Victoria (1987b). *Survey of Day Program Provision within Intellectual Disability Institutions.* Melbourne.

Community Services Victoria (1988a). *The St Nicholas Report (Abstract), The Evaluation of a De-institutionalisation Project in Victoria.* Melbourne.

Community Services Victoria (1988b). *The St Nicholas Report (Abstract), The Evaluation of a De-institutionalisation Project in Victoria.* Melbourne.

Community Services Victoria, (1988). *Ten Year Plan for the Redevelopment of Intellectual Disability Services. Final Report,* Melbourne.

Community Services Victoria (1989). *Community Living Support Services Program Description.* Melbourne.

Community Services Victoria (1990). *Case Management Guidelines, Intellectual Disability Services.* Melbourne.

Community Services Victoria (1992a). *Mayday Hills Transition and Training Needs Analysis. Melbourne.*

Community Services Victoria (1992b). *Training Centre Day Programs, Report on Survey Findings.* Melbourne.

Community Services Victoria (1992c). *IDS Client Services Practice Manual.* Melbourne.

Community Services Victoria (1992d). *Training Centre Day Programs, Report on Survey Findings.* Melbourne.

Conway, M. F. (1992). "Disability and Legislation: The relationship between changing policy and changing practices", *Australia and New Zealand Journal of Developmental Disabilities,* Vol 18, No. 2, 65-73.

Cook, T. D. and Campbell, D. T. (1979). *Quasi-experimentation: Design and analysis for field settings.* Houghton-Mifflin, Boston.

Cook, T. D. and Reichardt, C. S. (eds) (1979). *Qualitative and Quantitative Methods in Evaluation Research.* Sage Publications, Beverly Hills, CA.

Crissey, M. S. (1986). "The Legacy of the Residential Institution", in Crissey, M. S. and Rosen, M. (eds). *Institutions for the Mentally Retarded.* Pro-ed, Texas, USA.

Crossley, R. and McDonald, A. (1981). *Annie's Coming Out.* Penguin, Richmond.

Cullari, S. (1984). "Everybody is Talking About the New Institution", *Mental Retardation.* Vol. 22. No 1, 28-29.

Cummins, R. A., Baxter, C., Hudson, A., Polak, S. and Romeo, Y. (1992). "The Community Living Support Service: An Operational Overview", *Australian Disability Review,* No. 3.

Cummins, R. A. (1993). "On Being Returned to the Community: Imposed Ideology versus Quality of Life", *Australian Disability Review,* 2, 64-71.

Dalley, G. (1992). "Social Welfare Ideologies and Normalisation", in Brown, H. and Smith, H. (eds). *Normalisation; A Reader for the Nineties.* Tavistock/ Routledge, London and New York.

Dalton, G. W. and Lawrence, P. R. (eds). (1979). *Organisational Change and Development.* Richard D. Irwin, Inc., Illinois.

Davis, G. F., Deihmann, K A. and Tinsley, C. H. (1994). "The Decline and fall of the Conglomerate Firm in the 1980s: The Deinstitutionalization of an Organisational Form", *American Sociological Review,* Vol 59, August, 547-570.

Denzin, N. K. (1978). *The Research Act.* McGraw-Hill, New York.

Denzin, N. K. (1989). *Interpretive Interactionism.* Sage Publications, Newbury Park, CA.

Dokecks, P. R., Anderson, B. J. and Strain, P. S. (1992). "Stigmatization and Labelling", in P. James, L. Stedman, Donald J. and Neufold, G. Ronald. (eds). *Deinstitutionalisation.* Syracuse University Press, New York.

Elks, M. A. (1994). "Valuing the Person or Valuing the Role? Critique of Social Role Valorization Theory", *Mental Retardation,* Vol 32, No 4, 265-271.

Emerson, E. (1992). "What is Normalisation", in Brown, H. and Smith, H. (eds). *Normalisation: A Reader for the Nineties.* Tavistock/Routledge. London and New York.

Emery, F. E. and Trist, E. L. (1965). "The Causal Texture of Organisational Environments.", *Human Relations,* Vol. 18., 21-32.

Emery, F. E. and Trist, E. L. (1973). *Towards a Social Ecology.* Plenum Press, London.

Emy, H. V. (1976). *Public Policy: Problems and Paradoxes.* Macmillan, Melbourne.

Evatt Foundation (1989). *State of Seige; Renewal or Privatisation for Australian State Public Service.* Pluto Press, Leichardt, NSW.

Gaylin, W. G. (1978). *Doing Good: The Limits of Benevolence.* Penthleon, New York.

Gilgun, J. F. (1994). "A Case for Case studies in Social Work Research". *Social Work,* Vol. 39, No. 4.

Glaser, B. G. and Strauss, A. L. (1967). *The Discovery of Grounded Theory,* Aldine De Gruyter, New York.

Goffman, E. (1987). *Asylums.* Penguin Books, London.

Green, D. and David, J. L. (1984). "A Research Design for Generalising From Multiple Case Studies". *Education and Program Planning,* 7, 73-85.

Greenhalgh, L. (1992). "Organisational Decline". (*Research in the Sociology of Organisations,* Vol 2), JAI Press, London, England.

Griffin, R. G. (1986). "Institutions are they legal?", in Crissey, M. S. and Rosen, M. (eds). *Institutions for the Mentally Retarded.* Pro-ed, Texas, USA.

Hage, J. and Aiken, M. (1976). "Program Change and Organisational Properties, A Comparative Analysis", *American Journal of Sociology,* 72, 503-519.

Hage, J. and Aiken, M. (1980). "Program Change and Organisational Properties", in Resniek, Herman and Rino, J. Patti (eds). *Change from Within.* Temple University Press, Philadelphia, pg. 159 ff.

Hannan, M. T. and Freeman, J. H. (1978). "The Population Ecology of Organisations", in Mayer, Marshall, W. and Associates, (eds). *Environments and Organisations.* Jossey-Bass, San Francisco.

Hannan, M. T. and Freeman, J. H. (1989). *Organisational Ecology.* Harvard University Press, Massachusetts.

Hannan, M. T. and Freeman, J. H. (1977). "The Population Ecology of Organisations.", *American Journal of Sociology,* Vol 82, No 5. 929-964.

Hasenfeld, Y. (1983). *Human Services Organisations,* Prentice Hall, Inc. New Jersey.

Health and Community Services, Victoria (1994). *Service Plan for Contracted Out Intellectual Disability Community Residential Services,* Melbourne.

Health Department Victoria (1992a). *Audit of Standards of Treatment and Care in Psychiatric Hospitals in the State of Victoria,* Melbourne.

Health Department Victoria (1992b). *Towards Excellence in Care: Future Directions for Health Services in Beechworth, Benalla.*

Heaney, S. (1991). *Seeing Things.* Faber and Faber, London.

Heclo, H. (1972). "Policy Analysis", *British Journal of Political Science,* Vol 2. 83-108.

Henderson, D. (1989). "Perestroika in the West", in Nieuwenhuyson, J. (ed), in *Towards Free Trade Between Nations.* Oxford University Press, Melbourne.

Hough, G. (1994). *The Re-direction of State Welfare,* Unpublished PhD Thesis, La Trobe University, Melbourne. Intellectually Disabled Person Services Act (1986).

Jones, A. and May, J. (1992). *Working in Human Service Organisations.* Longman Cheshire, Melbourne.

Jurkovich, R. (1974). "A Core Typology of Organisational Environments", *Administrative Science Quarterly,* Vol. 19, 380-394.

Kanter, R. M. (1977). *Men and Women of the Corporation.* Basic Books, New York.

Kanter, R. M. (1987). *The Change Masters.* George Allen and Unwin, London.

Katz, D. and Kahn, R. L. (1978). *The Social Psychology of Organisations.* 2nd ed. John Wiley and Sons, New York.

Kaufman, H. (1975). "The Natural History of Human Organisations", *Administration and Society*. 7, 131-149.

Keating, T. P. (1983). *Imperatives in Implementation*, Unpublished Master of Social Work Thesis. University of Melbourne.

Keating, T. P. (1994). *Differentiation and Integration in Health and Community Services*. Paper presented to the Public Policy Interest Group, Melbourne, February.

Keating, T. P. (1995). *Tools and Products; an examination of the application of unit costing to Acute Health, Adult Day Training Services and Pre-schools.* Paper presented to the Public Policy Interest Group, Melbourne.

Keating, T. P. (1997a). *Social Sector Agencies in the Changing Environment of Europe*. Paper presented at International Federation of Social Workers/ European Association of Schools of Social Work Joint European Regional Seminar/Conference, Dublin, 24-28 August 1997.

Keating, T. P. and Calder. R. (1997). "Rural Community Responses to Structural Changes in Health Care", in *Strengthening Health Partnerships in your Rural Community*. Proceedings of the National Rural Public Health Forum, Adelaide, October.

Kellehear, A. (1993). *The Unobtrusive Researcher, A Guide to Methods.* Allen and Unwin Pty Limited, St Leonards.

Kelly, P. (1992). *The End of Certainty*. Allen and Unwin, Sydney.

Klein, D. (1980). "Some Notes on the Dynamics of Resistance to Change: The Defender Role", in Resnick, H. and Patti, R. J. (eds). *Change from Within*. Temple University Press, Philadelphia.

Kouzes, J. M. and Mico, P. R. (1979). "Domain Theory: An Introduction to Organisational Behaviour in Human Service Organisations", *Journal of Applied Behavioural Science*, 449-469.

Lawler, E. J. and Bacharach, S. B. (1992). "Political Action and Alignments in Organisations", *Research in the Sociology of Organisations*, Vol. 2. JAI Press, London, England.

Lawrence, P. R. and Lorsch, J. W. (1967). "Differentiation and Integration in Complex Organisations", *Administrative Science Quarterly*, Vol. 12, 1-47.

Lawrence, P. R. and Lorsch, J. W. (1986). *Organisation and Environment*, 2nd ed. Harvard Business School Press, Boston.

Lewis, M. (ed). (1979). *Research in Social Problems and Public Policy.* JAI Press, Greenwich.

Lindenberg, S. M. and Schreuder, H. (eds). (1993). *Interdisciplinary Perspectives on Organisation Studies*. Pergamon Press, Oxford.

Lippitt, G. L., Langseth, P. and Mossop, J. (1985). *Implementing Organisational Change*. Jossey-Bass, San Francisco.

Lister, M. (1991). *Ministerial Statement: Report of the Task Force Investigation Aradale Hospital and Residential Institution*. Health Department Victoria, Melbourne.

Lord, J. and Hearn, C. (1987). *Return to the Community, The Process of Closing an Institution*. Centre for Research and Education in Human Services, Ontario.

Lowman, J., Menzies, R. J. and Palys, T. S. (1987). *Transcarceration: Essays in the Sociology of Social Control.* Gower Publishing Co., Aldershot, U.K.

March, J. G. and Simon, H. A. (1958). *Organisations*. John Wiley, New York.

Markiewicz, A. (1988). *The changing position and location of the Social Work Profession within a State Government department: Community Services Victoria.* Unpublished Master of Social Work thesis, University of Melbourne.

Martin, E. W. (1992). "Human Service Organisations: An Australian Perspective.", *Social Policy and Administration,* Vol. 26, No 4, 320-335.

Mayer, M. W. and Associates (1980). *Environments and Organisations.* Jossey-Bass, San Francisco and London.

Menoluscino, F. J. and McGee, J. J. (1981). "The New Institutions: Last Ditch Arguments", *Mental Retardation.* Vol. 19. No. 5, 215-220.

Metcalfe, J. L. (1985). "Systems Models, Economic Models and the Causal Texture of Organisational Environments: An approach to macro-organisational theory", *Human Relations,* Vol. 27, 639-663.

Miles, M. B. and Huberman, A. M. (1984). *Qualitative Data Analysis.* Sage, Beverly Hills.

Miles, R. H. (1980). *Macro Organisational Behaviour.* Goodyear, Santa Monica.

Mintzberg, H. (1979). *The Structuring of Organisations.* Prentice-Hall International, Inc., Englewood Cliffs, New Jersey.

Morgan, G. (1980). "Paradigms, Metaphors and Problem Solving in Organisational Theory", *Administrative Science Quarterly,* 25, 605-622.

Morgan, G. (1986). *Images of Organisations.* Sage, Thousand Oaks, CA.

Motamedi, J. K. (1976). "Adaptability and Capability: A Study of Social Systems, Their Environment, and Survival", in Bennis, W. G., Benne, K. D., and Chin, R. (eds). *The Planning of Change, 4th ed.* Holt, Reinhart and Winston Inc., Fort Worth, USA.

Neuman, W. L. (1991). *Social Research Methods.* Allyn and Bacon, London.

Osborne, D. and Gaebler, T. (1993). *Reinventing Government.* Plume, New York.

Paterson, J. (1991). Foreword, *Annual Report 1990/91.* Community Services Victoria, Melbourne.

Paterson, J. (1992). "Evaluation of Welfare Programs: Facts, Outcomes and Black Holes", in *Evaluation Journal of Australia.* Vol. 4., No. 2.

Paterson, J. (1993). *Beyond Case Payments: A New Paradigm for Australian Health & Welfare.* EPAC Discussion Paper, October.

Paterson, J. and Hardy, B. (1991). *Review of Disability Services Head Office Functions.* Community Services Victoria, Melbourne.

Patti, R. J. (1980). "Organisational Resistance and Change: The View from Below", in Resnick, Herman and Rino, J., Patti (eds). *Change from Within.* Temple University Press, Philadelphia.

Patton, M. Q. (1990). *Qualitative Evaluation and Research Methods,* 2nd ed. Sage Publications, Newbury Park.

Pearson, G. (1975). *The Deviant Imagination.* Macmillian, London.

Perrin, B. and Nirje, B. (1985). "Setting the Record Straight: A Critique of some frequent misconceptions of the Normalisation Principle", *Australian and New Zealand Journal of Developmental Disabilities,* 11: 69-74.

Pfeiffer, D. (1994). "The Americans with Disabilities Act: Costly Mandates or Civil Rights?", *Disability and Society,* Vol. 9, No. 4, 533-542.

Picton, C., Cooper B. and Owen L. (1996). *Evaluation of the Relocation of the Aradale and Mayday Hills Clients.* Human Resources Centre, La Trobe University, Melbourne.

Porter, D. O. and Olsen, E. A. (1976). "Some Critical Issues in Government Centralisation and Decentralisation", *Public Administration Review*, 36, 72-84.

Preston, L. E. (1977). "Strategy - Structure - Performance: A Framework for Organisational/Environment Analysis", in Thorelli, Hans B. (ed). *Strategy & Structure = Performance*. Indiana University Press, Bloomington and London.

Provencal, G. (1989). *Characteristics of a Successful Community Living Program and Support Services*. Yungaburra Foundation, Melbourne.

Pullen, W. (1993). "Strategic Stocks: Managing Discontinuous Change", *International Journal of Public Sector Management*, Vol. 6. No. 1. 30-39.

Pusey, M. (1991). *Economic Rationalism in Australia*. Cambridge University Press, Sydney.

Rassaby, A. and Hall, A. (1986). *Normalisation and Principles of Legal Liability*. Office of Intellectual Disability Services, Melbourne.

Rein, M. (1983). *From Policy to Practice*. Macmillan. London.

Resnick, H. and Patti, R. J. (eds) (1980). *Change from Within*. Temple University Press, Philadelphia.

Rimmer, J. (1984). *The Report of the Committee on a Legislative Framework for Services to Intellectually Disabled People*. Health Department Victoria, Melbourne.

Rosenblatt, P. C. (1981). "Ethnographic case studies", in Brewer, M. and Collins, B. E. (eds). *Scientific Inquiry and the Social Sciences*. Jossey-Bass, San Francisco.

Rothman, D. J. (1980). *Conscience and Convenience; The Asylum and its Alternatives in Progressive America*. Little Brown, Boston.

Rothman, D. J. (1980). *Incarceration and the Alternatives in 20th Century America*. Washington, D.C. NILECJ.

Runyan, W. M. (1982). *Life Histories as psychobiography: Explanations in theory and method*. Oxford University Press, New York.

Sarantakos, S. (1993). *Social Research*. Macmillan, South Melbourne.

Schein, E. H. (1970). *Organisational Psychology*, 2nd ed. Prentice-Hall, Englewood Cliffs, New Jersey.

Schein, E. H. (1992). *Organisational Culture and Leadership*, 2nd ed. Jossey-Bass Inc., San Francisco, CA.

Schmidt, H. (1992a). "Generalism v Specialism in Human Services Management", *Social Policy and Administration*, Vol. 26, No. 3, 245-253.

Schmidt, H. (1992b). *Strategic and Structural Change in Human Service Organisations; The Role of the Environment*. Haworth Press, New York.

Schon, D. (1971). *Beyond the Stable State*. Basic Books, New York.

Scull, A. (1984). *Decarceration*, 2nd ed. Polity Press, Cambridge.

Scull, A. (1993). *The Most Solitary of Afflications*. Yale University Press, New Haven.

Self, P. (1993). *Government by the Market*. Macmillan, Hampshire.

Simmons, H. G. (1992). *From Asylum to Welfare*. National Institute on Mental Retardation, Ontario.

Simon, H. A. (1976). *Administrative Behaviour*, 3rd ed. The Free Press, New York.

Sinson, J. C. (1993). *Group Homes and Community Integration of Developmentally Disabled People*. Jessica Kingsley Publishers, London.

Solomon, S. (1987). *The Role of Interest Groups and Policy Change Networks in the Transfer of functions from the Victorian Health Administration to the Welfare Administration.* Unpublished Master of Arts Thesis, University of Melbourne.

Starbuck, W. H. and Hedberg, B. L. (1977). "Saving an organisation from a stagnating environment", in Thorelli, Hans B. (ed). *Strategy & Structure = Performance.* Indiana University Press, Bloomington.

Steer, M. and Annison, J. E. (1992). "Creative Approaches: Disability Policy Evaluation.", *Policy Issues Forum*, December.

Stretton, H. and Orchard, L. (1994). *Public Goods, Public Enterprise, Public Choice.* Macmillan, Hampshire.

Swan, N. and Patterson, J. (1995). *Reforming the Health Care System, The Health Report, ABC Radio National,* 27 November.

Taylor, S. J. and Bogdan. R. (1984). *Introduction to Qualitative Research Methods* 2nd ed. John Wiley and Sons, New York.

Terreberry, S. (1976). "The Evolution of Organisational Environment", in Bennis, W. G., Benne, K. D. and Chin, R. (eds). *The Planning of Change,* 4th ed. Holt, Reinhart and Winston Inc., USA.

Thiele, R. L., Paul, J. L. and Neufeld, G. R. (1977). "A Perspective for Deinstitutionalisation program Development", in Paul, J. L. (ed). *Deinstitutionalisation.* Syracuse University Press, New York.

Thompson, J. D. (1962). "Organisations and Output Transactions", *American Journal of Sociology,* Vol. 63, 309-324.

Thompson, J. D. (1967). *Organisations in Action.* McGraw, Hill, New York, USA.

Thompson, J. D. and McEwan, W. (1958). "Organisational Goals and Environment: Goal Setting as an Interactive Process", *American Sociological Review,* 23, 23-31.

Tichy, N. M. (1983). *Managing Strategic Change, Technical, Political and Cultural Dynamics.* John Wiley & Sons, New York.

Tyne, A. (1992). "Normalisation: From Theory to Practice", in Brown, H. and Smith, H. (eds). *Normalisation; A Reader for the Nineties.* Tavistock/Routledge. London.

Upper Murray Regional Consultative Council (1989). *The Future of Services for Persons with an Intelectual Disability,* Wodonga.

Victorian Council of Social Services and the Office of the Public Advocate (1992). *Double Disadvantage, Housing for People with a Disability in Victoria.* VCOSS, Melbourne.

Wallace, J. (1989). *Pleasant Creek Training Centre, Stawell, Report to the Director General of Community Services Victoria. Community Services Victoria,* Melbourne.

Watson, S. D. (1994). "Applying Theory to Practice, A Prospective and Prescriptive Analysis of the Implementation of the Americans with Disabilities Act", *Journal of Disability Policy Studies,* Vol. 5, No. 1, 1-24.

Whetten, D. A. (1980). "Sources, Responses and Effects of Organisational Decline", in Kimberly, J. R and Miles, R. H. (eds). *The Organisational Life-Cycle.* Jossey-Bass, San Francisco.

Whitehead, S. (1992). "The Social Origins of Normalisation", in Brown, H. and Smith, H. (eds). *Normalisation; a Reader for the Nineties.* Tavistock/Routledge, London and New York.

Wolfensberger, W. (1972). *The Principle of Normalisation in Human Services.* National Institute on Mental Retardation, Toronto.

Wolfensberger, W. (1975). *The Origin and Nature of our Institutional Models.* Human Policy Press, New York.

Wolfensberger, W. (1980). "The Definition of Normalisation: Update, problems, disagreements and misunderstandings", in Flynn, R. J. and Nitsch, K. E. (eds). *Normalisation, Social Integration and Community Services.* University Park Press, Baltimore.

Wolfensberger, W. and Thomas, S. (1983). *PASSING: Program Analysis of Service System Implementation of Normalisation Goals.* National Institute on Mental Retardation, Toronto.

Wolfensberger, W. (1994). "The Growing Threat to the Lives of Handicapped People in the Context of Modernist Values", *Disability and Society*, Vol. 9, No. 3, 395-413.

Woodward, J. (1965). *Industrial Organisations: Theory and Practice.* Oxford University Press, London.

Yarmolisky, A. (1975). "Institutional Paralysis", *Dedalus*, 194, No. 1, 61-67.

Yin, R. K. (1989). *Case Study Research: Design and Methods* 2nd ed. Sage Publications, Newbury Park, CA.

Zaltman, G., Duncan R. and Nolbeck, J. (1973). *Innovations and Organizations.* John Wiley & Sons, New York, USA.

Zucker, L. G. (1983). "Organisations as Institutions", *Research in the Sociology of Organisations*, Vol. 2. JAI Press, London.

Index

For Product Safety Concerns and Information please contact our EU
representative GPSR@taylorandfrancis.com Taylor & Francis Verlag GmbH,
Kaufingerstraße 24, 80331 München, Germany

Printed and bound by CPI Group (UK) Ltd, Croydon, CR0 4YY
08/05/2025
01864360-0003